DE HAVILLAND AND HATFIELD

1910-1935

DE HAVILLAND AND HATFIELD

1910–1935

JOHN CLIFFORD

FONTHILL

Geoffrey de Havilland in his new Hatfield office in 1935.
(© *Emil O Hoppé, Corbis Corporation*)

Fonthill Media Limited
Fonthill Media LLC
www.fonthill.media
books@fonthill.media

First published in the United Kingdom and the United States of America 2015
Reprinted 2020

British Library Cataloguing in Publication Data:
A catalogue record for this book is available from the British Library

ISBN 978-1-78155-360-2

Typeset in 10 pt on 13pt Sabon LT
Printed and bound in England

Contents

In memory of my father-in-law, John Brand (1927–2014), who was always welcoming, encouraging, and full of great practical advice.
I never tired of his stories.

Acknowledgements

This book is the product of generous co-operation between a large number of people. The sheer variety of documents and images, supplied from private collections and by photographers, provides ample evidence of this. I am very grateful to all of you, and I am delighted to mention particular individuals, groups and organisations without whom this book would not be what it is.

I wanted to properly set the historical scene, and to provide the contrast of life in Hatfield before and after de Havilland arrived in the early 1930s. My first thanks on this subject go to John Brindle, Brian Lawrence, and to other members of the Hatfield Local Historical Society. Justine Taylor, of the Honourable Artillery Company, provided the information I needed to complete the story of Vincenzo Lunardi and the first airborne landing in England. Chris Reynolds, of Hertfordshire-Genealogy.co.uk, provided invaluable material, especially relating to Victorian Hatfield. I found so many clues to follow in the great work of Owen Davies, Susan Hall, Julie Moore, Daphne Knott, Jane Toyne, Helen Tyler, and others. They have brought together priceless collections of community memories on the University of Hertfordshire's herts.ac.uk/Heritage-Hub and Hertfordshire County Council's OurHatfield.org.uk. I am also grateful for their personal support. I also want to thank Julie Regan-Startling and the staff at Hatfield Library, who made my own research so much easier than it might have been.

Hatfield's industrialisation and expansion first came with the railways. I am grateful to Roger Taylor, John Alsop, Rudi Newman, John Darnton, and their friends at the Smallford Station Project for helping me to cover this important subject properly. It was also important to describe the town's early experiences of aviation before de Havilland arrived, including during the First World War. In any case, it turns out that a number of the primitive aircraft seen by Hatfield's inhabitants were de Havillands. My biggest thanks for being able to cover this period adequately go to Paul Hare, who has been particularly generous with his archive on the Royal Flying Corps. I needed a lot of help with the airship raids, which I gratefully received from Tom Morgan of HellfireCorner.co.uk, Rod Filan of EarlyAeroplanes.com, Andreas Krug of Luftschiff.de, Kim Braun of Oldenburg

University, and the Zeppelin Museum's Friederica Ihling, Sabine Betzler-Hawlitschek, and Barbara Waibel.

I discovered so many themes, running in parallel with the development of both de Havilland and Hatfield, that this book has turned into a social commentary as much as anything else. The early days of commercial aerial photography are particularly fascinating. My thanks go to Katy Whitaker, Elizabeth Freshwater, and their colleagues at English Heritage for helping with some great material from the Aerofilms Collection. I could never have compiled a complete account of Hatfield's part in air racing between the Wars without expert research and advice from Terry Mace of aFleetingPeace.org and Andrew Dawrant of the Royal Aero Club Trust. An unexpected area of interest was the relationship between Hatfield Aerodrome and the film studios at Elstree and Welwyn. Jaume and Elisa Giro, Bob Redman, and Massimo Moretti were a big help with this. Those who could afford to fly in the 1920s and 1930s may have been privileged, but they were also pioneers who took great risks. Thanks go especially to Michael Traynor for helping me to piece together the sad tale of Sicele O'Brien.

And finally to the subject of the de Havilland Aircraft Co., and to those who were either part of the story when the Hatfield factory was operating or are, today, preserving such a proud past. Philip Birtles, who worked with chief test pilot John Cunningham, has been exceptionally generous with his photo collection. Ian Grace, of the de Havilland Flying Club in the USA, has kindly shared with me some great material from his father's time with the company at both Stag Lane and Hatfield. Ralph Steiner, Geoff Follett, and their colleagues at the de Havilland Aircraft Heritage Centre at Salisbury Hall, near London Colney, have been a great support. My hope is that this book will bring valuable publicity to their cause. Roger de Mercado and his fellow former-apprentices of the de Havilland Aeronautical Technical School Association have provided me with a lot of essential information. Another great source of de Havilland-related archive material has been Hatfield's Mill Green Museum, and I have received valuable assistance from staff members Rosemary Lee-Bapty, Julie Godden, and Jenny Oxley. Malcolm Fillmore's databases are unmissable for tracking down the histories of individual aircraft, and he has also been very kind in answering my endless questions. Stuart MacKay, of the de Havilland Moth Club, has been most helpful with his infinite knowledge and experience.

My greatest appreciation on this point goes to Janic Geelen of NZaviationpress.co.nz and Dave Robinson. I could not have fully pieced together the developments in aviation from contemporary sources relating to de Havilland and Hatfield without Dave's tireless research and support, or his amazing period magazine archive. He has been a constant support throughout the entire project. Janic's willingness to share his huge knowledge of de Havilland history and the MacRobertson air race, his patience with my never-ending questions, his generosity in sharing his extensive archive, and his time in reviewing the entire book are beyond my thanks.

This book would not be so well-illustrated without generous financial support from two sources: Eisai Europe Ltd, whose EMEA Knowledge Centre in Hatfield stands on the site of the original factory; the Hatfield branch of the Alliance to Reward Initiatives & Social Enterprise (ARISE Hatfield)—founded by Land Securities Group plc and supported by the Galleria shopping centre, Hatfield House and the University of Hertfordshire. I am most grateful to all those who helped me to secure this valuable sponsorship. I would particularly like to thank the artist Marek Radomski, who kindly granted me permission to use his side-profiles of de Havilland aircraft. Barry Guess, of the BAE Systems archive at Farnborough, has also been most helpful with guidance on using many images that originated with de Havilland.

Finally, special thanks go to those who have made this whole experience bearable. Living in Norfolk and working in Hatfield meant a lot of travelling and staying away overnight. Sam and Rebecca Wheatley and their family welcomed me into their home every week for the entire time I was writing the book, and provided me with a most pleasant and comfortable environment in which to work. I greatly value their friendship and kindness. My wife, my parents, and my mother-in-law have also been very kind and supportive, reading every word of the book with a careful eye.

John Clifford
Norfolk, August 2014

Foreword

The story of pioneering aviator Geoffrey de Havilland, and the aircraft company he founded, is one of the foremost aviation success stories of the 20th century. From the most tentative beginnings grew one of the world's leading aircraft manufacturers. Knowingly or otherwise, we have all benefited in many ways from de Havilland's legacy—from the rise of air power in the First World War, to the emergence of commercial and private aviation in the inter-war years, to the unequalled Mosquito (the world's first multi-role combat aircraft) during the Second World War, and to the dawn of the jet age, with military fighters and the world's first commercial jet airliner (the Comet). We should also not forget that the vast majority of pilots during the Second World War trained on de Havilland Tiger Moths, fitted with de Havilland Gipsy engines, and well over 100,000 de Havilland propellers were fitted to RAF aircraft during that conflict.

But it was the heady twenties and thirties that were undoubtedly the 'golden years' for de Havillands, when a small wooden two-seater, named 'the Moth', emerged from the Stag Lane sheds in 1925 and transformed aviation for all time. Pioneers such as Jim Mollison, Amy Johnson, Jean Batten, and so many others used de Havilland Moths to 'trail blaze' and set records across the globe, while Sir Alan Cobham opened up new commercial routes across the continents. All of this was achieved in tiny, open-cockpit biplanes—something to think about these days, while we sip our gin and tonic and watch a movie as we jet our way, effortlessly, from one side of the world to the other.

With his helper Frank Hearle, and an engine built to his own design, Geoffrey de Havilland had flown his first successful aeroplane from a field at Seven Barrows, in Hampshire, in 1910. Design work at Farnborough followed, resulting in a series of highly successful First World War fighter, bomber, and trainer designs—but, after the Armistice, the world of aviation pivoted to the opening up of commercial air services and the new world of private aircraft ownership. By 1920, de Havilland had leased land at Stag Lane, Middlesex, and the fledgling de Havilland Aircraft Company was born. But by the late twenties the airfield was coming under increasing pressure from suburban housing development, and de Havilland began a search for a more open area in which to relocate his company. He found and purchased fields at Hatfield, Hertfordshire, that were considered suitable—the great trek from Stag Lane to Hatfield was put in motion.

The history of the de Havilland Aircraft Company and its aircraft are well-documented, and has been covered in numerous publications over the years. But, in this book, John Clifford has achieved something new: he has placed the company firmly in the context of the Hatfield area, outlining the rich history of Hertfordshire. In 1930, the first element of the de Havilland enterprise to be relocated to the new Hatfield aerodrome was the de Havilland Flying School, followed by the London Aeroplane Club and the de Havilland Aeronautical Technical School, all of which benefitted from new, modern premises while the new aircraft factory was under construction. The move was finally completed in 1934, leaving only engine manufacture in the old Stag Lane works—now engulfed by neat new streets of suburban housing that completely swallowed the old airfield.

The move proved to be a highly successful one, and during the thirties the large new aerodrome at Hatfield was a hive of aviation activity of all varieties. In addition to the test-flying and delivery of new aircraft, the London Aeroplane Club became a prominent social centre. The RAF Flying Club provided more activity, and pilot training by the de Havilland School of Flying increased rapidly as the RAF expansion plan addressed the need to train more pilots as the clouds of war gathered once again. Through the thirties, de Havillands regularly fielded their latest products in the annual and prestigious King's Cup air races, hosted at Hatfield, which drew crowds of thousands and provided tremendous publicity for the company's products.

Although I now live and work in Seattle, I have a close connection with de Havilland's. My father joined DH's as young apprentice in 1920, when the company was first established at Stag Lane, and retired after the War, having managed the production of just over 3,000 Mosquitos at Hatfield between 1941 and 1945. In 1942 he married a nurse (my mother), and she joined DH's as an industrial nurse, at DH's No. 2 factory at Leavesden. Their wartime stories of DH's would fill another book! I grew up nearby, with the sight and sound of DH Trident airliners overhead on flight-test from Hatfield, not to mention the roar of Blue Streak missiles being tested in the test bed on the aerodrome.

Last month, on a visit to England, I visited the old aerodrome at Hatfield for old time's sake. The visit was tinged with sadness for me, as so much of the old works that I remember from my childhood has now been obliterated by a modern business park and a shopping centre. The historic runway, from which rose so many new aircraft, is long gone. However, some of the original DH buildings have been preserved, and the names of new access roads that now criss-cross what was the old aerodrome recall some of the famous DH aircraft types, executives, designers, and test pilots that will forever be a part of the history of Hatfield. Hopefully, locals and visitors alike will long be reminded of the history that was made under their feet.

Ian Grace
Chairman, de Havilland Flying Club, USA
August 2014

Introduction

All of the streets around Hatfield Business Park today are named after famous aircraft, pilots, designers, and executives of the de Havilland Aircraft Co., which occupied and expanded its operations on the site from 1930. The factory was owned by British Aerospace from 1977 and closed in 1993—BAE Systems still owns the site today.

A few original buildings remain: de Havilland's global headquarters 'Admin Block', and the canteen and restaurant block of 1934, used as Hatfield police station since 2009, and the factory gatehouse; the personnel block, built during the Second World War; and the 1950s flight hangar, now a health club and hotel. The other notable building nearby is the Comet hotel of 1936. The rest of the site was redeveloped from the late 1990s with commercial buildings, homes, and the de Havilland Campus of the University of Hertfordshire.

Many people will be aware of the significance of some of the street names on and around the Business Park, such as Tiger Moth Way, Mosquito Way, Comet Way, and Trident Place. But what about Bishop Square, Clarkson Court, Cunningham Avenue, Dragon Road, Gypsy Moth Avenue (it should be 'Gipsy'), Halford Court, Hearle Way, Queen Bee Court, Waight Court, and Walker Grove? What went on at Hatfield Aerodrome in the early years? Who visited, by land or air? How did the factory come to be built there? What effect did this have on the town, and how soon did the worsening international politics of the 1930s touch Hatfield, because of the factory's presence?

This is the story of de Havilland in Hatfield, during the 'Golden Years' of aviation.

1

Before Powered Flight

> When I was still very young ... looking out of the same window listening to the sounds of a fête a mile away in Nuneaton.... Suddenly a great balloon rose up from the town, climbing steadily and fast and high into the sky. Fascinated, we watched it until it finally disappeared in the far distance and at a great height ... we would talk occasionally about flying and the practicability of man one day conquering the air.
>
> *Geoffrey de Havilland*

Successive Conquests

The Old-English 'Scir' or 'Shire' of Hertford was a territory created in AD 959, administered from a wooden motte-and-bailey castle built at Hertford in AD 912–913. The name 'Hertford' comes from 'heort ford' in Anglo-Saxon, meaning a place where deer cross a river—in this case the River Lea. The 'hart', or stag, remains the symbol of the Shire, which included the early Anglo-Saxon settlement of 'Haethfeld' or 'Heathtfield', just to the south-west of the river.

During (or perhaps before) Roman times the area had been settled by the Belgae tribe, who were from an area of Western Europe that includes the modern country named after them. After the decline of Roman Britain, land to the east of the Lea was settled from the sixth to the eighth centuries by the East Saxons—becoming the kingdom of Essex. From AD 825, Essex came under the control of the West Saxons—the kingdom of Wessex. Land to the west of the Lea, including Heathfield, was within the Angle kingdom of Mercia, which stretched away to the north-west and covered the English Midlands. Many minor place names in the area end with the Old-English word 'Hyde'. This referred to a piece of land, varying from 60 to 120 acres, considered necessary to support one extended family.

The Viking invasions of the ninth century brought Essex and Mercia, plus the other Angle kingdoms of Northumbria and East Anglia, under the rule of the Danish 'jarls', or 'earls'. Only Wessex was able to maintain a resistance. Under

King Alfred the Great, the West Saxons pushed the Danes back to an agreed border line in AD 886. This followed the River Lea at its southernmost end, and stretched north-westwards along the old Roman road of Watling Street, as far as the Welsh border. Territory to the north and east of the line was called the 'Danelaw'.

Wessex continued the re-conquest in the early tenth century, under Alfred's son Edward the Elder. They pushed north and east into Danish Mercia and East Anglia, building fortresses like the one at Hertford as they went. Edward's son, Æthelstan, completed the re-conquest by defeating Danish Northumbria in AD 927. He united the Anglo-Saxon-Danish kingdoms under one monarchy for the first time, becoming the first King of 'Englaland' (Land of the Angles). King Edgar the Peaceable, grandson of Edward the Elder, created the Shire of Hertford and appointed a 'Scirgerefa'—later spelled as Shire Reeve or 'Sheriff'—as its governor. Edgar gave 5,000 acres, including Haethfeld, to the Abbey of Ely in AD 970. The Danes would only respect the Danelaw line as long as they received the 'Danegeld' tax from the Anglo-Saxons beyond it. Haethfeld had to contribute its share, half of which was paid by the Abbey.

After the Norman Conquest of 1066, the English shires and earldoms continued to form the network of regional government. Being under the control of French-speaking Norman lords such as counts, each area was referred to in Old French as a 'conté' or 'county', hence the 'County of Hertfordshire'. The Doomsday Book was compiled by the Normans in 1086 for calculating taxation. According to the Anglo-Saxon Chronicle, the Normans 'sent men all over England to each shire to find out what or how much each landholder had in land and livestock, and what it was worth'. Hetfelle, as the Normans pronounced it, is named as a 'terra' (land) held by the 'Abbatis de Ely'. North Mymms, just to the south, is described as a Danish settlement.

King William I granted Hertford Castle and nearby lands to one of his Norman supporters, Peter de Valoignes, who was appointed as sheriff of both Hertfordshire and Essex. The Doomsday Book records other lands given to Valoignes in Norfolk, Suffolk, Cambridgeshire, and Lincolnshire. The Sieur de Havylland, another of William's knights, is not recorded in The Doomsday Book as holding property in England, so it would seem that he returned to his lands in Normandy after the Conquest. Other de Havyllands are found in later medieval documents, and

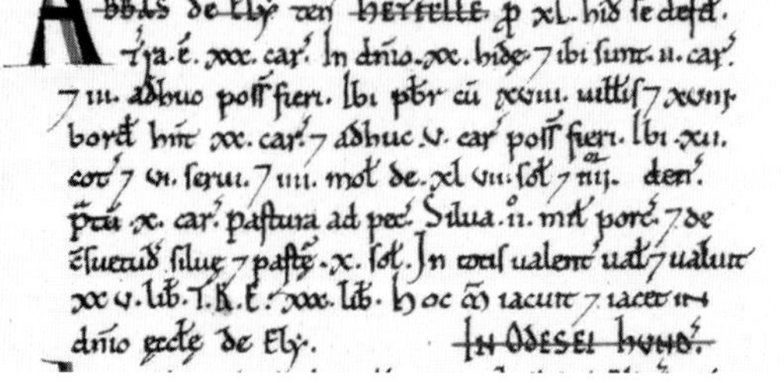
TERRA ABBATIS DE ELY

Hetfelle is recorded in the Doomsday Book of 1086 as "*terra*" (land) which belongs to the 'Abbatis de Ely'. (*Professor John Palmer and George Slater, University of Hull*)

held positions of authority in Guernsey. Peter de Valoignes' successor, Robert de Mancell, rebuilt Hertford Castle in stone between 1170 and 1174; part of this still stands.

Centuries of Peace

The Bishopric of Ely was created in 1109, and the property of Hatfield was transferred from the Abbot to the Bishop. The town became known as 'Bishop's Hatfield', which is still the name of the Church of England parish today. A palace was built for the Bishop in the thirteenth century, and the parish church, dedicated to St Etheldreda and first built in wood, was founded by monks from Ely in 1285. The original Anglo-Saxon form of the saint's name was Æthelthryth. She was an East-Anglian princess and Queen of Northumbria; in the AD 670s, she became Abbess of Ely. The spelling of her name was later Latinised as 'Aldreda', and then re-Anglicised as 'Aldrey', from which the medieval French form of 'Audrey' arose. The tower of the present church building dates from the fifteenth century.

In the late fifteenth century, a new bishop's palace was built on the site of the original by Cardinal John Morton, Bishop of Ely and Lord Chancellor to King Henry VII. Hatfield became the property of King Henry VIII in 1538, during the Protestant Reformation, in exchange for lands given to the Bishopric of Ely that were made available from the Dissolution of the Monasteries. Elizabeth had been kept under house arrest at Hatfield by her sister Mary, but inherited the estate from Edward VI when she herself became queen. While sitting under an oak tree in the Palace's Great Park in 1558, news was brought to her that she had become Queen following Mary's death. She held her first council in the palace's Great Hall. The only surviving wing is still used today for Elizabethan-style banquets.

King James I inherited the royal estate at Hatfield on Elizabeth's death in 1603. However, he preferred the Theobalds estate of his Lord Treasurer, Robert Cecil, just beyond the south-east corner of Hatfield's parish, between Cuffley and Cheshunt. Cecil was a supporter of the King in those politically turbulent times, and agreed to an exchange; he was given a succession of titles, becoming the first Earl of Salisbury in 1605. The Old Palace had fallen into a poor state of repair, so Cecil demolished most of it and had Hatfield House built on the site between 1607 and 1612. Its plan is the shape of the letter 'E', for Elizabeth, and it contains many fine examples of Jacobean craftsmanship. The House has entertained royalty and other important visitors many times, including the diarist Samuel Pepys in the 1660s.

James Cecil, Lord Chamberlain to King George III and Lord Lieutenant of Hertfordshire, was given the new title Marquess of Salisbury in 1789 for his services to the British Government. His son, James B. W. Cecil, second Marquess of Salisbury, married Frances Mary Gascoyne in 1821 and added her surname to his. To commemorate the visit to Hatfield by Queen Victoria and Prince Albert

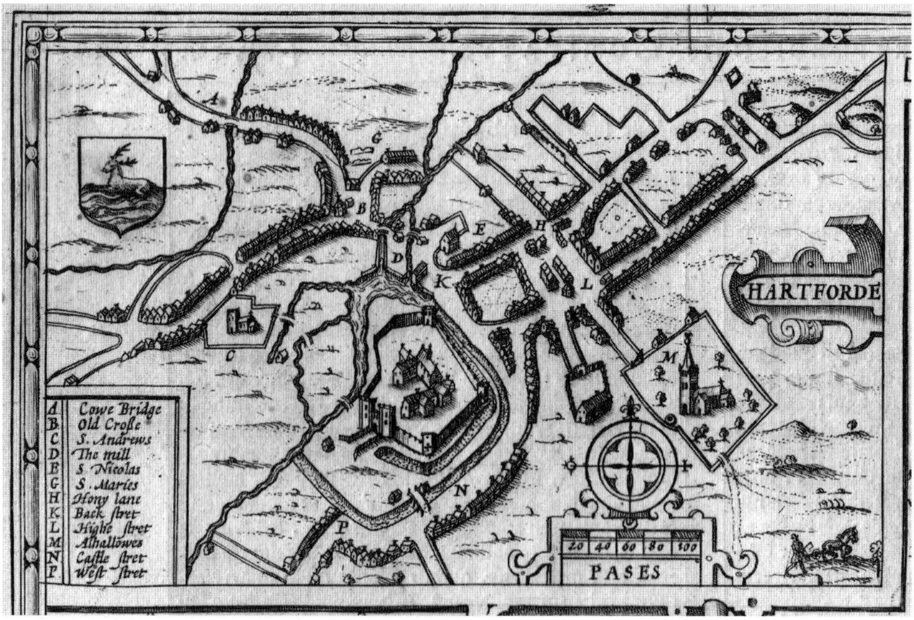

Detail from John Speed's map of Hertfordshire, first published in 1611, showing Hertford Castle. It is the only known map to show the castle still standing. (*Courtesy of Gillmark Antique Maps*)

in 1846, the second Marquess had a spire added to St Etheldreda's tower, which was completed in 1847. Robert A. T. Gascoyne-Cecil, the third Marquess, became Chancellor of Oxford University. More importantly, he was Prime Minister three times between 1885 and 1902, and was the last member of the House of Lords to hold the office.

Hatfield house remains the home of the Marquesses of Salisbury to this day, and has featured in many films including: *Batman*, *Shakespeare In Love*, *Sleepy Hollow*, *Tomb Raider*, *Charlie & the Chocolate Factory*, *Elizabeth: The Golden Age*, *Sherlock Holmes*, *The King's Speech*, and *Harry Potter & the Deathly Hallows*.

The Great North Road

The north-south road that passed through Hatfield was a route between London and the North from the twelfth century. Due to the deterioration of the old Roman road (Ermine Street), the principal route from the seventeenth century was the one that went through Hatfield. From that time onwards it became known as the 'Great North Road'. Horse-drawn mail coaches used it in the nineteenth century.

Under the Ministry of Transport's road numbering scheme of 1921, the 'Old

A late-Victorian engraving of Hatfield town showing St Etheldreda's, with its spire added, in 1847. The clock tower of Hatfield House is visible in the background. The spire was added in 1847 but, structurally, it was not a success and it would be removed in 1930. (Our Own Country: Vol 2, *Cassell Petter Galpin & Co, 1890, via hertfordshire-genealogy.co.uk*)

Postcard of Hatfield House, mailed in 1905 but first printed in 1886—when Robert Gascoyne-Cecil, 3rd Marquess of Salisbury, was Prime Minister for the second of his three terms. (*hertfordshire-genealogy.co.uk*)

North Road' was designated as the A10, the Great North Road as the A1, and the old Watling Street as the A5. Hatfield's bypass, built in 1927 and running up the west side of the town, was the northern end of the A555 Barnet Bypass. In 1954, to encourage through-traffic away from Barnet, Potters Bar, Hatfield, and Welwyn, the A1 was re-designated as the A1000, and the Barnet Bypass became the A1. From 1962, 24 miles of the A1 through Hertfordshire were gradually upgraded to Motorway standard as the A1 (M). This included the construction of the Hatfield Tunnel in 1986, which bypasses Comet Way by taking the A1 underground for 1,531 yards.

The First Landing in England

Captain Vincenzo Lunardi was Secretary to Prince Caramanico, the Neapolitan Ambassador to England. Lunardi was caught up in the balloon-flying craze that had been started in France by the Montgolfier brothers in 1783. He and his associate, George Biggin, decided to give a flying demonstration with a balloon made of oiled silk panels, which was coloured red and blue. They secured permission to use the training ground of the Honourable Artillery Company in Finsbury, near Moorfields in London, as the starting point for their attempt of 15 September 1784.

The balloon was inflated with hydrogen, which was produced by the reaction of zinc with sulphuric acid—then known as 'oil of vitriol'. Lunardi was unable to take off with Biggin, so he decided to ascend accompanied by a dog, a cat, and a caged pigeon. The wind took them north over Hertfordshire; the cat became distressed, so Lunardi descended. He landed in a corn field near North Mymms and Welham Green, on the Great North Road, about 2 miles south of Hatfield—a stone's throw from where much of this book was written. This was the first landing place of a manned flight in England. A stone in Welham Green, at the junction of Dellsome Lane, Parsonage Lane, and Huggins Lane, commemorates the event. It is known as Balloon Corner to this day.

Lunardi left the cat in the care of a local woman—the inscription on the 'Balloon Stone' says that he also handed her the dog, whereas other accounts don't—and set off again over Hatfield Park. He eventually landed at Standon Green End, Thundridge, near Ware, 24 miles from his starting point. Another 'Balloon Stone' marks this spot. He then exhibited the balloon at the Pantheon on Oxford Street, in London. This scene was recreated by Alexander Korda in his 1936 dramatised documentary, *Conquest of the Air*, which was commissioned by the Air Ministry of the British Government. Laurence Olivier played Lunardi, who described himself as the 'first aerial traveller in the English atmosphere'.

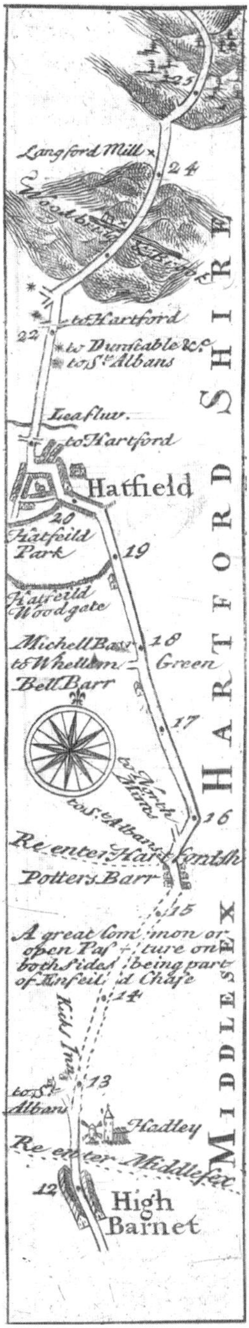

Left: Detail from a 'strip map' by Owen & Bowen, 1720—the Great North Road from Barnet through Potters Bar, Welham Green, and Hatfield, included in the first true pocket road book in the world. These were based on John Ogilby's Britannia atlas of 1675—the first maps of Britain to use a fixed distance of 1,760 yards for the mile, to a constant scale of one inch per mile. (*Courtesy of Gillmark Antique Maps*)

LUNARDI'S BALLOON.

Above right: Capt. Vincenzo Lunardi and his air balloon. On 15 September 1784, he ascended from the training ground of the Honourable Artillery Company in Finsbury, near Moorfields, in London. He descended near North Mymms and Welham Green, making the first landing in England, about 2 miles south of Hatfield. (*Robert Chambers*, Book of Days, *1864*)

The Railways

The Great Northern Railway Act of 1846 was proposed to Parliament during the railway mania of the 1840s. After negotiation with land owners such as the second Marquess of Salisbury, the GNR's first 20 miles—with bridges, cuttings, and tunnels—were built by 1849. A London terminus was opened at Kings Cross in 1852. The next stations included Finsbury Park, Potters Bar, Welham Green, and (at 17.7 miles out) Hatfield. A 'Newtown' had been built, in readiness, in 1848, which became the centre of Hatfield's twentieth-century expansion. Because Newtown was built 'way out west' of the old town, it was nicknamed 'California', a well-known destination during the Gold Rush of 1849.

The second Marquess also took the opportunity to re-route the Great North Road to its present position, outside his estate, following the line of the railway. A short road viaduct was later built to connect Hatfield House with the railway station, so that Lord Salisbury could be taken between the two, with dignity, in his carriage. While he was Prime Minister, the third Marquess had his own train as well. The Hall family had a grand home, Hill House, built next to the viaduct. They had been living in Hatfield for over 100 years, and had recently become relatives of the Guernsey de Havillands through marriage.

Hatfield was also the junction with a branch line to St Albans, built with GNR support and opened in 1865. The line headed briefly north-west from Hatfield station, but quickly turned south-west between Birchwood, Roe Green, and Ellenbrook—although this was all farmland then.

Continuing west, past Smallford and after a short stretch of countryside to Hill End, the Hatfield & St Albans Railway (H&StAR) entered St Albans with a station on London Road. The Midland Railway (MR) main line from London St Pancras, which opened in 1868, crossed over the branch line at this point, and added its own station at St Albans with services to Luton and beyond. The branch line ended at St Albans Abbey station, which was built in 1858 as the terminus for services from London Euston via Watford. This competition for London services meant that the H&StAR was never viable for connecting to services to Kings Cross. It was absorbed by the GNR in 1883.

Hatfield was also the starting point for GNR services to Luton, Dunstable, and Leighton Buzzard, and also to Hertingfordbury and Hertford. In 1868, a track was laid from Hatfield, alongside the GNR main line, for a few miles to the north as far as Welwyn. From there, the Luton line branched off westwards and the Hertford line eastwards. These branch lines had been built by the Hertford, Luton & Dunstable Railway, and opened between 1858 and 1860. They were soon absorbed by the GNR in 1861.

Many of the locomotives that pulled trains back and forth on these lines were designed by Patrick Stirling, Henry A. Ivatt, and H. Nigel Gresley. Stirling was the GNR's Locomotive Superintendent until his death in 1895. Ivatt was his

Postcard of Smallford station, on the Hatfield & St Albans Railway branch of the GNR, mailed in 1904. The locomotive is possibly a Class G2 0-4-4WT, designed by Patrick Stirling. The dark structure at this end of the platform is an outdoor iron urinal. (*The John Alsop Collection*)

Postcard of Hatfield station, printed in the early 1930s but first published in 1904. The GNR train is being hauled by a Class E1 2-4-0 locomotive, developed from a Stirling design by Henry A. Ivatt. (*The John Alsop Collection*)

successor, and retired as chief engineer in 1911. He was followed by Gresley, as chief mechanical engineer.

The GNR ended just after Doncaster. Beyond this was the North Eastern Railway (NER) and North British Railway (NBR). Together, they became known as the 'East Coast Main Line'. Under the Railways Act of 1921, they would be merged from 1923 as the London & North Eastern Railway (LNER). The GNR built an additional branch line from London to Stevenage, via Cuffley and Hertford, in 1910. This started carrying passenger traffic from 1924, from which time Hatfield was no longer the main rail route to Hertford.

A station was built for the new town of Welwyn Garden City in 1926. Gresley would live at Salisbury Hall, near London Colney, from 1931 until 1937, and would lead LNER locomotive development until his death in 1941. During the War a private 'halt' would be built on the St Albans branchline at Lemsford Road, in 1942, to help de Havilland employees get to work without using cars. Passenger services on all three branchlines would end in the 1950s, and freight traffic would cease in the 1960s.

Ordnance Survey map of Hatfield in 1925. The branchline to St Albans turns away from the East Coast Main Line and heads south-west, past Newtown. The land between Newtown and Harpsfield Hall, to the left of the map, would become Hatfield Aerodrome from 1930. (© *Crown Copyright—Old Maps & Ordnance Survey, www.old-maps.co.uk*)

2

Encounters with Early Aeroplanes

'I'm afraid I don't know much about aeroplanes anyway, and almost no theory at all,' I said lamely. 'I shouldn't worry about that,' O'Gorman replied cheerfully. 'Very few people know anything really reliable about them. It's still mostly a matter of trial and error.'

Geoffrey de Havilland, November 1910

Hatfield Gliders

Flight magazine was launched in January 1909. The 17 April 1909 edition contained an article about the Aero Club League's display of models of powered aircraft and gliders. These were shown at the Olympia exhibition centre in West Kensington, London. One of the models represented the Wright Flyer, which had achieved the world's first controlled, powered flight in 1903. Other models were provided by Blackburn and Short Brothers, and one was of a Voisin machine used by Henry Farman. Another of the models was named as the *Hatfield*, a 'Biplane with arched surfaces concave to each other. The tail is similarly arranged.'

There was great interest in aviation around the country in the early days of powered flight. In their 15 January 1910 edition, *Flight* magazine had to publish this disclaimer: 'Owing to the great mass of valuable and interesting correspondence which we receive, immediate publication is impossible, but each letter will appear practically in sequence and at the earliest possible moment.' A letter published in the 28 May 1910 edition of *Flight* revealed that active national interest included a J. McC. Clive of Hatfield, who commented on wing design. Had he contributed the *Hatfield* model at the Olympia show? He had now constructed 'a small glider with the dropping wing-tip, and found it almost uncapsizable ... [it] not only increases stability, but is almost totally unaffected by wind gusts'. This was the first time that the town was mentioned in this historic and long-running publication.

There are ancient reports from around the world of 'heavier than air' structures (without the use of a balloon) that could lift a man, such as kites. But modern glider design, to which Mr Clive was contributing, began in the nineteenth century. Sir George Cayley successfully flew a model glider in 1804, and published his work *On Aerial Navigation* in 1809–10. This was original research, conducted on his estate in Yorkshire, on aerodynamic lift, drag, and thrust, and discussed designs of fuselage, wing, tail, and control surface structures. Cayley started achieving brief 'hops' with manned gliders in around 1849. All aeroplanes designed since are based on the principles he identified. Many other pioneers followed Cayley's principles and achieved increasing success. In America, the Wright brothers experimented with gliders before installing an engine in their Wright Flyer. In 1911, they removed the engine from one of their later designs and resumed glider experiments.

Meanwhile...

Two pages before Mr Clive's letter, another letter was published on the power and weight of an aero-engine, built by the Iris Motor Co. to the writer's own design. He had recently displayed the engine at the Olympia Aero Show, where Frederick Handley Page had kindly made room on his stand. Other exhibitors included Blériot, Farman, Short Bros, and A. V. Roe, with his new *Avroplane*. Short's had become the world's first aircraft factory when they built Wright Flyers under licence in 1908.

The correspondent was a 27-year-old engineer who had salvaged his engine from the wreck of his *Biplane No.1*, after its one and only flight of about 100 feet (33 m) in December 1909. His name was Geoffrey de Havilland. He had been busy in a workshop on Bothwell Street in Fulham, west London, designing and building the aircraft with help from his friend Frank Hearle. It was a biplane, with the engine driving two propellers at the back that pushed the aircraft through the air.

Geoffrey was the second son of Reverend Charles de Havilland, rector of the parish of Crux Easton, in north-east Hampshire. Here and at his maternal grandfather's estate—Medley Manor in Oxfordshire—Geoffrey enjoyed nature while growing up, with an interest in moths and other insects. His older brother was Ivon, their sisters were Ione and Gladys, and their little brother was Hereward. They were half-cousins to two Hollywood actresses—the sisters Olivia de Havilland and Joan Fontaine (Joan took her step-father's name). Reverend de Havilland and the sisters' father were half-brothers.

It was Ivon who was with Geoffrey when they saw the balloon rise out of Nuneaton in the 1880s. They later enjoyed experimenting with electrics, steam engines, cars, and motorbikes. In 1896, when they were aged 17 and 14, they installed a coal-powered Brush Electrical Engineering Co. dynamo to provide electric lighting for their father's rectory. They later replaced it with a Crossley oil-fired generator. Ivon worked for Brush in Loughborough, and Daimler in Coventry. He got married and became chief designer at the Iris Motor Co. in

Willesden, north-west London, introducing his brother to his colleagues. Ivon's 'Iris' car design received acclaim at the 1905 Olympia Motor Show; sadly, he was too ill to attend the show. Weakened by overwork, he died from influenza on 3 December that year.

Geoffrey studied at the Crystal Palace School of Engineering. His apprenticeship was with Willans & Robinson, a steam engine and turbine manufacturer in Rugby. In 1905, he worked as a draughtsman in Birmingham for the Wolseley Tool & Motor Car Co. Ltd. John D. Siddeley was their London sales manager, and soon became managing director. In 1906, de Havilland joined the London design office of the Motor Omnibus Construction Co. Ltd (MOC), where he met Frank Hearle. They left MOC in 1907 to start working on *Biplane No.1*, lodging together with Ione as their housekeeper. For expenses, they borrowed £1,000 (£105,000 today) from de Havilland's maternal grandfather, Jason Saunders, who was a former Mayor of Oxford. A. V. Roe visited their workshop, and they visited his. In May 1909 Geoffrey de Havilland married Louise Thomas. 'Louie' had been governess to the younger children and a companion-help to their mother; she stitched the aircraft's dope-stiffened cotton panels on her Singer sewing machine. Frank and Ione would marry in December 1914.

They completed the machine in a shed originally intended for aviation pioneer John T. C. Moore-Brabazon. This was at Seven Barrows, below Beacon Hill, on

Geoffrey de Havilland's wife, Louie, stitching the aircraft's cotton panels on her Singer sewing machine. The expression on Louie's face may be due to the fact that the fabric was pre-stiffened with doping fluid. (*The Norman Eastaff Collection*)

Lord Carnarvon's Highclere estate in north-east Hampshire. In Egypt, in 1922, Lord Carnarvon would discover Tutankhamun's tomb with Howard Carter. Highclere Castle is now internationally famous as the filming location for TV's *Downton Abbey*. Brabazon was an early member of the Royal Aero Club, with Charles S. Rolls and the Short brothers. In May 1909, he had made the first powered aeroplane flight by an Englishman in England in his Voisin. He visited the shed with Lord Carnarvon, and took an interest in de Havilland's progress.

Seven Barrows was 3 miles north of Crux Easton. Revd de Havilland hid behind a shed, unable to watch his son's first attempt at flight, so Frank and Hereward were the only witnesses. Geoffrey and Frank then built the similar *Biplane No.2*, and returned to Seven Barrows for the first successful flight in September 1910. Geoffrey grew in confidence and started taking passengers, including Louie and their eight-month-old son, Geoffrey Jnr.

Above: The wreck of the de Havilland *Biplane No.1*, December 1909. It needed more than piano wire and bicycle wheels. (*The Norman Eastaff Collection*)

Below: Biplane No.1's Iris-built engine after its 'maiden crash', in the shed at Seven Barrows, in north-east Hampshire, where the aircraft had been assembled. (*The Norman Eastaff Collection*)

The Royal Aircraft Factory

Balloons had preceded aeroplanes in military use, although even balloons had not been considered by the British military until nearly 100 years after Lunardi's first ascent in London, and landing near Hatfield, in 1784. The School of Ballooning, established in 1878, was renamed as the Balloon Factory in 1897. By 1906 it had moved to Farnborough Common, near Aldershot in Hampshire. It was known as His Majesty's Aircraft Factory from 1911, reflecting a new focus on aeroplanes. The Factory's main purpose was research. It was not officially authorised to build its own designs, so its early creations used parts from other aircraft and were dubiously described as 'repairs'.

Mervyn O'Gorman, the Factory's Superintendent until 1916, founded the science of aeronautics in Britain. He was an Irish motoring pioneer, and published *O'Gorman's Motoring Pocket Book* in 1904. He was also active in the Royal Automobile Club, becoming its vice-president. He would also be involved in producing *The Highway Code* of 1931, still published today as a guide for driver behaviour on British roads. Frederick M. Green was the Royal Aircraft Factory's chief design engineer. He had left Daimler in 1909 and begun government research for developing military aeroplanes. He had worked with de Havilland's brother Ivon at Daimler, and had known Geoffrey since then.

Green met de Havilland and Hearle at the Olympia Motor Show in November 1910. At Green's suggestion, de Havilland sold his *Biplane No.2* to the Factory for £400 (£41,000 today) and asked O'Gorman for a job; the aeroplane was the first to be owned by the British Government. Samuel F. Cody, an American, and A. V. Roe had retained ownership of the previous machines to be tested. Cody had made the first flight of a powered aeroplane in Britain in 1908, with his British Army Aeroplane No.1.

The Factory took de Havilland on as a designer and test pilot in early 1911. He only accepted the job on the condition that Hearle was also taken on. He then moved to Farnborough with his wife and young son, Geoffrey Jnr. The Factory modified and re-designated his aircraft as the F.E.1, as it was similar to designs by the Farman brothers—French aviation was more advanced at the time. The 'E' stood for 'Experimental'.

Circuit of Britain Air Race of 1911

The skies around Hatfield witnessed some notable flights in the twenty years before de Havilland established its Aerodrome to the west of the town. The first *Daily Mail* Circuit of Britain air race, with a prize of £10,000 (£1m today), was held in July–August 1911. The competitors started on their 1,010-mile adventure at Brooklands, in Surrey. Aircraft that competed were built by Blackburn, Blériot, Breguet, Bristol, Cody, Deperdussin, Morane, and Nieuport.

Geoffrey de Havilland sits in his *Biplane No.2*, being inspected by Frank Hearle, in early 1911. It had been renamed by the Royal Aircraft Factory as the F.E.1 after he sold it to them –the first military aircraft owned by the British government. (*RAE 051, the Norman Eastaff Collection*)

An Austrian pilot, Lt Heinrich Bier, entered with a monoplane designed by his fellow countryman Ignaz Etrich, and built by the Lohner-Werke factory in Vienna. The bird-like aircraft was named the 'Taube', meaning dove or pigeon—or 'Renntaube' in this case, meaning 'racing pigeon'—and had warping wing tips for changing direction. It was the only aircraft in the race to carry a passenger.

Section 1 of the race was from Brooklands to Hendon. Section 2 was much longer, stretching 345 miles to Edinburgh, with the first control point at Harrogate, after 182 miles. A direct course from Hendon to Harrogate took the competitors over the 3 miles of countryside through which the railway branch line ran between Hatfield and St Albans.

The Army Manoeuvres of 1912

At the Royal Aircraft Factory in 1911, Geoffrey de Havilland developed the B.E.1 biplane, which had a 'tractor' propeller at the front to pull it through the air. He was assisted by Frederick Green and a promising young draughtsman named Henry Folland. They used a Wolseley V8 engine from a wrecked 'pusher' Voisin, although they later exchanged it for a Renault V8. The 'B' referred to the aircraft's Blériot-like layout. Other 'reconstructions' and blatantly new designs soon followed.

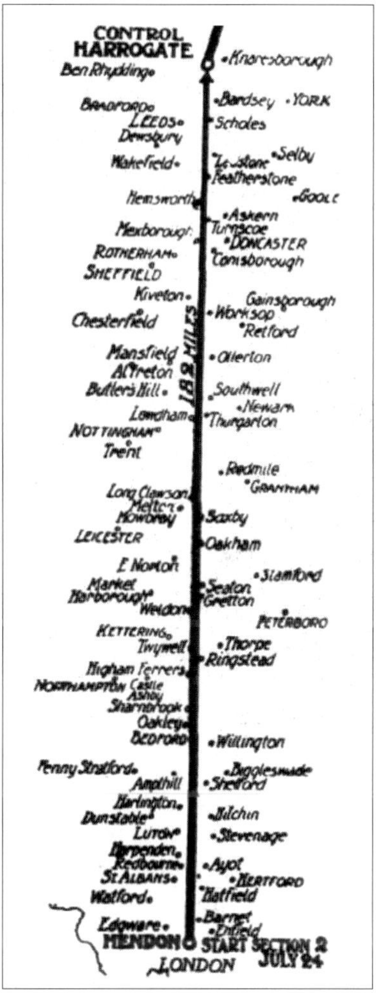

Right: Daily Mail Circuit of Britain—Section 2, 24 July 1911, from Hendon on to the first control point at Harrogate—shown in *Flight*, two days before the race. The route took competitors over the 3 miles of countryside between Hatfield and St Albans. (Flight, *via aviationancestry.com*)

Below: The wreck of the Etrich Taube monoplane, flown by Lt Heinrich Bier in the *Daily Mail Circuit of Britain* air race of 1911. He was forced to land heavily at Codicote, 6 miles north of Hatfield, and retired from the race. (*Courtesy of Tom Brearley*)

The Royal Flying Corps (RFC) was established in April 1912 with army and naval branches. In June, de Havilland reached an altitude of 10,560 feet in the B.E.2, the first of many records set with his aircraft. Maj. Frederick M. Sykes, the first commander of RFC's army branch, was his passenger. The B.E.2 was also the best-performer in the Army Aeroplane Competition that August. Three thousand would be built for the RFC. However, the Competition was officially for privately owned aircraft, and Cody's entry was given first prize. A. V. Roe, Deperdussin, Blériot, Breguet, Bristol-Coanda, Farman, Handley Page, and Vickers also entered aircraft.

Large-scale exercises in September 1912 involved tens of thousands of regulars and reservists. Based near Cambridge, Blue Force 'defended London' against Red Force, which approached from the East-Anglian coast. Hatfield was just to the south-west of the zone designated for infantry, cavalry, and artillery movements. On 2 September, a large group of men and wagons of the Army Service Corps and Royal Field Artillery spent an hour in the town, at around midday, to rest and feed their horses. They then continued to Standon, north of Ware, where they encamped for the night.

The RFC's army aeroplanes and airships, based at the Royal Aircraft Factory, conducted reconnaissance flights over the action. Maj. Charles J. Burke, one of the first army officers to consider military uses for aeroplanes, was the first commanding officer of RFC 2 Sqn; he flew the B.E.1 in the manoeuvres. Cody also flew his aircraft, as did de Havilland—the two pioneers had become good friends. With encouragement from Maj. Sykes, de Havilland joined the RFC Special Reserve (with the rank of 2nd Lieutenant) in order to take part. He flew a French Deperdussin monoplane, and also the B.E.2—a development of the B.E.1 that used a Renault V8 from the start. A Maj. Hugh M. Trenchard, who had served with the army in Africa and learned to fly with the Bristol Flying School at Brooklands, in July, was an aerial observer in the manoeuvres.

On 6 September, Major Burke was heading for Thetford, in Norfolk, with an RFC Captain as a passenger in the B.E.1. However, they had to find flat, open ground near Hatfield to make a landing—the first aircraft ever to do so. It was not uncommon for 'those magnificent men in their flying machines' to claim involuntary landings in the grounds of country houses when they were actually lost, or hoped to meet pretty girls, or to be invited to stay for lunch or tea. But Burke's reason was genuine on this occasion. According to the *Hertfordshire Mercury* for 7 September:

> Many of the inhabitants of Hatfield had their first near view of an aeroplane ...' Biplane 201' in a meadow belonging to Mr James Peart, of Woodhall Lodge, close to the GNR main line, shortly after 8 o'clock in the morning ... compelled to alight owing to the control wires of the steering gear becoming fouled. The officers ... at once telephoned to Aldershot for assistance.

Map of the army manoeuvres in 1912, from the *Souvenir and Official Programme*, published by Gale & Polden Ltd of Aldershot. Hatfield was just outside the south-western boundary. (*Cambridgeshire Collection, Cambridge Central Library*)

RFC pilots and observers gathered in Cambridge for the army manoeuvres in 1912. 2nd Lt Geoffrey de Havilland is seated at the far left. Major Frederick M. Sykes, first commander of the RFC's army branch, is seated at centre-right. (*The Paul R. Hare Collection*)

Postcard of the Royal Aircraft Factory B.E.1, designed by Geoffrey de Havilland and Frederick Green—only one example was built. It was flown by Major Charles J. Burke in the army manoeuvres of 1912. (*The Paul R. Hare Collection*)

Major Burke made a forced landing at Woodhall Farm, Hatfield Hyde, with fouled control wires. While they were waiting for a mechanic to arrive from Aldershot, sixty men, women, and children were photographed in front of the B.E.1. In the centre is William Horsey, a butcher in Fore Street, with his granddaughters Edith and Dorothy. Behind them is the embankment of the East Coast Main Line. (*Hertfordshire Libraries*)

The Pearts of Woodhall Farm, Hatfield Hyde, to the north of the town, were tenants of the Hatfield House estate. The area would become part of the new town of Welwyn Garden City, construction of which began in 1920. William Horsey had a butcher's shop in Fore Street, and used his horse and cart to quickly get up to Woodhall Farm, where a crowd was gathering. Sixty men, women, and children were photographed in front of the B.E.1—Horsey was in the centre, with his granddaughters Edith and Dorothy. George Bayliss, a signwriter in the town, and his son Ernest, were also there for the photograph, as were Harold Dunham, Johnny Moore, Eric Pegram, Cyril Dean, Bert Canham, and Les Graves. The crowd was certainly large by the time Burke attempted to take off again. The *Mercury* account continued:

> ...a sergeant mechanic arrived during the day and remedied the defect. About six o'clock in the evening the airmen attempted to proceed on their journey. Finding, however, that the oil pump of their Renault engine was not working satisfactorily they came to earth again in one of Mr Hunter's fields at Pear Tree farm ... the officers ... put up at the Red Lion Hotel. At five o'clock next morning they were up, and a successful ascent was made about seven o'clock.

The morning that Major Burke landed at Hatfield, Capt. Patrick Hamilton and Lt Atholl Wyness-Stuart were heading for a landing ground at the north-Hertfordshire village of Willian. At 7.10 a.m. their Deperdussin, which had come second in the army competition, disintegrated and fell, from at least 500 feet, into a field behind the George & Dragon pub in Graveley, just north of Stevenage. A Bristol-Coanda monoplane crashed four days later. These were the RFC's first fatal crashes; Geoffrey de Havilland immediately flew the B.E.2 to inspect one of the crash sites. The airmen were buried as selfless heroes. In response to public scepticism about the safety of flying, Major Burke stoically commented to the press, 'We fly when it is our duty to fly'. Consultations that included Green and de Havilland suspended the Military's use of monoplanes for the next twenty years. Frank Hearle left the Royal Aircraft Factory in 1912 to join Deperdussin. Cody would also be killed along with his passenger, cricketer William Evans, when his *Hydro-biplane* disintegrated at about 200 feet on 7 August 1913.

Geoffrey and Louie's second child, Peter, was born in 1913. That year, the 19-year-old Hereward de Havilland, who had himself joined the RFC, introduced his older brother to Frank B. Halford. Also aged 19, Halford learned to fly at Brooklands, and due to his natural talent he soon became an instructor there. Hugh Trenchard became Commandant of the Central Flying School in 1913, and it was at this time that de Havilland received a 'note' from Maj. Trenchard, '...asking if I knew anything about some army blankets that were missing. I replied rather tersely that I knew nothing about the blankets and had given mine in.' Both Trenchard and Halford would develop links with Hatfield in later years.

2nd Lt Geoffrey de Havilland at Farnborough in 1913, in the Royal Aircraft Factory B.E.2 in which he set a British altitude record of 10,500 feet (3,219 m) and flew in the army manoeuvres the previous year. He had developed the aircraft from the B.E.1, replacing its Wolseley V8 engine with a Renault V8. (*The Paul R. Hare Collection*)

The First World War

In January 1914, Geoffrey de Havilland was virtually ordered to join Farnborough's new Aeronautical Inspection Department. Halford also joined as an enthusiastic engine inspector, and was given the honorary rank of Lieutenant in the RFC at the end of the year. Despite still flying, de Havilland longed to return to designing. George Holt Thomas was founder of the Aircraft Manufacturing Co. (or 'Airco') at Hendon, in north-west London. He wanted a future for his company that involved more than just building Farmans under licence. When de Havilland offered to design aircraft for Airco, Holt Thomas liked the idea of competing with A. V. Roe, Blackburn, Bristol, Handley Page, and Short Bros for Government contracts. The deal was done, and de Havilland became Airco's chief designer and test pilot in July 1914. They leased a hangar from Claude Grahame-White's nearby London Flying Club. The de Havilland family moved to Edgware, also nearby.

Trenchard replaced Sykes as commander of the RFC's army branch on the outbreak of the First World War in August 1914. Geoffrey de Havilland was called up to join 2 Sqn, which was still commanded by Major Burke. For two weeks de Havilland flew anti-submarine patrols along the east coast of Scotland, using Blériot monoplanes. The War Office then recalled him to London, to continue his design work for Airco, but he was retained in the Reserve and was promoted to the rank of Captain, which he would hold for the rest of his life. Halford also briefly served with the RFC in France, but he too was recalled to engineering work. Major Burke returned to the army in 1916. Promoted to Lieutenant-Colonel, and commanding a battalion of the East Lancashire Regiment, he was killed on 9 April 1917—the first day of the Battle of Arras.

Geoffrey de Havilland met Hugh Trenchard when he visited the Front in France, and also at Farnborough. Their mutual respect grew through discussing improvements to de Havilland's designs. Trenchard also shared his thoughts with General W. Sefton Brancker, who would play a leading role in developing civil aviation in the 1920s. The designs that de Havilland produced for Airco were the first to use the initials of his surname; they would account for almost a third of the aircraft used by Britain and the US during the First World War. The DH.2 'pusher' helped to end the 'Fokker Scourge' against Allied aircraft. In fact, the next plane to come down at Hatfield might have been an Airco DH.1 or DH.2. William 'Bill' G. Walby, born into a long-standing local family of butchers, was aged around 6 at the time:

> We had some excitement one day when a plane came down in a field behind the Wrestlers Pub. It was an open framed plane with two wings and the propeller behind the pilot's seat. The pilot was hurt and was taken to St Albans hospital by Mr Canham, landlord of the Gun Inn, in a horse and trap.

The fast, Rolls-Royce Eagle V12-powered DH.4 of 1916 was the most successful single-engined day-bomber of the First World War. It was also produced in the US in large numbers. The DH.9 of 1917 was developed from the DH.4. The DH.9A had a Liberty engine from the US, and would form the 'backbone' of the RAF in the 1920s. DH.4s and DH.9s served with many other world air forces.

3

The First World War in Hertfordshire Skies

> ...all these cherished dreams and ambitions were shattered by Britain's declaration of war with Germany...we carried out our curious missions obediently and without question—as did so many others...
>
> *Geoffrey de Havilland*

Early Airship Raids of the First World War

On the evening of 8 September 1915, three German Navy airships (L11, L13, and L14) left their bases in north-west Germany. Only L13, commanded by Kapitänleutnant Heinrich Mathy, got beyond Cambridge, and proceeded over Buntingford and Ware. Mathy's attack across London that night was the most successful the War, making him a legend. The 109 casualties included twenty-two deaths. One sixth of the total air raid damage to Britain during the War was inflicted in that one attack.

On the night of 13–14 October 1915, the same three Zeppelins, plus L15 and L16, set off from their bases. From Cambridge, they turned south over Hertfordshire. They were fired at by mobile anti-aircraft guns, and dropped bombs in retaliation. L13 was again commanded by Mathy. When they got back to base, Mathy's report for the airship's 'Kriegstagebuch' or 'KTB' (war flight log) included that 'enemy counter-action was carried out by a battery and searchlights in Enfield. The position was covered by four explosive bombs [50-kg]; the enemy ceased to fire, one of two spotlights extinguished.' According to the time of 10:05 recorded in the KTB, they were actually twenty minutes beyond Enfield, just south of Hatfield, in the Potters Bar area.

In L15, Kapitänleutnant Joachim Breithaupt responded similarly and accurately to ground fire near Broxbourne, and then continued over Potters Bar and Barnet. Oberleutnant-zur-See Werner Peterson was commanding L16, which bombed Hertford with 18 explosive and 30 incendiary bombs. There were twenty-four casualties, including nine fatalities. The fleet then bombed the London area. L15

Postcard of German naval personnel bidding farewell to Kapitänleutnant Heinrich Mathy, who is in the front gondola of Zeppelin L13. On the night of 13–14 October 1915, they dropped four bombs in response to ground fire just south of Hatfield. (*Courtesy of Rod Filan*)

Another angle of L13, which Heinrich Mathy directed over Buntingford and Ware on the evening of 8 September 1915 before reaching London. His attack that night caused twenty-two deaths, and one sixth of the total air-raid damage to Britain during the whole of the War. (*Archiv Andreas Krug, www.luftschiff.de*)

was fired at by a Royal Naval Volunteer Reserve anti-aircraft battery, based at the Honourable Artillery Company's training ground—from where Lunardi's balloon had taken off 131 years before.

Zeppelin *v.* de Havilland

On 31 March 1916, 2nd Lt Alfred de Bathe Brandon helped ground fire to bring down L15, in his de Havilland-designed, Royal Aircraft Factory B.E.2c biplane. This was a more stable version of the B.E.2, which could be flown 'hands and feet off'. Brandon won the Military Cross.

On the night of 2–3 September 1916, sixteen German airships (the largest force of the War) headed for London. Twelve were Kriegsmarine (navy) Zeppelins, and four were Schütte-Lanz from the Luftstreitkräfte (air arm) of the Deutsches Heer (army). One of the Luftstreitkräfte airships that night was the Schütte-Lanz SL.11, its crew of sixteen commanded by Hauptman Wilhelm Schramm. They bombed London Colney, South Mimms, and north London.

Photo developed from one of hundreds of glass plates taken at the Schütte-Lanz assembly hall in Leipzig. SL.11 is shown under construction, which started on 10 April 1916. It first flew on 1 August, entered Luftstreitkräfte (army air arm) service on 12 August, and was destroyed over Hertfordshire on 3 September. The hall collapsed in 1917. (*Nachlass Johann Schütte, Bildarchiv Stadtmuseum, Oldenburg*)

At around 2.30 a.m., SL.11 was shot down by 2nd Lt William Leefe Robinson of 39 Sqn, RFC, based at Suttons Farm near Hornchurch, Essex. The squadron had been formed the previous April for the very purpose of 'Home Defence' against Zeppelin raids. Leefe Robinson was using the new Brock-Pomeroy incendiary ammunition onboard his B.E.2c.

Thousands in London, Essex, and Hertfordshire watched SL.11 plummet. The blaze lit up Hatfield's night sky, and was visible from Cambridge, 35 miles to the north. Cheering and singing of the national anthem broke out. The wreckage landed behind the Plough Inn in Cuffley, 6 miles from Hatfield, at the south-east corner of the parish and district boundary; it was the first enemy aircraft shot down over Britain. Werner Peterson's L16_was also in the fleet. Passing directly over Hatfield, they witnessed the end of SL.11 and were caught in the glow, so they jettisoned their bombs over Essendon and climbed to safety. Robinson received the first Victoria Cross for action in Britain. A Pathé Gazette newsreel shows wreckage from SL.11 being displayed to the public at the Honourable Artillery Company grounds.

On the night of 23–24 September, Werner Peterson returned with L32. Frederick Sowrey, also of 39 Sqn, emptied three drums of the new ammunition into L32, which crashed in Essex. The crew members were buried in a local churchyard. Sowrey was awarded the Distinguished Service Order (DSO). The same night, Alfred Brandon again assisted ground fire to force L33 down in Essex. The crew survived. Brandon was awarded the DSO.

On the night of 1–2 October Heinrich Mathy was commanding Zeppelin L31, among eleven other airships. L31 crossed the Suffolk coast and continued over Essex. Passing over Harlow and into Hertfordshire, it headed north to Buntingford; then south-west, between Knebworth and Welwyn; and then east, toward Hertford and Ware. A final change of course brought L31 over Cheshunt, where it dropped fifty bombs—damaging over 300 properties.

2nd Lt Wulstan J Tempest then arrived in another 39 Sqn B.E.2c with incendiary ammunition; he had to fly through anti-aircraft fire from ground batteries that shared his purpose. Around midnight, watched by tens of thousands of cheering onlookers following the searchlights, the fireball that had been L31 roared down onto Potters Bar's Oakmere Park, 4 miles south of Hatfield. Tempest, too, received the DSO.

In June 1917 L48 was shot down by four British aircraft, and crashed in Suffolk. Again, the whole crew perished and were buried nearby. L48 was the fourth and last airship to be shot down over Britain solely by the RFC.

The Ones That Got Away

Zeppelin L55 drifted over Hatfield on the night of 19 October 1917, with Kapitänleutnant Hans Kurt Flemming in command. It was among thirteen of the

Postcard of soldiers attending to a 240-bhp (177-KW) Maybach engine, amid the wreckage of SL.11 at Cuffley. Destroyed by 2nd Lt William Leefe Robinson (inset) in the early hours of 3 September 1916, it was the first enemy aircraft shot down over Britain. (*Courtesy of Rod Filan*)

Postcard showing the cockpit of 2nd Lt William Leefe Robinson's de Havilland-designed Royal Aircraft Factory B.E.2c. Note the Lewis gun, loaded with the new Brock-Pomeroy incendiary ammunition that he used to destroy the Schütte-Lanz SL.11. (*The Paul R. Hare Collection*)

new 'high-climber' Zeppelins that were tasked to attack English cities. However, bad weather—not anticipated by German naval meteorologists—scattered the fleet. Disorientated, Flemming ordered bombs to be dropped on Hull; they were, in fact, south of Peterborough. He then ordered their remaining sixteen explosive bombs, totaling 2,200 lbs, to be dropped on Sheffield—although he later decided it was Birmingham. They were actually following the East Coast Main Line, between Hitchin and Hatfield. They caused minor damage, and slight injury to one man.

After bombing Hertford, L52 made it safely home to Germany. Others bombed London, leaving 33 dead. Protected by the bad weather, L55 crossed the English coast near Hastings—British disappointment would be discussed in Parliament. But L55 had not escaped. Thinking they were above Dover, they were actually over the Western Front. Other airships were forced down by French aircraft and ground batteries. L55's crew noticed incoming attacks, and Flemming ordered an ascent to climb out of range. They reached 7,300 m, a record for airships, exceeding their safe ceiling of 6,500 m and causing a loss of hydrogen. Jettisoning all ballast, she crossed the German front line still in excess of 7,000 m, but her descent was uncontrollable. Low enough to read a railway station sign, 200 miles from home, and low on fuel, L55 landed heavily in a forest clearing near Tiefenort, in Germany. Badly damaged, she had to be scrapped, and the crew set about dismantling her themselves. The German navy had lost five airships during what would be their last large-scale raid.

In the final raid of the War, on 5 August 1918, L70 was shot down off the Norfolk coast, near Wells-next-the-Sea, by Maj. Egbert Cadbury and his gunner, Maj. Robert Leckie, in their Airco DH.4. None of the Zeppelin's twenty-three crew members survived, including Peter Strasser, the Kriegsmarine's chief commander of Zeppelins.

The brand new Zeppelin L55 in autumn 1917, at Ahlhorn naval air station in north-west Germany. It bombed countryside between Hitchin and Hatfield on the night of 19-20 October. On the return journey, it ascended to a record-breaking but unsafe altitude to escape attacking aircraft over France, and then crashed near Tiefenort in central Germany. (*Courtesy of Rod Filan*)

Hertfordshire's Zeppelin Legacy

The nineteen naval crew members of L31 were buried in the same Potters Bar cemetery as their army comrades from SL.11. A *Topical Budget* news film shows soldiers carrying the coffins of the crew from SL.11 (wrongly identified as L21), followed by a graveside service—of which locals took a dim view. An initiative to improve relations in 1931 resulted in an annual official German remembrance ceremony in the cemetery, which was held until 1939. In the 1960s, the remains of all four airship crews would be moved to the German Cemetery at Cannock Chase, Staffordshire.

Leefe Robinson was posted to France in 1917 as a Flight Commander. His Bristol F.2 Fighter was forced down in combat with Albatros D.IIIs led by 'The Red Baron', Manfred von Richthofen. Leefe Robinson's health deteriorated in custody and, after returning to England, he died in the 1918 influenza epidemic. A memorial to him stands near where SL.11 crashed. Robinson Close, in Hornchurch, is on the site of Suttons Farm airfield. In 2010, a Class 313 train was named *Capt. William Leefe Robinson VC*, to mark the centenary of the extension to the Great Northern Railway that included Cuffley. The village football team is nicknamed *The Zeps*.

Members of the Royal Flying Corps help to bury the sixteen crew members of SL.11 at Mutton Lane cemetery, in Potters Bar, on 8 September 1916. This was 4 miles south of Hatfield. The crew members of L31 were buried beside them. (*Origin unknown*)

Frederick Sowrey was posted to Flanders in 1917, as a flight commander with 19 Sqn. He became a fighter ace, won the Military Cross, and went on to command 143 Sqn. He died in 1968. Wulstan Tempest was promoted to Major, survived a posting to the Western Front, and left military service in 1921. Two streets in Potters Bar—Wulstan Park and Tempest Avenue—honour his memory. He lived until 1966.

A Brave New World

The RFC's naval branch had been separated to form the Royal Naval Air Service (RNAS) in 1914. On 1 April 1918 the Royal Air Force (RAF) was created through a re-amalgamation, independent of both the army and the navy. Maj.-Gen. Hugh Trenchard, knighted in the New Year's Honours, was appointed as Chief of the Air Staff. The naval branch would be known as the Fleet Air Arm from 1924.

In 1917, the Government had decided to restrict the Royal Aircraft Factory to its original research remit, and to leave design and manufacturing to private companies. This was in response to a campaign led by the Member of Parliament for East Hertfordshire, Noel Pemberton-Billing. He had founded his own aircraft company in 1913, which named its products as 'Supermarine'. It became known as Supermarine Aviation Works Ltd after he left it in 1916. Several senior staff left the factory including Fred Green, who was by then a Major in the RFC. He became chief engineer at Siddeley-Deasy, which was led by John Siddeley since 1912. To avoid confusion with the RAF from 1918 onwards, the Factory was renamed as the Royal Aircraft Establishment (RAE)—a name it retained for the next seventy years.

The third of the de Havilland's three children, John, was born in 1918. He was described by his father as 'the great naturalist' of the family. He inherited his father's love of the outdoors, and became an expert on insects, birds, and wild animals. With Hereward, all five of the de Havilland men would fly at Hatfield Aerodrome. In 1919, the family moved to Stanmore in Harrow, north-west London, where Geoffrey would live for the rest of his life.

Siddeley-Deasy was acquired in 1919 by Sir W. G. Armstrong Whitworth & Co., which had created an aircraft division in 1912. They renamed their acquisition as Armstrong Siddeley Motors, with John Siddeley as managing director; the aircraft division would become a separate company in 1920. Fred Green would stay with Armstrong Whitworth Aircraft until his retirement in 1933. A. V. Roe & Co. would also enter its next chapter in 1920, when it was bought by Crossley Motors. Also in 1920, Harry Hawker would create H. G. Hawker Engineering, acquiring the assets of the bankrupt Sopwith Aviation Co., with Tom Sopwith as one of his partners. All of these companies would cross de Havilland's path, not least at Hatfield. Hawker would be killed in 1921, when his Nieuport Goshawk crashed at Hendon.

4

Civilian Flying in the 1920s

> Every new means of transport since the industrial revolution has had its romantic period, this usually occurring between the first experimental days and the time when it becomes accepted by the masses and develops into big business...For the aeroplane it followed the First World War.
>
> *Geoffrey de Havilland*

Aerofilms and Airco

Founded in 1919, Aerofilms Ltd was the UK's first commercial aerial photography company. Starting with sideways-looking 'oblique' cameras, they created the largest aerial photographic archive of Britain's changing landscape up to 1939. In June 1920, they compiled a 'Herts Regional Report', including photographs of Hatfield town centre, its Great Northern Railway (GNR) station, and Hatfield House.

Geoffrey de Havilland described the years following the First World War as aviation's 'romantic period'. Civilian flying had resumed in 1919. The principle of civilian aircraft registrations had been established in 1910, at an international conference in Paris, but the War had postponed its implementation. The first flight of a registered civilian aircraft in Britain was made by a de Havilland-designed Airco DH.9, with the temporary code of K-100. Unfortunately, the flight ended in a crash.

Airco produced 300 aircraft each month during the final year of the War, which ended in November 1918. In December George Holt Thomas claimed that his company was the largest aircraft manufacturer in the world. The Hendon factory employed more than 7,000 workers, using the latest machinery and techniques.

The Paris conference had allocated the G- prefix to Britain, which now introduced the G-Exxx series for powered aeroplanes. K-100 would have been G-EAAA if it had not been written off. It was registered to Aircraft Transport & Travel (AT&T), the UK's first airline, created by Airco. AT&T started the first daily international air service in 1919—London to Paris—and also won the first

British civil air-mail contract that year. The first Paris flight was made by DH.9B K-109, flown by Henry 'Jerry' Shaw with George Pilkington—of the famous glass company—as a passenger. This was a civilianised DH.9A (ex-RAF serial H9277), with a two-passenger cabin and Siddeley Puma power—a development of the Beardmore Halford Pullinger engine of 1916, which Frank Halford had created from an Austro-Daimler unit.

Aerofilm's offices were initially in Hendon, at Claude Grahame-White's London Flying Club. He was their Chairman, and they hired the club's aircraft. They then used Stag Lane Aerodrome in Edgware, north-west London. This was home to the London & Provincial School of Flying, owned by flying instructors W. T. Warren and M. G. Smiles. Aerofilms hired K-109 from Airco, which was soon re-registered as G-EAAC. They also hired Airco pilots, including Alan Cobham. Their photographs documented the countryside, industry, towns and villages, archaeological sites, historic buildings, and the upgrading of the national road network. Postcard manufacturers bought the images.

In around 1920 aerial joy rides were being given for five shillings, from a field south-west of the town on Briars Lane. Bill Walby had just turned eleven, and his remaining sister Nancy was still under five; his brother and two other sisters had been among Hatfield's victims of the influenza pandemic of 1918–20. They had all died in the same week, aged between seventeen months and seven years.

> Dad took Nancy and I ... Mum followed later. As there were only two seats Dad took Nancy up and I followed later with somebody else. It was grand, the wind from the propeller blowing through your hair, and we were able to look over the side of the cockpit. When mum got to the field she said, 'Where is Bill?' Dad pointed and said, 'Up there!' She nearly had a fit.

The Birth of de Havilland and The King's Cup

The Aircraft Disposal Co. (ADC, or 'Airdisco') was established in 1920, by Frederick Handley Page and others, to convert War surplus aircraft for the civilian market. The British Treasury would receive half of the profits. Large military contracts ended, and Airco became unprofitable. It was sold to the Birmingham Small Arms Co. (BSA) in 1920, and was liquidated by the year's end. AT&T also closed down, so Aerofilms needed a new 'partner'.

With significant capital from George Holt Thomas, de Havilland bought some of Airco's assets and formed the de Havilland Aircraft Co. in September. The new company rented two large wooden sheds at Stag Lane Aerodrome, and developed them as a factory. They also used two wooden huts as their general and design offices.

Several Airco employees joined de Havilland. Frank Hearle, head of Airco's experimental department from 1917, became the new Works Manager. He had

Looking north to Hatfield and its station on the Great Northern Railway (GNR) in June 1920. This photo by Aerofilms was part of their 'Herts Regional Report', and was published in the 1927 Hertfordshire Regional Planning Report by town planning consultant W. R. Davidge. (© *English Heritage, Aerofilms Collection, image EPW001650*)

Hatfield town centre, looking north-east, in July 1920. The gas works is at bottom right. St Etheldreda's spire—removed in 1930—is just above centre-right. Hatfield House is at top right. (© *English Heritage, Aerofilms Collection, image EPW005054*)

joined Airco from Vickers, where he had set up their Brooklands factory at Weybridge, in Surrey, to produce B.E.2s under licence for the War Effort. Engineer Charles Walker became Chief of Stressing and Aerodynamics. Wilfred Nixon, company secretary, had been a financial administrator at both Airco and the Royal Aircraft Factory. Airco's Sales Manager, Francis E. N. St Barbe, became the new Business Manager. Designer Arthur E. 'Ernie' Hagg became head of the new drawing office, which Ronald E. Bishop joined as an apprentice in 1922. Alan Cobham continued as a test pilot. The production workforce of around forty-five included a small group of women in the fabric and doping shop.

In 1921 the de Havilland Aeroplane Hire Service was created to bring in additional income, using ten DH.9Bs and DH.9Cs (three-passenger cabin). The Service's first pilot was its manager, Alan Cobham, who continued to fly for Aerofilms. Other Aerofilms flights were piloted by Capt. Hubert Broad, de Havilland's new chief test pilot. That year, Aerofilms added vertical photography for surveys and mapping.

Warren and Smiles then asked De Havilland to buy the site or leave. Vital capital was provided by 23-year-old Alan S. Butler, whose family wealth had come from mining in Rhodesia. In 1920 he had formed the Butler Aerial Survey Co. (Newfoundland) Ltd in Canada, employing ex-RFC survey pilot Maj. Harold Hemming. Having returned to England, Butler also ordered a new aircraft from de Havilland, to be designed to his requirements. This was the DH.37, de Havilland's first aircraft for private ownership. It first flew in 1922, and was powered by a Rolls-Royce Falcon. Named 'Sylvia' after Butler's sister, the DH.37 was registered as G-EBDO. In December Cobham flew it to Constantinople (Istanbul). The company was also able to develop Stag Lane with a new, steel-framed factory. It was built by Archibald D. Dawnay & Sons Ltd, whose headquarters were on Steelworks Road, Battersea, in south London.

Sir Sefton Brancker, who was made an Air Vice-Marshal after the RAF was formed, was appointed as Director of Civil Aviation in 1922. Under his

Airco DH.9C G-EAAC, with its fellow fleet members in the de Havilland Aeroplane Hire Service, used by Aerofilms for its aerial photography flights from Stag Lane after the demise of Airco. G-EAAC may have been the aircraft they used to photograph Hatfield in 1920. Alan Cobham flew it to third place in the King's Cup Circuit air race in 1922; it would be based at Hatfield from 1930. (*BAE Systems, via Philip Birtles*)

chairmanship, the Royal Aero Club's Racing Committee created the annual King's Cup Circuit of Britain Air Race to encourage development of light aircraft. It would be the highest-profile event in light aircraft racing for many years. Frank Barnard, in DH.4A G-EAMU, was the 1922 winner, beating twenty other competitors at Croydon, Surrey. Cobham was third in G-EAAC, now a DH.9C of the Hire Service. Butler was fifth, in his DH.37.

The de Havilland School of Flying

In 1923, de Havilland opened their School of Flying at Stag Lane. The Air Ministry required basic training and flying opportunities for RAF Reserve officers. Armstrong Whitworth, Beardmore, Blackburn, Bristol, and de Havilland were awarded the initial school management contracts. These would employ, as instructors, members of the Reserve of Air Force Officers (RAFO), who had previously completed a four-year short service commission as pilots in the RAF. First to open was the de Havilland school. The chief ground engineer was Bob Hardingham, who would move to Hatfield with the school in 1930. Geoffrey de Havilland's three sons learned to fly with the school, and also joined the RAF Reserve.

Cobham was second in the 1923 King's Cup at Hendon, in DH.9J G-EBEZ—another Hire Service aircraft. Its Armstrong Siddeley *Jaguar* radial had been temporarily replaced with a Napier Lion. He was beaten by Frank Courtney, in an Armstrong Whitworth Siskin. Broad was third, in DH.9C G-EBGT. Frank Barnard, again in DH.4A G-EAMU, was fourth. Harold Hemming was fifth, in Butler's DH.37. That year Cobham also made a 12,000 mile (17,700 km) tour of Europe and the Mediterranean, in the Hire Service's DH.9C G-EBCZ. G-BGT was named *Nulli Secundus* ('second to none'), after Britain's first powered military aircraft—one of the airships built in 1907 at the Army Balloon Factory at Farnborough, with assistance from Geoffrey de Havilland's old friend Samuel Cody.

War had necessitated the granting of contracts to various manufacturers, but inferior designs were now being accepted just because it was one manufacturer's 'turn'. Over-regulation and official interference added to the frustration, so de Havilland concentrated on the growing civilian market. Four days after the maiden flight of the prototype DH.50, G-EBFN, Alan Cobham flew it to the Gothenburg Exhibition in Sweden, where it won a civilian aircraft competition. Herman Göring competed, with a Junkers J10. Seventeen years later, Göring would send another Junkers to 'visit' Hatfield.

G-EBFN joined the Hire fleet. Sponsored by Sir Charles Wakefield, founder of Castrol, Cobham used it to win the 1924 King's Cup at Lee-on-the-Solent in Hampshire. Alan Butler, chairman of de Havilland from that year, was third in his DH.37. Aerofilms' artwork department modified images for their clients' promotional purposes. They also did it for themselves, and produced an image of a DH.9A with the pilot and photographer painted in more visible positions. They also 'borrowed' the identification letters from Cobham's race-winning DH.50. From 1924 to 1926, Cobham made several long-distance flights in DH.50s: with Sir Sefton Brancker to India; pioneering new routes for Imperial Airways, to countries such as South Africa; and in an aerial survey of Australia. He was knighted in 1926.

In 1925, the de Havilland Hire Service closed. Two of its DH.9s, G-EAAC and G-EBEZ, continued with the flying school, and were soon re-engined with Armstrong Siddeley Jaguars as DH.9Js. Aerofilms was acquired by the Aircraft Operating Co. Ltd (AOC) that year, which had its own fleet of DH.9s. AOC had been founded by Harold Hemming in 1923, with Alan Butler as chairman. They expanded Aerofilms' operations and moved its headquarters back to Hendon, but its flights from Stag Lane continued. Also in 1925, Ordnance Survey awarded its first aerial photography contract to AOC for global surveying and map-making.

The London Aeroplane Club

Encouraged by Sir Sefton Brancker, the Royal Aero Club's Light Aeroplane Club scheme was created to promote national 'air mindedness' by subsidising flying clubs and schools. At Hearle's suggestion, de Havilland founded the London Aeroplane Club at Stag Lane in 1925. Many of the clubs were equipped with the new Cirrus-powered, two-seater DH.60 Moth, the first example being G-EBKT. Its folding wings were convenient for storage and towing behind a car. With a locker for luggage and tools, it was a big hit with private owners and commercial users. A world-wide flying club 'movement' would be built on the affordability and reliability of the Moth.

Frank Halford had set up his own engine design business in 1923. Geoffrey de Havilland asked him to create the Cirrus from a First World War Renault unit. This was put into production by ADC which, by 1925, had sold 2,000 ex-First World War airframes and 3,000 engines, generating over £2.5m (£257m today) in profits.

Parts of the 1925 King's Cup course were similar to the *Daily Mail* race of 1911, taking competitors once more over the countryside and railway between Hatfield and St Albans. Frank Barnard won again, this time in a Siskin. Harold Hemming flew Butler's DH.37 into third place at the Croydon finish. Fog ruined the race for most, including Geoffrey de Havilland, in Moth G-EBKU, and Alan Cobham, in Moth G-EBKT, again sponsored by Wakefield. They both had to put down near St Albans.

1926 was Hubert Broad's year with Moth G-EBMO at Hendon. The course took competitors between Hatfield and Hertford. Sir Charles Wakefield sponsored Broad's entry on this and eight further occasions.

Hubert Broad tows a Moth, with its wings folded, on a public road, behind a 'Bullnose' Morris Oxford Tourer. (*BAE Systems*)

Photo signed by Geoffrey de Havilland and sent as a greeting to the Royal Aero Club 'With best wishes for Xmas 1925'. It shows himself, and his wife Louie, at Stag Lane in the second prototype DH.60 Moth, G-EBKU. He flew the aircraft in the 1925 King's Cup, as did Alan Cobham in the first prototype, G-EBKT. The course took them near Hatfield, but they were both forced to land near St Albans due to fog. However, Maj. Harold Hemming—flying Alan Butler's DH.37—claimed third place. (*London News Agency Photos Ltd/BAE Systems, via the Royal Aero Club Trust, 0254-0002*)

Hubert Broad won the 1926 King's Cup (at Hendon) with Moth G-EBMO. The course took competitors between Hatfield and Hertford. (Flight, *via Philip Birtles*)

In 1927, at Hucknall in Nottinghamshire, former Hire Service pilot Capt. Walter L. Hope won the King's Cup in Moth G-EBME. He had founded Air Taxis Ltd at Stag Lane in 1926. Broad had to retire his DH.71 Tiger Moth monoplane prototype, G-EBRV. Geoffrey de Havilland had built its stressed plywood fuselage around Hubert Broad's shoulders, to maximise aerodynamics. Butler also had to retire the Cirrus II-engined Moth X prototype, G-EBQH. However, Lady Mary Bailey—a newly qualified pilot—used G-EBQH to set a world altitude class record of 17,283 feet. Louie de Havilland was her passenger for the flight from Stag Lane. Lady Bailey was the daughter of Derry Westenra, Fifth Baron Rossmore of County Monaghan in Ireland. She had married South-African millionaire Abe Bailey in 1911. In a second DH.71, G-EBQU, Broad set a 100-km world closed-circuit class record of 186.47 mph from Stag Lane.

The de Havilland Aeronautical Technical School was established at Stag Lane in 1928. It was the first organisation to provide training for the Ground Engineer's licence in the repair and maintenance of civil aircraft. Courses were then added on aircraft design and production engineering. Geoffrey de Havilland considered 'the most pleasing and romantic aspect' of life at Stag Lane to be the presence of many women. Britain's most famous female pilot, Amy Johnson, joined the London Aeroplane Club in 1928 and learned to fly and navigate. She was taught partly by First World War 'Ace' Capt. James Valentine Baker, the club's chief flying instructor

The de Havilland factory and Aerodrome at Stag Lane, Edgware, in around 1927—with urban development getting closer. Moth G-EBPR of the Flying School is flying in. Of the two aircraft in the centre, the right-hand one is Moth G-EBRI, owned by the Duchess of Bedford. She kept it at Woburn, where she had a private air strip. In the foreground are DH.9C G-EBGT—flown into third place by Hubert Broad in the 1923 King's Cup—and Moth G-EBRY, both also flying school aircraft. G-EBGT would move to Hatfield, with the school, in 1930. (*BAE Systems, via Ian Grace and the Norman Eastaff Collection. Restored by Rod Filan)*

at the time. She gained most of her early experience with Moths. She would soon follow in the 'flight paths' of Lady Bailey, who flew that year, in Moths, from Stag Lane to South Africa and back.

Wally Hope beat 35 other entries to win the King's Cup again that year, at Brooklands, Surrey, flying G-EBYZ—the prototype DH.60G Gipsy Moth. Frank Halford's Gipsy engine was commissioned and manufactured by de Havilland to replace the Cirrus, marking the beginning of the company's own aero-engine production. Of the thirteen Moths that entered the race, nine finished in the first twelve places. Amy Johnson's friend, Winifred E. Spooner, a Stag Lane 'graduate' from 1927, was the first woman to win a prize when she came third in Moth G-EBOT. Broad, de Havilland, and Butler were fourth, fifth, and sixth—all in Moths.

The 1927 International Radio-Telegraph Conference had revised the aircraft registration system. Britain continued to use the G- prefix, but re-started its sequence with G-AAAA—the format that continues to this day. The aircraft to receive the first of the new registrations was Geoffrey de Havilland's own DH.60G, in 1928. Also in 1928, Mr and Mrs de Havilland took a Gipsy Moth to a new altitude class record of 19,980 feet. In December Mr & Mrs Butler flew to set another world class record of 119.8 mph over a 100-km closed circuit.

Aerofilms returned to Hatfield to photograph the town and its station (LNER since 1923) in August 1928, and again in November. By 1929, AOC and Aerofilms together employed 170 staff. Aerofilms acquired a few aircraft of their own, including DH.60X Moth G-EBZT. It was registered at Stag Lane, first to AOC in 1928, and then to Aerofilms in 1929.

The 1929 King's Cup at Heston, west London, took the forty-one entrants directly over St Albans. Twenty-one of them were Moths. Fg Off. Richard L. R. Atcherley won in a Gloster Grebe, with Flt Lt George H. Stainforth as navigator. Fourteen of the Moths were placed from second to twenty-second. Wally Hope and Alan Butler were third and fourth, in Gipsy Moths. Winifred Spooner was fifth in another. Geoffrey de Havilland flew G-AAAA, fitted with a coupé canopy, to ninth place, with Geoffrey Jnr on board. He nearly killed them both, in thick cloud, when the course took them over the Cumbrian Mountains. Alan Butler's wife Lois was fourteenth, in his coupé model. With so many Moths competing, de Havilland provided maintenance support around the 1929 course, with Capt. Clement A. Pike carrying spares in G-EAAC—one of the DH.9J conversions. The flying school's Jack Tyler (in yet another Moth) did likewise, but they weren't needed. After service in the RFC and RAF, 'Clem' Pike had joined the de Havilland drawing office in 1922 and became an instructor with the School of Flying in 1927.

Atcherley and Stainforth were members of the RAF High Speed Flight team for the 1929 Schneider Trophy, held on 7 September at Calshot, where Southampton Water opens into the Solent. Stainforth's Napier Lion-engined Gloster VI seaplane was withdrawn from the race, which was won by their team mate, Fg Off. H. Richard D. Waghorn, in a Rolls-Royce R-powered Supermarine S.6. Amy Johnson, who had gained her pilot's licence on 6 July, watched from a bobbing boat. The next day Stainforth used the Gloster to set a world air speed record of 336.3 mph. However, Sqn Ldr Augustus Orlebar raised the mark two days later, with the S.6, to 357.7 mph. Atcherley, Orlebar, and Waghorn would enter the 1930 King's Cup. Most of these people would visit Hatfield Aerodrome over the next few years.

Despite opposition from Lt Cdr Harold E. Perrin (secretary of the Royal Aero Club since 1903 and of the London Aeroplane Club) and from the new chief flying instructor, Maj. Herbert G. Travers, Amy Johnson also learned to service and repair aircraft and engines. Under the care and protection of Stag Lane's chief engineer Jack Humphreys, she became the first female ground engineer to be licenced by the Air Ministry on 10 December 1929.

Looking north-west to Hatfield House, with the north of the town beyond, photographed by Aerofilms in August 1928. The horseshoe-shaped housing development is Stonecross Road. The farmland beyond that was later developed as Crawford Road, and is immediately to the north-east of the land that became Hatfield Aerodrome in 1930. (© *English Heritage, Aerofilms Collection, image EPW022351*)

Hatfield station and the Great North Road, photographed by Aerofilms on 5 November 1928—very possibly using Moth G-EBZT. (© *English Heritage, Aerofilms Collection, image EPW025382*)

Aerofilms' Moth G-EBZT, first registered at Stag Lane in 1928 to Aerofilms' parent company, AOC, and then to Aerofilms in 1929. It is seen here over Harrow, north-west London, in November 1928. The camera is looking north, towards Hertfordshire. The de Havilland family had lived at Stanmore, in Harrow, since 1919. Geoffrey would live there for the rest of his life. (© *English Heritage, Aerofilms Collection, image EPW025539*)

Left to right: School of Flying instructor Clem Pike, chief engineer Charles Walker, tennis player Lilí Álvarez, the Secretary of State for Air Sir Samuel J. G. Hoare, and his wife, Lady Maud Hoare, with Geoffrey de Havilland in 1928. (*BAE Systems*)

Outgrowing Stag Lane

Production, maintenance, training, and flying activities at Stag Lane were all increasing. Suburban development nearby was also increasing, and Edgware's village character was becoming a thing of the past. Geoffrey de Havilland remembered, 'When we first began manufacturing aircraft at Stag Lane in 1920, there was only one small house near the aerodrome.' He kept his Ford Model T in a farm building. An underground station, surrounded by fields, had opened in 1924, enabling more people to commute into central London. This meant a rapid growth of housing and local infrastructure.

By 1929 de Havilland employed 1,500 people. Of every 100 aeroplanes in Britain, around 85 were Moths. Some were also licence-built in Australia, Canada, the USA, Norway, France, and Finland. The company itself was also rapidly becoming international. They had businesses in Australia (Melbourne) from 1927—founded by Hereward de Havilland—Canada (Toronto) from 1928, and India (Karachi) from 1929. They would add South Africa (Johannesburg) from 1930. Stag Lane would continue to be a significant site for de Havilland for some years to come, but the company needed somewhere with more room—on the ground and in the air.

AOC and Aerofilms were taken under Government control from 1940, in the creation of the Allied Photographic Interpretation Unit at Medmenham. The two companies became part of the Hunting Group in 1942. The Aerofilms archive was bought by English Heritage in 2007, in partnership with the Royal Commission on the Ancient and Historical Monuments of Wales and Scotland. Aerofilms' most-seen picture was their vertical survey photo of modern London, used for the end credits of long-running BBC drama *Eastenders* until 2009.

In 1931 Aerofilms sold G-EBZT to Nordisk Luftfoto, an aerial photography company in Denmark. Its last known owner was the Danish artist, Baron Erik Mauritz Von Plessen, from whom the Germans confiscated the aircraft in 1943. (*Aerofilms image A3921, via the Norman Eastaff Collection*)

5

Space to Spread Their Wings

> For many months, we looked for a suitable site, doing a lot of reconnaissance by Moth along most of the main roads leading out of London, the most hopeful being to the north. Eventually, we found an area near Hatfield that looked good from the air, a large, level area of farmland bordering the main road. The farmer was prepared to sell at a reasonable price ... Although not beautiful, the country around our new aerodrome was very pleasant, and of course it possessed a greater sense of spaciousness than Stag Lane ever had.
>
> *Geoffrey de Havilland*

A New Home for the de Havilland School of Flying

Hatfield is just 18 miles from central London. The area spotted from the air was to the north-west of where the A1057 Hatfield-St Albans road was crossed by the Barnet Bypass, later named Comet Way. The 'Clockhouse' hotel and its clock tower, later known as the 'Stonehouse', was built at the new junction, as was Waters Garage, with its car sales showroom.

The farm in question was over 400 acres, centred on Harpsfield Hall in the St Albans rural parish of St Peters. The Hall had been owned by the Gape family of St Albans from 1676 until the 1920s. The Gapes were mayors of St Albans fifteen times between 1564 and 1829. John Gape, who lived at Harpsfield Hall, was a Member of Parliament for St Albans four times between 1679 and 1714. He was also High Sheriff of Hertfordshire in 1696. From 1863, the Sinclair family (from Scotland) lived at the Hall, albeit a later building, and farmed the land as tenants of the Gapes. They bought the property from the Gapes in the 1920s, but times were hard, and they decided to accept de Havilland's offer to buy some of the land in 1928.

John Stroud would spend his life in aviation promotion and publishing. He was 10 years old when his parents moved to Hatfield in 1929:

View of Hatfield Aerodrome in 1932, looking north. The northern end of the Barnet Bypass, built in 1927, runs up the centre of the picture and crosses the Hatfield & St Albans Railway (H&StAR) branchline. This is the view that commended itself to de Havilland for the establishment of their new aerodrome in the late 1920s. (*BAE Systems, via Philip Birtles*)

Harpsfield Hall in 1925. Now owner rather than tenant, farmer James Angus Sinclair stands in the doorway. (*Mill Green Museum, Welwyn Hatfield Museum Service*)

> ...we arrived in the early summer of 1929. At that time there was no aerodrome at Hatfield but aircraft were seen frequently overhead. One blustery day a dark blue Cirrus Moth was giving joyrides from a farm ... another Cirrus Moth also visited a farm nearby...
>
> The big event, although it seemed small at the time, was the landing of a Puss Moth on a farm one dull evening during the winter of 1929–30. This was in fact the arrival of Clem Pike when de Havilland was searching for a site for an aerodrome to relieve and ultimately replace Stag Lane. The farmer's name was, I believe, Hill....

Clem Pike was a founding member of the Guild of Air Pilots and Air Navigators, created in October 1929. The DH.80 *Puss Moth*, initially known as the *Moth Three,* was a high-wing cabin monoplane for which Halford designed the Gipsy III. If this was the aircraft that John Stroud saw it could only have been the prototype, first flown from Stag Lane by Geoffrey de Havilland on 9 September 1929. Its modern design would have certainly made an impression on anyone who saw it. The second example didn't fly until March 1930. Stag Lane would build 261 of them.

The farm where Pike landed was probably Roe Hyde, owned by Scottish sheep-farmer Alexander Campbell Hill. The Gapes had owned Roe Hyde since 1671. Hill had been another of their tenants, but he bought it from them in the mid-1920s while also being the tenant farmer of Roe Green North. He was one of several Scottish farmers who had moved to the area, taking up tenancies from the Hatfield House estate. They chose land next to the Great North Road and the East Coast Main Line for good access to the markets in London, where they sold their produce. However, the building of the Barnet Bypass and the widening of the St Albans Road cut through Roe Hyde, and Hill too now agreed to sell some of his land to de Havilland's chairman, Alan Butler.

The initial purpose of the Aerodrome was to provide a new home for the de Havilland School of Flying, which moved there in June 1930. Bob Hardingham continued as chief ground engineer at Hatfield. The London Aeroplane Club, with which the 20-year-old New Zealander Jean Batten was now learning to fly, remained at Stag Lane for another three years.

In 'Hatfield Memories', an article published in the December 1975 edition of *Air Pictorial*, John Stroud wrote:

> My next visit to the site must have been in about May or June 1930. The steel work was going up for the first hangars which backed on to the Barnet bypass....
>
> The original aerodrome was divided into two parts. The landing area was the northern part and it was separated from the southern area, which sloped downwards from the hangars, by a ditch containing a stream [the Ellenbrook]. Initially, the ditch was filled in at its western end but it was some time before this

> obstacle was finally removed and I once saw a Moth sitting with its wheels in the stream while its lower wings formed a bridge. The first buildings were a five-bay hangar, a 'club house' and offices, and later, on an 'island' site, a small office building with a fuel pump at each corner.
>
> The entrance to the aerodrome was via a narrow lane which ran from the Barnet bypass and along the eastern boundary to reach the farm. Beside the lane and opposite the aerodrome gate were a couple of cottages, one of which was occupied by the DH policeman—Tom Sayers, I believe. Beside the lane and beyond the club house was a sheep-fenced public enclosure in which I spent many hours when my efforts to get right in failed.
>
> From June 1930 the School was functioning at Hatfield with a fleet of Gipsy Moths for civil and general pupils and DH.9Js for RAF Reserve annual refresher courses.... The 9Js, which had red fuselages, wheels and struts, and goldish wings and tails, were G-EAAC, G-EBEZ, G-EBFQ, G-EBGT, G-EBTN and G-AASC ... fitted with Jaguar engines.... I can still remember the sound of those Jaguars and in particular the sound of G-EBTN which made a singing noise all of its own. G-EAAC was of special interest, having been the Aircraft Transport & Travel DH.9 K-109 (H9277) which Jerry Shaw flew from Hendon to Le Bourget on 15th July 1919, with the first charter passenger when international civil flights were allowed.... The chief flying instructor in those days was F/Lt R. W. (Bob) Reeve, and his staff comprised [George M.] Cox, [Eddie] Fulford, R. L. Palmer and Clem Pike. Rivers Oldmeadow was ground instructor. Most of the staff, especially Reeve, were very kind to me and after a while gave me fairly free access to the aerodrome and hangars. Oldmeadow even gave me a ride in his big green Bentley at the time when Bentleys and motor racing were synonymous...

The first Hatfield resident to be employed by de Havilland was 16-year-old Don Lawrence, who relayed his experiences in 2007:

> My father and uncle, who were agricultural contractors at Hatfield, secured a contract to do drainage, remove hedges and prepare the site ... to be ready by 1930 ... my father had come into contact with Bob Hardingham ... asked if there was a vacancy for a young lad ... all the other employees came out every day from Edgware ... four Ground Engineers, two aerodrome labourers whose job it was to swing the propeller for starting and keep the aircraft clean, a labourer to keep the hangar clean and make the tea and myself as a trainee Ground Engineer.... Very often before flying started, farm livestock which had broken through ... had to be rounded up.

Moth G-AAEO of the de Havilland School of Flying. (*The A. J. Jackson Collection*)

Tough times

C. Martin Sharp, assistant editor of *The Aeroplane,* would learn to fly with the London Aeroplane Club at Hatfield in September 1934. He would then join de Havilland in 1936 as their Director of Public Relations. Sharp held the position until 1960, when he published his history of the company, entitled *DH*. He described how in the early 1930s, despite appearances, de Havilland was struggling:

> In 1929 ... reports came of an unfortunate slump in American business.... The depression proved anything but temporary and spread throughout the world ... de Havilland business contracted...
>
> The company ... purchased open fields at Hatfield ... transferring the [Flying] school there in June [1930]. This expenditure and the increase of stock and work in progress due to slower sales deliveries left the company with an overdraft....
>
> A dozen long flights by Moths in 1930, many of them the outcome of training and planning at Stag Lane, brought spirit into the struggle, and so captured the public imagination that it was generally thought that de Havilland must be on top of the world.
>
> That was the year when a slip of a girl from Yorkshire, Amy Johnson ... made the first solo flight by a woman from England to Australia, taking 19 ½ days in a Gipsy Moth...

John Stroud saw Amy Johnson's DH.60G Gipsy Moth, G-AAAH, fly over Hatfield shortly before her Australia flight in May 1930. She had 'gone solo' for the first time less than a year before. Finance from her father was supplemented by civil aviation benefactor Charles Wakefield. He had just been made a Baron in the New Year's Honours, and took the title of Lord Wakefield of Hythe. Sir Sefton

Looking east to Hatfield Aerodrome in 1932. Harpsfield Hall is at centre-left. Immediately beyond the white Aerodrome buildings is Hatfield's 'New Town' area, built in 1848 in anticipation of the Great Northern Railway. Beyond that is the original town with Hatfield House just visible to the right of top-centre. (*BAE Systems, via Philip Birtles*)

Brancker, Director of Civil Aviation, was impressed by Amy's determination and encouraged Wakefield to support her. However, she was being kept waiting for a new aircraft designed and built by James Martin. He would form the Martin Baker Aircraft Co. Ltd in 1934, with Amy's old flying instructor Valentine Baker. They would become famous for the ejector seats that they are still producing today.

So Amy bought her Gipsy Moth from Wally Hope and named it *Jason*. Hope had modified it for long-distance flying, and had flown it to Kenya to photograph the Royal Tour of Central Africa for the *Daily Mirror*. He also advised Amy on spare parts for her 9,900-mile trip. She borrowed a parachute from Leslie W. Irvin. Irving Air Chute of Great Britain Ltd—a 'g' had been added to the company name by accident but they kept it—had their headquarters on Icknield Way, in Letchworth, north Hertfordshire.

In the end, she wasn't able to beat the record set in 1928 by Sqn Ldr Herbert J. L. 'Bert' Hinkler, with an Avro Avian, of 11,000 miles in 15 ½ days. In any case, the Australia-England record had been reduced in 1929 to 12 days, 14 hours, and 18 minutes over 12,000 miles. This was achieved in Fokker F.VII *Southern Cross*, by a crew that included Australian pioneers Sqn Ldr Charles E. Kingsford Smith and Charles T. P. Ulm. But Amy had certainly set an impressive women's record. In June, she was awarded the CBE and honorary membership of the Guild of Air Pilots and Air Navigators. In August Brancker and Baron Thomson of Cardington, who had replaced Sir Samuel Hoare as Secretary of State for Air in 1929, welcomed her home from Australia in front of 200,000 fans at Croydon. Popular songs were written about her and, in recognition of her achievement, de Havilland gave her Puss Moth G-AAZV, delivered on 15 September. She named it *Jason II*. Geoffrey de Havilland would have fond memories of her:

> I always liked Amy and we got on well together. She always used to come to see me to discuss her plans before setting off on a flight, bringing along her charts and itinerary. I never ceased to admire the thoroughness and care with which she prepared for her expeditions, and of course, her courage and skill in the air became a by-word.

The *Daily Mail* sponsored Amy to tour Britain with *Jason*, but she was unable to continue through September due to exhaustion. The newspaper donated the aircraft to the Science Museum in London, where it is still displayed today. The *Daily Sketch* and the *Sunday Graphic* raised money from their readers to buy her another Gipsy Moth, G-ABDV, which she named *Jason III*. In January 1931, bad weather would force her to abandon the aircraft in a Polish potato field—she was heading for Moscow, to discuss plans with the Russian authorities for a flight to Japan. She would achieve this in July-August 1931 with *Jason II*, accompanied by her mechanical mentor Jack Humphreys. Taking a route via Berlin, they reached Tokyo in under nine days.

Giant airships were also seen over Hatfield during their test flights in 1930. Short Brothers had acquired a site in 1916 near Cardington, Bedfordshire, on which to erect construction facilities for building airships. This was nationalised as the Royal Airship Works in 1919. The best-known giants flown from Cardington, the R100 and R101, resulted from a Government-funded competition. The R100 was built by the Airship Guarantee Co. at Howden Royal Naval Air Station, south-west of York. The company was a subsidiary of Vickers-Armstrongs, which had been formed in 1927 when Vickers merged with Sir W. G. Armstrong Whitworth & Co. However, John Siddeley had taken Armstrong Siddeley out of the group and also bought Armstrong Whitworth Aircraft. The Vickers-Armstrongs name was retained, although the company would usually be referred to as 'Vickers'.

Barnes N. Wallis, initially the chief engineer, employed a spirally-woven 'geodesic' wire support structure, first used in airships by Schütte-Lanz. He was assisted and then succeeded by Nevil Shute Norway, who had begun his engineering career in the de Havilland Design Office before moving to Vickers in 1924. R100's first flight was to Cardington, in November 1929, from where it made several trial flights—including a transatlantic return voyage to Canada in July-August 1930.

The De Havilland School of Flying, Hatfield Aerodrome in 1932. Harpsfield Hall is at top-centre. (*BAE Systems, via Reg Willoughby, DHAeTS Association*)

Vickers would use Wallis' geodesic principle for their Wellesley, Wellington, and other aircraft designs of the mid-late 1930s. During the Second World War, he would develop the bouncing bomb used in the 'Dambusters' raid, and also the Tallboy and Grand Slam deep-penetration 'earthquake' bombs. After the War he would work on supersonic designs and swing-wing technology.

The other air ship competition entrant was the R101, built at Cardington by an Air Ministry-appointed team. It made the first of its test flights a month before the R100 did so. The *Graf Zeppelin* visited Cardington while they were there. Until Zeppelin's ill-fated *Hindenburg* of 1937, the R101 was the largest aircraft ever built. John Stroud saw them over Hatfield:

> ...I saw both of them pass over on their first flights to London. By the time the R100 flew over I must have become known for my aviation interest because the whole school was turned out to see it and the headmaster asked me to explain why there was a line hanging from it.... On nine occasions I saw the R101 ... and the Graf Zeppelin twice.

Crashes and Fatalities

Tragedy struck British civil aviation in October 1930. On the evening of the 4th R101 left Cardington heading for Karachi, which was then in British India, with fifty-four passengers on board. Among them were Brancker and Lord Thomson. Almost immediately one of the R101's engines was shut down with oil pressure problems, and the weather was deteriorating rapidly. John Stroud witnessed her struggling over Hatfield 'in heavy rain and battling against the wind—it was very noisy and its vibration made the doors in the house rattle long before it came into sight.' She continued over Potters Bar and London, and left the English coast at Hastings, reaching the French coast over Point de St Quentin. Just after 2 a.m. on the 5th R101 entered a dive, hit the ground, and burst into flames at Allonne, near Beauvais in northern France. Forty-eight passengers and crew died—including Thompson and Brancker, who had done so much to create the opportunities in civil aviation that de Havilland had been able to make the most of.

The official enquiry team included John Moore-Brabazon, who had visited Geoffrey de Havilland at Seven Barrows in 1909. He had entered politics after leaving the Royal Flying Corps as a Lieutenant Colonel in 1918. Dr Hugo Eckener, head of Luftschiffbau Zeppelin GmbH, also joined the enquiry. The findings brought an end to 'lighter than air' civil aviation in Britain for many years, and R100 was scrapped. Lt-Col. Sir Francis C. Shelmerdine, who had worked at the Air Ministry in the 1920s and latterly as Director of Civil Aviation in India, was Brancker's successor.

The economic gloom was also continuing. Martin Sharp summed it up:

> 'We can say goodbye to 1930 without regret', Mr Butler remarked, 'and the question is—have we touched the bottom?' We had not.... 1931 was virtually unprecedented; for the professors it became a textbook example of the growing economic interdependence of nations...

Film studios had been developed at Elstree from 1927. Just 8 miles to the north, Hatfield was ideal for aerial filming, and many people involved with theatre and cinema were learning to fly. Director Walter Summers wrote the screenplay for the 1931 film, *The Flying Fool*, in which Henry Kendall played a pilot who infiltrates a gang of jewel smugglers. The opening credits acknowledge Imperial Airways, the French Air Union, and 'the de Havilland Aircraft Co. Ltd in the production of the aerial scenes in this film'. The *Times* for 7 January 1931, reporting on new British films, credited the de Havilland School of Flying in particular.

However, the *Times* also had to report that, during filming of a chase scene in *The Flying Fool* on 2 February, an Avro that had taken off from Hatfield crashed through the back gardens of a street in Brixton, south London. It had been chartered, with two Moths, by British International Pictures Ltd at Elstree Studios. Pilot Richard Bush's head smashed through the glass windscreen, and cameraman

Flight for 17 April 1931 described the Flying School as 'within easy reach of London ... admirably equipped with buildings which include large hangars and a well-appointed club lounge, smoking room and restaurant.... The aerodrome is large and the approaches good, while the surrounding country is also admirable for forced landings should these become necessary.' (*L N A Photos Ltd, Hatfield Aerodrome booklet, 1935—BAE Systems, via Roger de Mercado, DHAeTS Association*)

Stanley Rodwell, from Welwyn Garden City, broke ribs when he jumped out before impact. The camera was undamaged. Walter Summers was a passenger in one of the Moths and the 'villain', Wallace Geoffrey, was in the other—Summers had learned to fly himself before asking his actors to take to the air. When they saw the Avro in trouble, dropping out of sight through the clouds, they returned to Hatfield to get news, and then got airborne again to continue filming. The Air Ministry's Inspector of Accidents determined that the Avro's engine had suffered a fuel shortage.

Flying a transport plane, Kendall pursues the villains' car through a dangerous mountain pass—a School of Flying instructor was his double in the flying scenes. The *Welwyn Times* for 25 February describes the car as 'a Bentley specially designed by Sir Henry Birkin', which ends up going over the White Cliffs of Dover. In 1929 Birkin had bought one of Welwyn Garden City's new workshop facilities in Broadwater Road. Here, he developed the supercharged 'Blower' Bentleys in partnership with fellow racing driver W. Mike Couper.

In 1932 Birkin would develop *The Brooklands Race Game*—indoor racing of model cars—designed by Patrick G. Kennedy. Birkin set up Miniature Speedway Ltd at his workshops in Welwyn to produce metal cars and extruded rubber tracks for them to run on. The cars were 6 inches long and contained an electric motor. Contact brushes under the cars were guided by powered rails, and scale speeds of up to 150 mph were claimed. He set up demonstration tracks in various places, including one in the Hatfield Aerodrome clubhouse lecture rooms. Unfortunately, Birkin's would go into liquidation in 1933.

There were crashes at Hatfield, too. John Stroud, now aged 12, was among those who saw an aircraft crash fatally on 18 June 1931. It had flown from Blackburn's aerodrome at Brough, near Hull. The incident was reported in the *Times* the next day, with a misspelling of 'Harpsfield':

> An eye witness of the accident, Mr W. J. Grovestock of Hartsfield Hall Farm, who arrived at the spot a few minutes afterwards, said it was quite impossible to get anywhere near the aeroplane to help the occupants, whom he could see through the flames. There was, however, no sign of life from either of them.

The Times for 23 June reported on the coroner's inquest:

> The inquest on the bodies of Miss Sicele O'Brien, the airwoman, and Mrs Gordon Gallien, who were burned to death when an aeroplane piloted by Miss O'Brien crashed near Hartsfield Hall, Hatfield Herts. last Thursday night, was held at St Albans yesterday.
>
> Miss O'Brien ... won the first women's air race in this country, and in 1928 lost a leg in an aeroplane crash. Mrs Gordon Gallien ... was a great traveller and had been awarded a Diploma of the Royal Geographical Society for an expedition in Tanganyika...

The Royal Aero Club had awarded an Aviator's Certificate to Enid Merlin Gordon Gallien on 30 July 1930. Sicele O'Brien had received hers in 1926, and after the 1928 crash in her uninsured Moth she was keen to fly again. From 1929 she was organising aviation rallies and flying displays. She wrote several articles on private flying in 1929–30 for a publication known as *The Girl's Own Paper & Woman's Magazine*. These covered flying lessons, pilots' licences, costs of ownership, types of light aircraft, and aerobatics. Her April 1930 article was entitled, 'Keeping an Aeroplane of One's Own', in which she suggested that anyone could learn to fly. She assured readers that the wings of light aircraft such as the Moth 'can be folded or opened by a girl single-handed in less than two minutes', for storage in 'an average-sized garage'. If one could not 'establish a private aerodrome on one's own estate', she recommended one of the 'flying clubs springing up all over the country'. She even encouraged basic 'do it yourself' maintenance, 'if one has even a wee bit of a mechanical mind'. Sicele's licence had been renewed a few weeks before, and she launched a 'Buy British Goods' campaign, flying around Britain in an Imperial Airways aircraft. She gave lectures on the Empire and its products, and offered joy rides for members of the audience.

The Times continued:

> Dr Percy M. Brittain, of Hatfield, said that when he arrived at the scene of the accident the aeroplane was on fire, with two bodies inside. In his opinion death in each case was due to shock from burns.
>
> Arthur Potter, of Hatfield, timekeeper and night watchman at the De Havilland Flying School, said that at 8 p.m. on Thursday a two-seater biplane made a good

Publicity photograph showing how easily a Moth could be stored in a garage. G-EBSQ was first registered on 28 July 1927.

Photos of Miss Sicele O'Brien (left) and Mrs Enid Gordon Gallien from the Royal Aero Club's membership records. (*Royal Aero Club Trust*)

landing on the aerodrome. The machine was refilled, and later the pilot and her passenger had tea in the club room. When he was pushing the machine towards the petrol tank the pilot said, 'Don't lift too high, because I am rather heavy on the nose,' After he got the machine started Miss O'Brien went a few yards and called to him, 'You will have to come and help me, I can't turn this thing across there.'

He pointed out that the spot which Miss O'Brien indicated was not the one from which pilots usually took off, but Miss O'Brien appeared to be in a hurry. She began to taxi and went a considerable distance in comparison with what other pilots usually did before her machine left the ground.

'She left the ground about 18in, or 2ft,' the witness said, 'then dropped again, took on a little more speed, and eventually got off the ground and climbed against the wind. I thought that the trees were sheltering the wind, but when I saw that she was above the trees I was satisfied that she had got off all right. A gamekeeper who saw her take off suddenly cried to me, "Look, Arthur, she's down." I saw the machine spinning to the ground. The aeroplane struck the ground with her nose and burst into flame immediately. When she rose she turned right, which is against the rules of the aerodrome. The machine crashed just outside the aerodrome in a hayfield.'

Harry Albert Love, pilot in charge of the Hull Aero Club, said ... Miss O'Brien before leaving asked to have the rudder-bar in Mrs Gallien's seat adjusted so that Mrs Gallien could work it. Miss O'Brien would perhaps find difficulty in getting the machine out of a spin because of her artificial leg, and he thought she wanted the rudder bar adjusted so that Mrs Gallien could help her out of a spin.

The Deputy Coroner said he did not think there could be any blame attached to the pilot or the passenger. A verdict of 'Accidental death' was returned.

One last DH.9J was added to the School of Flying fleet in 1931. Despite being an old design, this one was brand new—the first of several aircraft built by the technical school apprentices to give them experience of building a complete aircraft. Meanwhile, one of de Havilland's most iconic aircraft was being created at Stag Lane, in response to a request from the RAF to modify the Gipsy Moth. They needed improved access to the front cockpit, usually occupied by the instructor, and the ability to escape from it while wearing a parachute. Frank Hearle worked with Fred C. Plumb and W. Douglas Hunter on moving the centre section of the upper wing forward, to place the struts ahead of the cockpit. To restore the aircraft's balance, they swept both wings back. They also added fold-down doors to the cockpit sides. After a number of 'trial and error' changes on a full-size mock-up, they produced drawings for the new model. It retained its DH.60 designation initially, but suffixed with 'T' for *Tiger*, re-using the name of the DH.71 monoplane racer of 1927. After further modifications the type was given the new number of DH.82, and Hubert Broad made its first flight on 26 October. Production of the Gipsy Moth continued at Stag Lane, and it would remain at the heart of British flying until the start of the Second World War.

Blackburn Bluebird G-AABF which crashed at Hatfield on 18 June 1931, killing its two occupants: Miss Sicele O'Brien and Mrs Enid Gordon Gallien. (*Krul Antiquarian Books, Hoofddorp, Netherlands*)

Looking west to Hatfield Aerodrome in 1932. St Albans Road comes from bottom-right, passes under the H&StAR branchline, and meets the Barnet Bypass at the Stonehouse junction, in the centre of the picture. (*BAE Systems, via the Norman Eastaff Collection*)

6

From Near and Far

> Turning to affairs at home: our new aerodrome at Hatfield referred to last year has been completely finished and is now one of the finest aerodromes in the country. There are excellent club premises with restaurant and sitting rooms for flying pupils and private owners, and we should be at all times very pleased to see shareholders and their friends there.
>
> *Alan Butler, de Havilland Annual General Meeting, 31 December 1931*

International Visitors

Moths of all variants were also used by many air forces around the world, some even in offensive roles. In 1928, both Iraq and Egypt had decided to add Flying Corps to their armies. From hundreds of applicants in each country, six Iraqi and three Egyptian officers were chosen for pilot training. The Iraqis came to the RAF College at Cranwell, in Lincolnshire, followed by attachments to various RAF squadrons. The Egyptians were trained at home by the RAF, before travelling to England for further training.

The first Iraqi aircraft unit consisted of five Gipsy Moths. Five of the Iraqi pilots flew the Moths from Hatfield on 8 April 1931, heading for Baghdad. An RAF officer was seconded to the Iraqi Government, and ferried a Puss Moth for King Faisal's personal use. Before the six aircraft took off, Frank Hearle, de Havilland's General Manager, presented them with a silver model of a Moth to commemorate the founding of the Iraq Flying Corps. The Iraqi Ambassador was present, among RAF and other dignitaries. John Stroud witnessed some embarrassment for the RAF:

> ...the Royal Iraq Air Force took off from Hatfield. I do mean the air force, the whole of it, because it comprised five immaculate silver Gipsy Moths and one Puss Moth, all wearing the new red, white, green, and black air force markings.... Three [Armstrong Whitworth] Siskins of No. 41 Squadron came to Hatfield for

the occasion and, after the departure of the Iraqis, tried to make their own. The first Siskin taxied across the recently filled-in ditch and promptly got bogged. A team with shovels and other forms of aid was at work by the time the second aircraft reached the site and it too got bogged. The third Siskin took a different route and got airborne.

In September 1931 de Havilland had won a contract to supply Egypt with ten Gipsy Moths. The British Government tried to send the first five aircraft to Alexandria by sea, but the Egyptian Government insisted that the Moths should be assembled in England and flown to Cairo. The ship had got as far as Gibraltar and was ordered to turn back. The five Gipsy Moths were then seen off from Hatfield on 23 May 1932 by the Egyptian Ambassador, their Minister for War, and army generals. The three Eyptian and two British pilots arrived at Almazah airport on 2 June, as heroes—to a huge reception.

The US Embassy in London had acquired a Puss Moth in 1931, for use by their naval attaché. The dark blue and silver aircraft was officially based at Hendon, but it was often seen at Hatfield.

The Iraq Air Corps' first pilots at Hatfield. They had just finished their training with the RAF, and were ready to fly home in their new Moths. They set off on 8 April and reached Baghdad on the 22nd, via France, Italy and Greece. (*CEGES/SOMA Collections, Brussels - No.596258*)

At de Havilland's AGM on New Year's Eve, 1931, Alan Butler suggested that more flying days were available there than at many other aerodromes nearer to London. Fuel pumps were installed on an 'island' filling station, about 40 yards in front of the hangars. This was built by Wayne Tank & Pump Co. Ltd of Newlands Park, near Crystal Palace, in south London. Heston had a similar facility. A long, swinging arm was positioned at each corner, carrying hoses for refuelling up to four aircraft at once. Wayne also installed an oil 'fountain'. Arthur Hagg was developing a new design based on the Tiger Moth, but with an enlarged fuselage to accommodate a three-seat passenger cabin. The pilot still sat in an open cockpit above. This was the DH.83 *Fox Moth*, first flown on 29 January 1932 by Hubert Broad. It became the first aircraft to earn a profit in commercial airline service without government subsidies.

From that winter, agents of Standard Telephones & Cables Ltd were available at Brooklands, Stag Lane, and Hatfield, to handle orders for ground station and aircraft radio equipment. They had their own Tiger Moth demonstrator at Hatfield. The Lady Margaret L. L. Loch, wife of Baron Edward Douglas Loch and daughter of William Compton, 5th Marquess of Northampton, started keeping her Gipsy Moth at Hatfield.

Robert 'Bob' J. Waight learned to fly at the School of Flying in early 1932. He would become assistant test pilot to Hubert Broad, and would later take over from him. Around the time Bob was training, the school started offering every civilian pupil experience of flying 'on instruments' in case of bad visibility, free of charge—expressly not to encourage risk-taking but rather for safety preparedness. This involved pulling a hinged hood over the trainee pilot so that they could see nothing but the instruments in the cockpit. Communication with the instructor was via 'air tube' earphones.

Prince Lennart of Sweden had flying lessons at Hatfield. The *Welwyn Times* for 10 March reported that:

> He is an apt pupil and is likely to become a first-class pilot in a very short time. He began his instruction on Tuesday last week, flying from Stag Lane in a Puss Moth, and took the controls under the direction of Mr Buckingham, one of the instructors ... the prince remarked that he found flying very fascinating, and that he enjoys it very much, expressing a wish to continue instruction immediately with daily flights. On Tuesday the prince flew with his instructor, and, taking the controls, made an excellent landing.

Hugh Buckingham had worked for de Havilland since 1926. He had learned to fly at Stag Lane with the School of Flying, and worked in technical and sales from 1929. With his fiancée—Miss Karin Nissvandt—Prince Lennart gave a rooftop film shoot in London to the Pathé Gazette, who entitled the film, 'The Happy Lovers'. The Prince is seen using his own cine camera to film his fiancée. He then chats in impeccably clipped English: 'I've just flown this morning.... I'm just taking my certificate now.' He confirms that he hopes to get his flying licence before the wedding. When asked whether they would fly on their honeymoon, he answers, 'Well, I don't know but I hope so.... Why not.... She loves it, much more than cars.' He admits that, on a windy day, 'It's a little bumpy. Awfully bumpy, isn't it?', and he gives the lady a chuckling nod. He continues, 'Well, I don't mind. I think it's alright ... at 5,000 feet, and then it's alright.' The couple were married on 11 March, without official Swedish consent—which meant that the Prince forfeited his royal titles.

The Trimotor aircraft that had taken Amy Johnson from Brisbane to Sydney, as part of her triumphal tour of Australia, was piloted by James 'Jim' A. Mollison. He too became a record-breaker in July-August 1931, flying from Australia to England, in a Gipsy Moth, in 8 days, 19 hours, and 25 minutes. He beat the previous time by two days and nearly four hours. This had been set just eight weeks before, in another Gipsy Moth, by Wg Cdr Charles Kingsford Smith, a former RAF light heavyweight boxing champion. Kingsford Smith would be knighted on 3 June 1932 for services to aviation.

John Stroud was present again when three more Puss Moths left Hatfield for Baghdad on 12 April 1932, destined for the Iraqi Flying Corp. Three of them were the first Puss Moths to be fitted with racks for carrying light bombs. The fourth was fitted out as an ambulance.

Jim Mollison and Amy became close, and in 1932 they decided to get married. The press called the couple 'The Flying Sweethearts'. In June Walter Summers wrote and directed a short film, *Dual Control*, in which Amy and Jim appeared as themselves. This was a publicity piece for Jim's planned solo flight across the

A still image from a Pathé Gazette film shot on a London rooftop, entitled *The Happy Lovers*. Prince Lennart of Sweden holds his own ciné camera, which he has just used to film his fiancée, Miss Karin Nissvandt. (*British Pathé Ltd*)

Atlantic in his new Puss Moth, G-ABXY, which he named *The Heart's Content*. Amy acquired Gipsy Moth G-ABVW from de Havilland, and named it *Jason IV*. The wedding took place on 29 July 1932. Lt-Col. Sir Francis C. Shelmerdine, Director of Civil Aviation, was their best man. They flew from Stag Lane to Scotland for their honeymoon, Amy in her new *Jason* and Jim in *The Heart's Content*. Don Lawrence remembered the couple visiting Hatfield with the Puss Moth.

Crossing the Atlantic from east to west was against the prevailing winds, causing higher fuel consumption and a longer flight time than in the other direction. Jim achieved the feat on 18 August—from Dublin to New Brunswick, Canada—in a little over thirty hours. It was the longest non-stop flight for a light aircraft to date.

The School of Flying Thrives

The School of Flying was 'community-minded'. In May 1932, the newly-formed Hertfordshire Aero Club, based at St. Albans, organised a charity event for the Wheathampstead Hospitals fête Committee, and the Hatfield school provided a flying display. Private pilots who wanted to attend were asked to land at Hatfield. They would repeat the display twelve months later.

John Stroud also witnessed the end of a flying school aircraft on 16 October 1932: 'I saw DH.9J G-EBGT spin into the ground and I well remember the silence after it hit and the dust and crows rising from the scene.'

But John's memories of those early days were mostly happy ones:

> The Moths and DH.9Js were normally lined up facing into the wind and none had brakes. I used to be allowed to put the chocks in ... wedged under the wheels ... remove them and hang on to the wingtips to swing the aircraft out of line—hanging on to a Jaguar-engined DH.9 is no easy task for a boy of eleven or twelve! I used to help push the aircraft in and out the hangars and on one great day I was allowed to ride back from the fuel pumps in the rear cockpit....
>
> In those early Hatfield days many of the visiting aircraft were club Moths ... including those of the London Aeroplane Club (yellow and silver), Midland Aero Club (green and silver), Cinque Ports Flying Club (white with zig-zag fuselage bands of brown and blue) and Herts and Essex Aero Club (brown and orange). The Brooklands School of Flying's dark blue and red Moths used to appear, also the orange and black Moths and Desoutters of National Flying Services ... all gold Moths belonging to Shell and the green, red and gold [Avro] Sports Avians ... of Shell-Mex.

Happily, it was not long before appearances were matched, once again, by stability and growth in the business, as described by Martin Sharp: '...1931–2 did see the

DH.9J G-EBEZ of the de Havilland School of Flying. It was flown into second place by Alan Cobham in the 1923 King's Cup. It moved to Hatfield with the School in 1930, and is seen here at the Hatfield fuel pumps. The aircraft was retired in 1933. (*The A. J. Jackson Collection*)

bottom of the depression...Things took a turn in October-December 1932, and the calendar year finished with a DH payroll 50 per cent larger than in January...1932–3 was easily the best in the company's thirteen years.' As previously mentioned, the de Havilland School of Flying was created at Stag Lane in 1923 in response to an Air Ministry requirement for basic RAF training and for flying opportunities for reserve officers. At de Havilland's annual dinner in December 1932, Alan Butler was delighted to confirm the renewal of the school's government contract for another four years. He also announced that Tiger Moths would replace the school's remaining DH.9Js.

Ten Tiger Moths were registered for the school on 6 February 1933, with registrations from G-ACDA to G-ACDK, and the DH.9Js were taken back to Stag Lane for disposal in March. Among the Tiger Moths, Fox Moth G-ACDD would be registered briefly at Hatfield. It had been intended for the Prince of Wales, but the order was cancelled and it was sold to a customer in Belgium at the end of March. Gipsy Moth G-AACZ was privately owned and kept at Hatfield from 1932 to 1935; Bob Reeve was its owner from March to July 1933. It was then registered to Dennis A. Rea, who would become a flying instructor at Brooklands. In May 1933 Alan Butler took a refresher course in blind flying, and the school gave flying lessons under a *Daily Express* scholarship scheme.

The young Jack Franklin had been flown to the Aerodrome on a local joy ride in 1932. He was admiring one of the DH.9s when he was approached by someone

Hatfield Aerodrome's buildings in 1932, looking east, with the Stonehouse junction beyond. In the centre foreground is a DH.9J. The light-coloured aircraft is a Puss Moth. The other dark-coloured aircraft are Gipsy Moths. The long line of houses at the top of the picture is Stockbreach Road. (*BAE Systems, via Philip Birtles*)

whom he considered to be 'one of the kindest men I have ever met'. It was the school's chief flying instructor, Bob Reeve, who had been with the company since 1925. '"Like to fly it?" he said. "Of course", I replied, "but I couldn't possibly afford it." "You get paid to fly this one," was his answer, and he told me about the Reserve of Air Force officers.' Jack joined the following year. An Air Ministry recruitment campaign, launched in December 1933, describes the training course that Jack experienced:

> Approximately 60 vacancies exist for entry into the Royal Air Force Reserve during the next few months for initial training in flying. The vacancies will be filled by direct entrants from civil life. Experience of flying is not necessary as a complete course of flying instruction is given at no cost to the candidate. Applicants, who would be entered ... in the rank of Pilot Officer, must not have reached their 25th birthday and must be physically fit and of good education ... The instructional course consists of 50 hours' flying which must be carried out in a maximum period of 3 months ... Entrants are required to do 10 hours' flying in the second half of their first year of service. Thereafter they must carry out 20 hours' flying annually within a maximum period of 20 days. Entrants are also

required to attend a short 4–6 day course at a R.A.F. unit in their second and subsequent years of service. Flying training is carried out at civilian flying schools, at present situated at Bristol, Brough (East Yorks), Hamble (Hants), and Hatfield (Herts).

The instruction is given by qualified flying instructors of the RAF Reserve and the types of aircraft used are the De Havilland 'Tiger Moth', Avro 'Cadet' and Blackburn B.2. The syllabus of instruction includes practice in air pilotage, aerobatics, 'blind flying', camera gun work and photography ... Candidates selected for interview are required to attend a selection board at the Air Ministry and to pass a medical examination prior to acceptance. Vacancies also exist ... for holders of Civil A licences. Candidates may be considered for this Class up to their 28th birthday, and are required to pass a flying test to demonstrate their ability to proceed direct to reserve training.

Clem Pike was usually Jack's instructor, but:

I occasionally flew with Eddie Fulford, who would tell his pupils on the approach to come in by the clock tower on the Stone House restaurant ... to see the time. A habit of another instructor, George Cox ... was to glide down on the approach over the veranda of the clubhouse, where pupils were waiting in deck chairs (what a leisurely life!) and when directly overhead he would lean out of the cockpit and bellow, 'Get ready "so-and-so"!' to ensure that the change-over to the next pupil could be made without stopping the engine.

One of the original batch of Tiger Moths, registered to the de Havilland School of Flying at Hatfield on 6 February 1933. It is seen here in the late 1930s, when the School's fleet had expanded. (*Royal Aero Club Trust, 0379-0047*)

> ...lectures took place in the clubhouse, where Flight Lieut Rivers Oldmeadow instilled into us the functions of the four-stroke engine and elementary navigation, and, having done that, would neatly vault off his one leg into his open sports Bentley, and thunder off. The clubhouse was managed by Bob Reeve's charming wife. [Farmer Sinclair's] daughter did clerical work in the Flying School.
>
> One of the problems which caused despair among the ground staff was sheep droppings on the aerodrome, which would whip up from the wheels to the underside of the main plane [wing] on take-off. Dried hard when airborne, it became almost impossible to scrape off, and this resulted in frequent replacement of fabric.

Jack would continue to maintain his flying hours at Hatfield. In 1937, he would join the newly created Volunteer Reserve (RAFVR).

In May 1933, the Iraqi Flying Corps returned to Hatfield to collect eight examples of the new DH.84 Dragon. John Stroud, now fourteen, was allowed inside one of them. Due to the immediate success of the Fox Moth, Arthur Hagg designed the DH.84 to a commission from Hillman's Airways. It was a twin-Gipsy biplane with a long cabin accommodating the pilot and six passenger seats. Initially named as the *Dragon Moth*, Hubert Broad had made the first flight in the prototype at Stag Lane on 12 November 1932.

Advert placed by de Havilland in the Punch *Almanack* for 1933. (*Courtesy of Jim Crowther*)

New DH.84 Dragons for the Iraq Flying Corps, at Hatfield, with Iraqi pilots ready to fly them to Baghdad on 5 May 1933. Harpsfield Hall is behind the trees at top-right. These were general-purpose aircraft with uses such as transport and aerial survey, but they were also armed with three machine gun positions and racks for sixteen 20-lb (9-kg) bombs. They arrived in Iraq on 13 May. (*Sport & General Press Agency Ltd—BAE Systems, via Philip Birtles*)

The Iraqi Dragons being lined up before unfolding their wings. (*Associated Press—BAE Systems, via Philip Birtles*)

7

The King's Cup comes to Hatfield

> Flying in the King's Cup Air Race was good sport, but after a few years of it I gave up all hope of winning and was content to share in the general excitement and derive satisfaction and interest from following a set course round England. Plenty of skill and care were demanded.... The throttle remained fully open from start to finish.
>
> *Geoffrey de Havilland*

While Hatfield was Developing

In 1930 Hanworth saw the largest ever King's Cup field, with eighty-eight starters. Miss Winifred Sawley Brown, in her Avro Avian, became the first woman to win the race. Crossley Motors had sold Avro to Armstrong Whitworth in 1928. A Hawker Tomtit, powered by an Armstrong Siddeley Mongoose, was sponsored by HRH the Prince of Wales—the future King Edward VIII. HRH Prince George sponsored his older brother's personal pilot, Flt Lt Edward H. Fielden, to fly one of Wally Hope's Air Taxis—DH.75 Hawk Moth G-AAUZ. This was powered by an Armstrong Siddeley Lynx. There were seven Puss Moths and thirty-seven Moths in the race. Such events were described as 'Moth-eaten', but only nine of them would be among the twenty entries credited with a final placing. Alan and Lois Butler were second and fourth, he in Gipsy Moth G-AAXG with a faired-over second cockpit—still flying today—and she in his Puss Moth, G-AAXL.

Five members of the RAF High Speed Flight entered. The 1929 Schneider Trophy winner Dick Waghorn was third, in a Blackburn Bluebird. Fg Off. Leonard Snaith's Comper Swift did not start. Richard Atcherley, the 1928 King's Cup winner, retired his Segrave Meteor at the start with fuel feed trouble—he and his twin brother, David (who competed in the 1931 and 1937 King's Cups, the latter at Hatfield), would become legends in the RAF. Augustus Orlebar was twentieth, in a Bluebird; Sqn Ldr Leonard H. Slatter retired his Bluebird during the race. Slatter had been sponsored by Lord Trenchard, Marshal of the RAF, who had retired on 1 January and was made Baron Trenchard of Wolfeton in the New Year's Honours.

Fielden was seventh, as he had been the previous year. Broad was ninth, in a Puss Moth, and Hope was tenth, in a single-seat Gipsy Moth. Winifred Spooner was fourteenth in a Southern Martlet. The Prince of Wales's Tomtit was eighteenth. Geoffrey de Havilland and Geoffrey Jnr (now aged 20) were both forced to retire—father in his own Puss Moth, G-AAXO, and son in the flying school's Gipsy Moth G-AASL.

At Heston, in 1931, forty entries included seventeen de Havillands. Fg Off. E. Cecil T. Edwards won, in a Bluebird, at his first attempt. A Simmonds Spartan was second. Puss Moths were third, fourth, seventh, and eighth. A Comper Swift was sixth. The best-placed Gipsy Moths could only manage tenth and eleventh. Nick Comper had joined Geoffrey de Havilland in the Airco design office in 1915, but was posted to France with the RFC Special Reserve, as a reconnaissance pilot, in 1916. After the First World War he remained in the RAF, studied aerodynamics, and became an engineering instructor at the RAF College at Cranwell, Lincolnshire. One of his pupils was Frank Whittle, who went on to invent the jet engine. Comper left the RAF in 1929 to form his own company. He competed in the 1926 and 1932 King's Cups. The Swift was his most successful racing design.

From forty-two starters at Brooklands in 1932, Wally Hope took his third win with the new DH.83 *Fox Moth*, G-ABUT—sponsored by designer Arthur Hagg. Edward Fielden was second, in a Comper Swift. Third place was taken by Sqn Ldr W. Leslie Runciman, Commanding Officer of 607 (County of Durham) Squadron, Auxiliary Air Force, who had also competed in 1930. His father was Walter Runciman, Member of Parliament for St Ives in Cornwall and President of the Board of Trade. Puss Moths also finished fourth, sixth, and eighth, the latter being Geoffrey de Havilland with his own G-ABGT. Hubert Broad was fifth, in Gipsy Moth single-seat racer G-ABVW. It was fitted with the new 'inverted' Gipsy IIIA, which was known as the Gipsy Major from 1933. Winifred Spooner was fifteenth, in a Gipsy Moth. Newly-married Amy Mollison then took G-ABVW on her honeymoon with Jim.

Hatfield Preparations for the 1933 Race

To set the scene, the DH.71 Tiger Moth G-EBRV—the single-seat, record-breaking monoplane that was built around Hubert Broad's shoulders in 1927—was used as a mounted display. Newly-extended hangars were made available to competitors on Friday 7 July, the day before the race. A fabric doping service was available from Cellon Ltd of Kingston-upon-Thames, south-west London. They had a service van at Hatfield over the two days, although ten of the eleven winners since the first race of 1922 had used Titanine dope. Competitors who had Irvin parachutes among their equipment could ask for assistance from de Havilland ground engineers, paid for by Irving Air Chutes.

Next to the clubhouse, a squash courts building and an open-air 'lido' swimming pool had just been completed in June, and these quickly became very popular. The

This photo of the extension to the Hatfield hangars was used in an advert in the *Welwyn Times* for 21 September 1933, placed by London-based company Archibald D. Dawnay & Sons Ltd. They had built the Stag Lane factory in the early 1920s, and they now supplied the steel for the extended Hatfield hangars from their factory in Welwyn Garden City. The architect was A. G. Stedhan. Construction was completed by another London company, Courtney & Fairbairn Ltd; the project began on 18 April, and was completed in ten weeks. The doors were supplied by Esavian Ltd of 171-181 High Holborn, central London. Esavian also supplied fittings for hangars at Heston, Speke, and Filton, near Bristol. (*Hertfordshire Libraries*)

pool, complete with diving board, was filled in early summer each year, and was continually replenished with up to 2,000 gallons an hour from an artesian well. It was also emptied and cleaned once a week, and was flood-lit from dusk.

For those flying into Hatfield on the Friday afternoon or early evening, a published letter from the Headmaster of Mill Hill School in Barnet, Maurice L. Jacks, asked them to avoid flying low near the school as it was their speech day. Although 10 miles (16 km) south of Hatfield, the school was on a straight line from Hendon, and flights from Croydon might also pass over. For the Saturday, Sir Christopher Bullock at the Air Ministry issued Notice to Airmen No. 43 of the year. This instructed pilots 'to avoid, as far as possible, landing at Hatfield Aerodrome between 0730 and 1930 … as competing aircraft will be taking off and landing continuously'. Any aircraft that wished to leave during the day was not allowed to take off without permission from the airfield control officer. Handley Page offered their aerodrome at Radlett to airborne visitors, from where a local bus company would take them the 9 miles (14.5 km) north to Hatfield.

Enclosures were provided from where spectators could get a good view of the start and finish. Ticket prices were 1*s* 6*d*, 2*s* 6*d*, and 5*s*. Unfortunately, the area

Newly extended hangars and marquees for the King's Cup on 8 July 1933. The hangars were made available to competitors the day before the race. (*Barratts Photo Press Ltd, the Norman Eastaff Collection*)

DH.71 Tiger Moth G-EBRV, the 1927 monoplane racer, mounted on a pole at Hatfield Aerodrome in the summer of 1933. (*Copyright acknowledged, via the A. J. Jackson Collection*)

reserved for those paying the top ticket price faced into the afternoon sun. Car parking was extra, at 2*s* 6*d*, but they could park right up to the railings—and if it rained, they could watch while sheltering in their vehicles. Motorcycles were also charged at 6*d*, or 1*s* 6*d* if they had a sidecar attached. If the weather held, there were plenty of chairs to enjoy the open air. On the Saturday morning, a large number of cars did indeed turn up. The clubhouse restaurant and bar did well to keep serving food and drinks all day long, although they struggled at times.

Car manufacturer Sir William Morris was there, sponsoring three Hawker Tomtits with new engines from his Wolseley Motors division. Geoffrey de Havilland had worked for Wolseley as a draughtsman in 1905. Sir William was accompanied by Wolseley MD William Cannell, and the joint MD of Hawker, Fred Sigrist. H. G. Hawker Engineering was renamed as Hawker Aircraft Ltd that year. Frederick Handley Page and Frank Halford were also there, as were de Havilland's chief engineer, Charles Walker, and General Manager Frank Hearle. Sir John Siddeley, knighted the year before, would present the Siddeley Trophy to the highest-placed private flying club entrant.

The contest would be held over four rounds, each over a triangular course. The four fastest competitors in each heat would go through to the next round. The first round would have six heats, beginning at 8 a.m.—the second round would have four heats. After two semi-finals, the final would be the thirteenth race of the day, ending in the late afternoon. There were thirty-five entries, of which thirteen were de Havillands. To make the drama of a close finish more likely, the slower aircraft set off first; the faster the known speed of the aircraft, the higher its 'handicap'. The decisions of the officials making the calculations were final.

Spectators who parked their cars up to the railings had a good view of the air racing. (Flight, *via aviationancestry.com*)

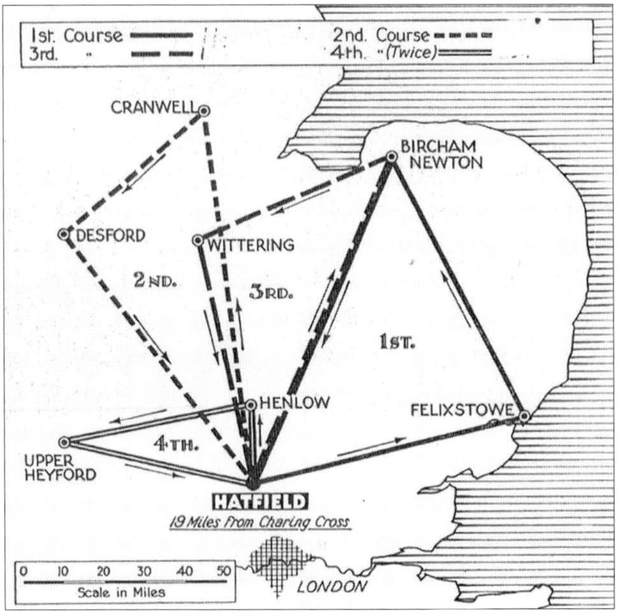

Stage courses for the King's Cup Race on Saturday, 8 July 1933. (Flight, *via aviationancestry.com*)

Round One

The course for the first round was 224 miles (360 km): east to Felixstowe on the Suffolk coast; up to Bircham Newton, in north-west Norfolk; and back down to Hatfield. British Pathé filmed Hon. Richard Westenra, Lady Bailey's brother, setting off in the first heat, side-by-side with Laurence Lipton in their Gipsy Moths, G-ACCW and G-ABVW. Lipton had acquired the latter from Amy Mollison in May 1933, and replaced the Gipsy Major engine with an older Gipsy III—but he retained the name *Jason IV*. Unfortunately, he was forced to land in a field near Ipswich with a shattered wooden propeller. Most of the other competitors were using Fairey metal airscrews. Westenra got through with his Gipsy Major-engined machine, finishing second, behind Capt. E. D. Ayre's Desoutter.

Cecil Edwards, the 1931 winner and now a Flight Lieutenant, was so fast in heat two that he arrived back at Hatfield ahead of some of the heat-one competitors. He was in his Pobjoy-engined Comper Swift. Caught off-guard, the *Flight* reporter and others abandoned their bacon and eggs so as not to miss other arrivals. Tom Campbell Black was next, in a Gipsy III Puss Moth. Leslie Runciman was third, in a Puss Moth. Capt. T. Neville Stack, the Lancashire Aero Club's chief flying instructor, was fourth—in a Pobjoy-Swift entered by Richard O. Shuttleworth, who was unable to fly it himself following a car accident. Stack had joined the Royal Flying Corps in 1917, and served in the RAF from 1921 to 1925, with his duties including a posting to Iraq. He had flown a Gipsy Moth to India in 1926, and had competed in the King's Cup in 1928, 1929, and 1930. 'Mad Jack' Shuttleworth was a racing driver and a collector of veteran cars and aircraft, which he repaired and displayed.

The line-up for the 8 a.m. start of heat one. A Southern Martlet is nearest to the camera, a Spartan Clipper is next, and Capt E. D. Ayre's Desoutter is beyond that—Ayre won the heat. (Flight, *via aviationancestry.com*)

An Arrow Active biplane was eliminated. It was sponsored by somebody who was used to winning—'Bentley Boys' motor-racing legend Woolf 'Babe' Barnato. Bentley had already won the Le Mans 24 Hours in 1923 and 1927 when Barnato and Bernard Rubin won in 1928. He won again, in 1929, with Henry 'Tim' Birkin—Bentleys took the next three places, too—and yet again in 1930, with Glen Kidston. Birkin won the 1931 race with Francis R. H. P. Curzon, 5th Earl Howe, in an Alfa Romeo.

Capt. Hubert Broad, the 1926 winner now competing for the eighth time, was first home in heat three, piloting DH.84 *Dragon* G-ACFG. He was followed in by another Pobjoy-Swift, flown by the 21-year-old Alexander A. D. Henshaw. Lady Bailey came fourth, and qualified for round two. The Pathé Gazette film also shows her taking off in her Gipsy Major Puss Moth, G-AAYA.

Geoffrey de Havilland, making his sixth attempt, and Capt. A. J. 'Bill' Styran both went in heat four. They each flew one of the new DH.85 Leopard Moths, G-ACHD and G-ACHC. They qualified for round two in first and second places. This was a high-wing, three-seater cabin monoplane, powered by the Gipsy Major and intended to replace the Puss Moth. It was the last aircraft that Geoffrey de Havilland designed himself, and he had made its first flight on 27 May 1933. Later that day he had flown it to Hatfield, and took Bob Hardingham on a flight. Hardingham remembered that 'somewhere over Luton [Geoffrey] got out of his front seat and joined me in the back'. The company advertised it as 'The sportsman's coupé on wings', and described the ease of flying it as 'Feet and hands off'. It was de Havilland's personal favourite, and he bought the prototype from the company—using it to commute between Stag Lane and Hatfield.

Haliburton H. 'Julie' Leech got through in a Gipsy III Arrow Active. Hawker test pilot Fg Off. Phillip E. G. 'Gerry' Sayer was eliminated in his Tomtit. Lois Butler, in a third Leopard Moth—with her husband in the cabin as navigator—won heat five. She had flown the aircraft for the first time just two days before. The *Flight* reporter was not at all sure that her Fairey adjustable pitch airscrew did not give her an unfair advantage; Styran also had one. Hawker chief test pilot Flt Lt P. W. S. 'George' Bulman was second, in another of the Tomtits. Carill S. Napier, son of the famous engine manufacturer Montague S. Napier, was too slow to qualify for round two in his Hendy 302A. He had also competed in the 1929, 1930, and 1931 races. Flt Lt Harry M. Schofield, 1927 Schneider Trophy RAF team member and a director of General Aircraft Ltd (GAL), had to retire his GAL ST-6 Monospar. He would fare much better next year.

Another Comper Swift (this one with a Gipsy Major) and the fastest entrant on paper, with a top speed of well over 170 mph, was flown in the last heat of round one by Flt Lt George H Stainforth, a member of the RAF High Speed Flight. The 1931 Schneider Trophy had been won by Flt Lt John N. Boothman, in Supermarine S.6B S1595. Stainforth flew the same aircraft two weeks later to regain the World Air Speed Record, at 407.5 mph (655.67 km/h), making him the first man to exceed 400 mph. In February 1933 Sir Malcolm Campbell had increased his Land Speed Record to 272.46 mph, after installing the same Rolls-Royce R engine that had powered the S.6B. Another High Speed Flight teammate, Augustus Orlebar, now a Wing Commander (he would reach the rank of Air Vice Marshal in the Second World War, but would die in 1943 aged 46), was among the spectators at Hatfield for the 1933 King's Cup. But none of this could help Stainforth, as his Swift had

Lois Butler sitting in front of her husband's DH.85 Leopard Moth, G-ACHB. She piloted it in the race, and Alan Butler was in the cabin with her as navigator—did well. The Pathé newsreel of the race shows Alan getting into the back seat. (*Planet News Ltd/Royal Aero Club Trust, 0398-0058*)

the highest handicap. Despite averaging 160.46 mph (258.24 km/h), he finished last in heat six—and he was no longer the Air Speed Record-holder. On 10 April, WO Francesco Agello had achieved 423.824 mph (682.078 km/h) in a Macchi MC.72.

The crank handle for the Napier Javelin in Capt. Edgar W. Percival's Gull was awkwardly positioned, and it refused to start. He had started the Percival Aircraft Co. in 1933. A big man from the crowd jumped onto the port wing, and cranked with all his strength; the engine fired and Percival was away, several seconds late. He could only manage fifth.

Heat six was won by Flt Lt John 'Jack' G. D. Armour, in another Javelin-Gull—entered by HRH Prince George. Flt Sgt George E. Lowdell was second, in the third Tomtit. Three-times winner and current Cup-holder Wally Hope was third, in a Gipsy III Swift. He can also be seen taking off in the Pathé Gazette newsreel; this was his sixth time in the competition. Air Vice Marshal Amyas E. Borton (Air Officer Commanding of the RAF's Inland Area since 1929) was fourth, in another Javelin-Gull. He had been a pilot and commander in the Royal Flying Corps during the First World War, and was promoted to senior ranks in the RAF in the 1920s. He served with distinction on the Western Front, in Palestine, and in Iraq, and was the first Commandant of the RAF College at Cranwell from 1923 to 1926.

The terrace in front of the clubhouse, from where the racing could be viewed in style with refreshments from the restaurant and bar. (Flight, *via aviationancestry.com*)

Round Two and the Semi-Finals

The course for heats seven to ten was 207 miles (333 km) long: up to Cranwell; across to Desford, in Leicestershire; and then down to Hatfield. Edwards won heat seven, followed by Ayre. Westenra was eliminated when Campbell Black overtook him, near the finish, to claim fourth. In heat eight, Henshaw and Broad took the first two places and Runciman was fourth. Neville Stack and Lady Bailey were eliminated; this was her fifth and last time in the competition. During the Second World War, she would be appointed as a Section Officer in the Women's Auxiliary Air Force.

The three Leopard Moths were together in heat nine with Bulman. Lois Butler got away quicker than Capt. Styran, but he caught her and finished second behind Geoffrey de Havilland. She claimed fourth behind Leech, so all three Leopard Moths qualified for the semi-final. Bulman was out; he had made the first flights of many Hawker aircraft since 1925, and would do likewise for the Hurricane in November 1935. He would become head of the Aircraft Testing Branch of the British Air Commission, in Washington DC, from 1941 to 1942. He would retire from Hawker in 1945, and never flew again.

Armour brought Prince George's Gull home first again in heat ten. Drama unfolded further back, when Francis R. Walker crashed his Gipsy III Swift a few miles north of Northampton—although he escaped serious injury. AVM Borton was third. Hope lost height, furiously pumping fuel through to his gravity tank to stop his engine dying. He pulled up with only 20 feet (6.1 m) to spare, and nearly caught Lowdell on the line—only to be eliminated.

The course for the semi-finals—heats eleven and twelve—was 195 miles (313 km) long: up to Bircham Newton; across to Wittering, in north-west Cambridgeshire; and then down to Hatfield. Campbell Black and Runciman were eliminated in the first semi-final, when Edwards, Ayre, Broad, and Henshaw secured their places in the final. In the other semi-final, yet again, de Havilland, Styran, Leech, and Mrs Butler came through in the first four places. Borton, Armour, and Lowdell could proceed no further. Borton would retire from the RAF that August, just before his 47th birthday. Lowdell would join Vickers as a test pilot in 1941 and would work with Alex Henshaw, flying Spitfires and Wellingtons. From 1943 he would be chief production test pilot at Weighbridge, flying their Viking, Viscount, Valetta, and Varsity airliners.

A de Havilland Home Win

The final was two laps of a 103-mile (165-km) circuit: up to Henlow in east Bedfordshire; over to Upper Heyford, in Oxfordshire; back over to Hatfield, and round again. Spectators witnessed the aircraft banking hard at the turning point over Hatfield Aerodrome as they began the final lap. With Leech and Broad flying the only biplanes, it was difficult to tell which of the other six—all high-wing monoplanes—was ahead. At about 6.30 p.m. dots on the horizon became distinguishable, as two Leopard Moths, split by a Comper Swift, led the group home.

After a total of 830 miles (1,337 km), Geoffrey de Havilland achieved victory in his prototype Leopard Moth: 'I flew the first one we built ... and had a great and pleasant surprise when I was able to come in first'. As with most winners before him, his fabric surfaces were doped with Titanine. On getting out of the cabin, the shy winner was lifted onto the shoulders of his supporters, including his sons Geoffrey Jnr and Peter, Wally Hope, and the School of Flying's chief instructor Bob Reeve—all captured in the Pathé newsreel.

Edwards crossed the line just seven seconds behind, with Styran twenty-three seconds later, and Ayre only seven seconds behind him. Leech followed nearly a minute later, with Lois Butler arriving after another half-minute. A further half-minute saw Broad finish in the Dragon. Young Alex Henshaw would have been seventh, but he crossed the line too high and had to double back.

The main prizes were presented by Ronald Gorell Barnes, 3rd Baron Gorell, Chairman of the Royal Aero Club since 1932. Handing the King's Cup to Geoffrey de Havilland, Lord Gorell said:

Geoffrey de Havilland is carried by Wally Hope—he has Geoffrey's right leg—and others in celebration of his King's Cup victory. Twenty-year-old Peter de Havilland has his father's left knee. (© *Bettmann Archive, Corbis Corporation*)

> I'm sure that not even those who took part will grudge the victory to that very good, old friend of the air, Captain de Havilland ... it gives me great pleasure to give you this cup, which you've won on your own ground.

Viscount Wakefield provided the cash prizes, as he had many times before. Geoffrey de Havilland received £250 (£15,600 today), plus £25 for the fastest time in the final, averaging 138.86 mph (223.47 km/h). Edwards' prize was £100 (£6,200 today), although nobody could find him when it was time for the ceremony. Styran was there to receive his £50. George Stainforth didn't end the day empty-handed, winning £25 for the fastest time in Round One. Hope received the same for Round Two with 157.95 mph (254.2 km/h), and so did Jack Armour for 154.25 mph (248.24 km/h) in the semi-final. Lastly, Sir John Siddeley presented his trophy to Alex Henshaw, representing the Skegness & East Lincolnshire Aero Club. He had only 'gone solo' for the first time in the last week of May! He would have an illustrious career as a test pilot. Hatfield would host the King's Cup for the next five years.

Tragically, Capt. Styran and two others were killed when he crashed a Javelin-Gull in fog at Sandhurst, Kent, in October 1933. Ironically, they were on their way back from northern France after attending the unveiling by Prime Minister Ramsay MacDonald and President Daladier of the memorial to the R101 airship disaster.

Capt. Geoffrey de Havilland receives the King's Cup for 1933 from Lord Gorrell, Chairman of the Royal Aero Club. (The Aeroplane, *via BAE Systems*)

8

The Flying Clubs Move In

> Such a large number of those actively interested in the theatrical or film profession have learnt, or are learning, to fly that they have decided to form a club of their own.... The flying headquarters will be at Hatfield Aerodrome and an inaugural Garden Party will be held there next Sunday.
>
> Flight, *22 July 1932*

The Stage & Screen Aero Club

Owners and pilots of private aircraft were soon also able to use the flying school building and Aerodrome as members of flying clubs. As if flying and aircraft ownership weren't glamorous enough, the first club to call Hatfield 'home' took things to new heights. The Stage and Screen Aero Club was established at Hatfield in July 1932, and acquired Gipsy Moth G-AADI from the de Havilland School of Flying. *The Times* for 25 July reported:

> The first meeting was held yesterday.... Captain Broad ... gave an exhibition of 'stunt' flying in a Tiger Moth, specially equipped with a petrol systems adapted for upside-down flying, and Flight-Lieutenant Comper flew the Comper Swift machine which the Prince of Wales entered for the last King's Cup race.

Puss Moth G-ABDH was demonstrated at the event by de Havilland agents Brian Lewis & Co. of Heston. Brian E. Lewis was a racing driver and had finished third at the Le Mans 24 Hours in a Talbot on 19 June, equalling his result from 1930. He would again be placed third in 1933, in an Alfa Romeo.

The club's president was the famous stage actor Sir Gerald H. E. B. Du Maurier. He had made his name in two plays by J. M. Barrie: *The Admirable Crichton* in 1902, and *Peter Pan, the Boy Who Wouldn't Grow Up* in 1904, in which he played both George Darling and Captain Hook. His daughter, author Dame Daphne Du Maurier, was born in 1907. He was knighted in 1922 for his services to drama.

The inaugural meeting of the Stage & Screen Aero Club at Hatfield, on 24 July 1932. Brian Lewis & Co of Heston, de Havilland agents, were there with Puss Moth 'demonstrator' G-ABDH. (Flight, *via aviationancestry.com*)

An American celebrity who Jack Franklin remembered seeing at Hatfield was 'Dorothy Hyson, the very pretty actress daughter of the well-known Dorothy Dickson'. She had made her London stage debut aged 12, in J. M. Barrie's *Quality Street*. She and her first husband—British film actor Robert Douglas—were both club members. Rogers and Hart would dedicate to her their 1935 song, *The Most Beautiful Girl in the World*—from their musical, *Jumbo*. She would work with Laurence Olivier and Raymond Massey, and was close friends with not only Noel Coward and John Gielgud but also Queen Elizabeth II and The Queen Mother. She would work as a cryptographer at the secret Bletchley Park code-breaking establishment during World War II, and would be very happily re-married to actor Anthony Quayle in 1947. She died in 1996, aged 81.

Other members of interest included actress and racing driver Eirane 'Paddie' Naismith, who gained her pilot's licence at Heston in August 1932. She would become Britain's first air hostess in 1934. Because of her red hair, in 1940 John Logie Baird would choose her as the first person to be seen in a transmitted colour television picture. Marjory Mars would be in the cast of *Brief Encounter* in 1945. Margaret Cory-Wright lived with her husband, Douglas, at nearby Mackerye End House, near Harpenden. Douglas was a First World War naval veteran, and would become chairman of the Chamber of Coal Traders. He would also be High Sheriff of Hertfordshire for the year of 1963.

In the summer of 1933, the Stage & Screen Aero Club held 'theatrical midnight bathing parties' and games of squash for the casts of While Parents Sleep and Ten Minutes Alibi. It was reported in *Flight* for 3 August that, one night in the previous week, 'a cool north wind at that hour rather checked their ardour'. However, the fun ended with 'a cheerful kipper, bacon and egg supper, and an impromptu dance.'

Above left: A postcard depicting Gerald du Maurier in 1905, while he was playing a part in Edward Bulwer-Lytton's play *Money*. Du Maurier founded the Stage & Screen Aero Club at Hatfield in 1932. (*Rotary Photo Co/Foulsham & Banfield Ltd, courtesy of Manuel Palomino Arjona*)

Above right: Postcard of American actress Dorothy Hyson—a member of the Stage & Screen Aero Club—photographed in around 1935 by Royal photographer Dorothy Wilding. (Picturegoer, *Series No. 7.85a*)

Those using the pool to escape from the daytime heat that week included Hubert Broad, Air Chief Marshal Sir John M. Salmond—Chief of the Air Staff and successor to Lord Trenchard—and W. Linsday Everard, Member of Parliament for Melton Mowbray, in Leicestershire, and owner of Everards Brewery. He was also president of the Leicestershire Aero Club, which was based at his private airfield at Ratcliffe Hall, on the Nottinghamshire border. By the following week, the Stage & Screen Aero Club had received 180 membership applications.

Stage & Screen hosted a garden party on 29 September, with a gymkhana and fair. Many celebrated actors and actresses ran various side shows. Prominent Hatfield residents also attended. The event included a 'Grand Giggle' theatrical performance in one of the hangars. Money was raised for the Actors' Orphanage Fund, of which Sir Gerald was the president, later known as the Actors' Charitable Trust. Edgar Percival was there with one of his Gulls, as was Standard Telephone & Cable's Tiger Moth. Spectators were also able to watch routine flights being

The open-air 'lido' swimming pool and squash courts building, constructed next to the clubhouse and completed in June 1933. The pool was continually replenished from an artesian aquifer, and was warmed by steam injection. (Flight, *via aviationancestry.com*)

DH.71 Tiger Moth G-EBRV, topping a sign advertising the Stage & Screen Aero Club's 'Theatrical Garden Party' on 29 September 1933. (*BAE Systems*)

The 'Balloon Stone' in Welham Green, about 2 miles south of Hatfield, near where Capt. Vincenzo Lunardi made the first landing in England in 1784. He had ascended from the Honourable Artillery Company's training ground in Finsbury, London, carrying a dog, a cat, and a caged pigeon. After handing the distressed cat to a local woman, he continued over Hatfield Park and landed at Standon Green End. Another Balloon Stone marks that spot. (*Photographer: Wesley Clifford*)

Original postcard depicting the destruction of the Schütte-Lanz SL-11 airship over Hertfordshire, in the early hours of 3 September 1916.The view from Hatfield was much like this. (*The Tony Chew Collection*)

AIRCO D.H.2 5964 - Maj. Lanoe G. Hawker, dowódca 24 Dywizjonu RFC; Francja, listopad 1916.
AIRCO D.H.2 5964 of Maj. Lanoe G. Hawker, Commander of No.24 Squadron RFC; France, November 1916.

Geoffrey de Havilland's Airco DH.2 design, which helped to end the 'Fokker Scourge' of the First World War. One of these, or its DH.1 predecessor, may have been the 'open framed plane with two wings and the propeller behind the pilot's seat' which Bill Walby saw crash in a field behind the Wrestlers Pub, early in the War, when he was around six years old. (*Marek Radomski*)

DE HAVILLAND D.H.82A Tiger Moth (G-ADCA) - Szkoła Lotnicza De Havillanda; Hatfield, 1933.
DE HAVILLAND D.H.82A Tiger Moth (G-ADCA) of The De Havilland School of Flight; Hatfield, 1933.

DH.82 Tiger Moth, of the first batch to be registered to the de Havilland School of Flying, at Hatfield on 6 February 1933. It is still flying today. (*Marek Radomski*)

The DH.88 Comet in which Charles Scott and Tom Campbell Black won the England–Australia race of October 1934. The race was sponsored by Sir MacPherson Robertson, to celebrate the centenary of the founding of the State of Victoria and its capital, Melbourne. The aircraft was completed at Hatfield and test flown for the first time just eleven days before the race. (*Marek Radomski*)

DH.60 Gipsy Moth G-AAWO, first registered on 2 May 1930—the colour scheme is similar to that worn by the first de Havilland School of Flying aircraft to take up residence at Hatfield, in June of that year. It is seen here on 7 May 2013 at Daedalus Airfield, Lee-on-the-Solent. G-AAWO has been owned by the Reid family since 1955. (*Photographer: Richard Davies*)

Above left: Jim Mollison's Puss Moth G-ABXY, which he acquired in June 1932 and named *The Heart's Content*. Recreated here at Hatfield in Microsoft Flight Simulator X. (*Scene composed by Peter Dodds, buildings by Toby Vickers, aircraft by Milton Shupe, and colour scheme by Damian Radice*)

Above right: Lord Trenchard in his uniform as Metropolitan Police Commissioner, a position he held from 1931–35. He was president of the RAF Flying Club at Hatfield from 1933. This cigarette card was the eleventh of fifty-four depicting personalities 'In the Public Eye' in 1935. To ensure further sales, the answer to the question on the bottom on the card could be found on the twelfth card. (*Godfrey Phillips Ltd*)

DH.82 Tiger Moth G-ACDA is an original member of the de Havilland School of Flying's fleet, registered to them at Hatfield on 6 February 1933. It is seen here at the 29th International Moth Rally in 2011. (*Photographer: Mike Gill*)

Tiger Moth G-ACDA at the Little Gransden Airshow, in Cambridgeshire, on 30 August 2009. The aircraft has been owned by Jonathan Turnbull since 2013. (*Photographer: Alan Gray*)

G-AOEI was built at Hatfield in 1939, and served with 81 Squadron in France in 1940. It is one of a pair of Tiger Moths owned and operated by the Cambridge Flying Group, at the city's airport, since the mid-1970s. They wear the livery of the London Aeroplane Club. G-AOEI is seen here at Compton Abbas airfield, in Dorset, on 3 July 2010. (*Photographer: Tony Gordon*)

Tiger Moth G-AOBX was built at Hatfield in 1939, and wears the livery of the London Aeroplane Club. It has been owned by the David Ross Flying Group since 2000, and is a member of the Tiger 9 Display Team. It is seen here at the International Moth Rally on 15 June 2008, held at RAF Halton. (*Photographer: Ben Allsup*)

The steel-glass lantern structure of the navigation beacon which stood on the roof of the aerodrome squash courts from mid-1933. It was removed in 1988, when the old building was demolished to make way for the building in the background—the MacLaurin building, on the University of Hertfordshire's de Havilland Campus. The beacon was stored at North Weald airfield in Essex for many years, before being restored and returned to Hatfield in 2011. In the foreground is one of the University's Heritage Trail boards, which give the history of the site. (*Photographer: Carol de Solla Atkin*)

Original poster for the first King's Cup air race to be hosted at Hatfield, which was also the venue for the event over the next five years. (*Origin unknown*)

Desoutter G-AAPZ, first registered on 4 June 1930, which Capt E. D. Ayre flew to fourth place in the King's Cup at Hatfield on 8 July 1933. It is seen here on 13 August 2011, at Old Warden Aerodrome in Bedfordshire. The aircraft is an original member of the Shuttleworth Collection, having been owned by Richard Shuttleworth in the 1930s. (*Photographer: David Whitworth*)

Comper Swift G-ACGL, registered on 30 May 1933 to Alex Henshaw—who flew it to eighth place in the 1933 King's Cup. The aircraft is seen here on display at the RAF Museum at Cosford, in Shropshire. (*Photographer: Flickr username NTGpictures*)

DH.80 Puss Moth G-ABLS was first registered on 7 May 1931, and was flown to ninth place in the 1934 Hatfield King's Cup by Owen Cathcart Jones. It is seen here at the Sywell Airshow on 19 August 2012. (*Photographer: Nick Jennings*)

Puss Moth G-ABLS at Popham Airfield, in Hampshire, on 13 April 2009. It has been owned by Richard Seeley since 2006. (*Photographer: Neil Randell*)

Monospar ST-10 G-ACTS, winner of the 1934 King's Cup. This cigarette card was the seventeenth in the 'Aeroplanes (Civil)' category, a 'Series of 50 selected by the editor of *The Aeroplane*'. (*John Player & Sons*)

The Art Deco-style, 'Administration Block' headquarters, designed for de Havilland by architects James M. Monro & Son, of Glasgow, and built by Holland Hannen & Cubitt in 1934. The company's global administration was conducted from here. The building was renovated for use as Hatfield police station, which opened on 26 March 2009, and is seen here on 27 April 2010. The office block in the background is 5 Trident Place, on the Everything Everywhere campus, which was opened in 2001. Its exterior uses materials coloured to match the old building. (*Photographer: Claire Parfrey*)

The de Havilland factory gatehouse of 1934, seen here on 27 April 2010. The building was renovated in 2008. (*Photographer: Claire Parfrey*)

Artwork presented in 1954 to de Havilland employees who had completed twenty years' service, having started with the company in the year that Comet G-ACSS won the MacRobertson race. (*BAE Systems, via the Norman Eastaff Collection*)

DH.88 Comet G-ACSS in Shuttleworth's Hangar One workshop at Old Warden, seen here on 24 September 2011. (*Photographer: Peter Cox*)

Comet G-ACSS at Old Warden, in Bedfordshire, where it has been part of the Shuttleworth Collection since 1965. It is seen here at the Shuttleworth Autumn Air Display on 4 October 2009. (*Photographer: Rob Feeley*)

DH.80 Puss Moth G-AAZP, first registered on 4 June 1930 and flown by Diana Guest in the King's Cup that year. For the 75th anniversary of Jimmy Melrose's flight in the England-Australia MacRobertson race of 1934, the aircraft was marked to represent Jimmy's Puss Moth, VH-UQO. He named it *My Hildegarde*, after his mother. It is seen here on 4 October 2009, at the Shuttleworth Collection's Old Warden Aerodrome in Bedfordshire. (*Photographer: Andrew Scrutton*)

G-AAZP has been owned by Tim Williams since 1982. To commemorate the 50th anniversary of Jimmy Melrose's flight in the MacRobertson race, Tim and Henry Labouchere flew the aircraft from Mildenhall to Melbourne between 21 October and 15 December 1984, sponsored by British Aerospace. It is seen here at Houghton Hall, in Norfolk, on 13 September 2009. (*Photographer: Peter Hudson*)

The last DH.83 Fox Moth to be built (partly at Stag Lane), transported by road to be completed at Hatfield. It received its Certificate of Airworthiness on 22 October 1934, and was exported to New Zealand, where it was registered as ZK-ADI on 29 January 1935. It is seen here on New Zealand's South Island, at the Warbirds over Wanaka air show on 16 April 2006. (*Photographer: Chris Finney, Contrabandit Photos*)

Fox Moth ZK-ADI was rebuilt in the UK in the mid-1980s, and returned to New Zealand in 1997. It has been part of the Croydon Aircraft Co. collection at Old Mandeville Aerodrome, on New Zealand's South Island, since 2002. (*Photographer: Hugh McCall*)

Above and below: One of 335 de Havilland Dominies (the RAF version of the Dragon Rapide) built in 1944 by Brush Coachworks, in Loughborough, and originally given the RAF serial HG724. In 2009, it was finished to represent a 1935 aircraft, G-ADDD, including its luxurious interior. The original was registered to royal pilot Flt Lt Edward Fielden on 4 March 1935, for use by the Prince of Wales. It was delivered to Hendon on 8 June, became the first aircraft to carry a reigning British monarch on 22 January 1936, and was a founding member of the Kings Flight, on 21 July of that year. The aircraft is seen here on 18 May 2012, at Warbirds Over the Beach at Virginia Beach. It has been owned by Lewis Air Legends, in San Antonio, Texas, since 2013. (*Photographer: Norman A. Graf*)

DH.90 Dragonfly G-AEDU—still flying today—which came off the Hatfield production line in December 1935, and was initially registered to Lindsay Everard MP as G-ADXM. It has been owned by the Norman Aeroplane Trust since 1997, and is seen here at Duxford on 23 January 2014. (*Photographer: Tony Clarke*)

As chairman of the Royal Aero Club's Racing Committee, Lindsay Everard entered this Dragonfly in the 1936 and 1937 King's Cups at Hatfield. He kept it at his private airfield at Ratcliffe Hall until it was commandeered by the RAF in 1940. It is seen here at Duxford Flying Legends on 13 July 2008. (*Photographer: Andy Cutler*)

Actress, racing driver, and pilot Paddie Naismith was a member of the Stage & Screen Aero Club, seen here at their 'Theatrical Garden Party' on 29 September 1933. She would become Britain's first air hostess in 1934, and the first person to be seen in a transmitted colour television picture in 1940. (*The Alfieri Collection, Topham Picturepoint —TopFoto.co.uk, EU002790*)

made by staff, and members of the de Havilland School of Flying and the other clubs that had moved in by then.

Hosting the RAF

The RAF Reserve Flying Club was established at Hatfield in 1933. This enabled both reserve officers and civilian volunteers to maintain their flying time at the rate of £1 per hour (£62 today). They could also volunteer to do aircraft maintenance at Hatfield, supervised by de Havilland ground engineers.

Robert E. G. Brittain had joined the RAF Reserve while finishing his studies at Oxford in 1931. He was told to report to Hatfield that summer for flying training, along with others from Oxford and Cambridge. The new pilots then wanted to remain in contact with each other more often than their annual two weeks' training would allow. In 1932, Fg Off. Brittain secured approval from Sir Christopher L. Bullock, Permanent Under-Secretary at the Air Ministry, to form an official club for RAF Reserve officers. Alan Butler happily offered de Havilland's support, including housing and maintenance of the club's aircraft at Hatfield.

Brittain invited around 500 reservists who had trained at Hatfield to join the club. The response encouraged him to extend the invitation to another 1,500 members of the reserve across the country, including the Oxford and Cambridge University Air Squadrons. The response was overwhelming. Replies from around the world included offers to work as instructors, ground engineers, and as the secretary.

Senior figures who accepted invitations to lead the club included Lord Trenchard as president. The vice presidents were: Capt. Geoffrey de Havilland;

Sir Christopher Bullock; Air Cdre Christopher L. Courtney, the RAF's Director of Training; Grp Capt. Robert Leckie, Superintendent of the RAF Reserve; Lt-Col. F. C. Shelmerdine, Director of Civil Aviation; William F. Forbes-Sempill; Lord Wakefield of Hythe; and Sir Henry 'Harry' E. Brittain, journalist, politician, and Fg Off. Brittain's father. Chief flying instructor of the de Havilland School of Flying, Bob Reeve, was a member of the club's committee.

Lord Trenchard had accepted the post of Metropolitan Police Commissioner in October 1931, a position he would hold until 1935. Grp Capt. Leckie had shot down Zeppelin L22 over the West Frisian Islands in 1917, and L70 off the Norfolk coast in 1918; he later supervised the development of civil aviation in Canada.

Sempill's father, John, was 18th Lord Sempill and 9th Baronet of Craigievar, in Scotland. William was usually referred to as the Master of Sempill. He had served with the Royal Flying Corp and Royal Naval Air Service in the First World War. In the 1920s he had assisted with the development of the Imperial Japanese Naval Air Service, including sharing plans for the new purpose-built British aircraft carriers. In 1926 he was rightly suspected of passing secrets to the Japanese, but he was not prosecuted due to his high profile and his royal connections (his father was *aide-de-camp* to King George V), and to avoid official embarrassment. Nonetheless, he served as chairman of the Royal Aeronautical Society and as its president from 1927 to 1930, advising other countries on the creation of their naval air services. On 4 September 1930 he flew from Brent Reservoir, in north-west London, to Stockholm, in a Gipsy Moth fitted with floats—1,040 miles, in a record 12 hours. Mitsubishi Heavy Industries employed him as a consultant from 1932.

The club gradually acquired a fleet of Gipsy Moths. Their first was G-AAEO from the School of Flying, which became surplus when the school's new Tiger Moths arrived. Overhauled and painted silver with a red, dark blue, and light blue tail, it was handed over to the club on 23 May 1933. In June the club obtained permission from the Air Ministry for its RAF officers to wear service parachutes—they would not have enough for civilian members and guests until January 1934! They also acquired a 'pistol' camera for members to practice aerial photography with.

The club's official opening took place at Hatfield on 22 July 1933. This commenced with Grp Capt. Leckie's wife 'launching' G-AAEO, which was wearing the club's new badge on its fuselage. Charles S. H. Vane-Tempest-Stewart, 7th Marquess of Londonderry and Secretary of State for Air since 1931, arrived in a Hawker Tomtit—he had a pilot's licence.

Regular RAF and Auxiliary Air Force units that provided flying displays included No.1 (Fighter) Squadron and No.600 City of London (Bomber) Squadron. Instructors from the Central Flying School and various civilian-run schools also took part. The aircraft included Avro Cadets and Tutors, a Blackburn B.2, a Fairey Firefly of the Belgian *Aviation Militaire*, Hawker Furies, a Saunders Roe A17 *Cutty Sark*, and Tiger Moths. The record-breaking Danish parachutist Anton 'John'

Aircraft gathered at Hatfield for the RAF Reserve Flying Club's inaugural display on 22 July 1933. (The Aeroplane, *via aviationancestry.com*)

The RAF Reserve Flying Club's founding members in front of their first aircraft, Gipsy Moth G-AAEO. Fg Off. Robert Brittain is third from the left. (The Aeroplane, *via aviationancestry.com*)

Tranum made a descent. Music was provided by the Band of the Home Aircraft Depot, Henlow. Many spectators stayed on to use the swimming pool, have dinner, and dance.

The air display was not the only large-scale military aviation activity involving Hatfield during July 1933—from the 17th to the 20th, 'Air Exercises' gave RAF staff and squadrons practice at working together as units. This included The Observers Corps and the 1st Anti-aircraft Searchlight Battalion of the Royal Engineers. 'Northland' was defended by thirteen fighter squadrons using Hawker Demons, Furies, and Bristol Bulldogs. Reconnaissance flights were made by Westland Wallaces and Hawker Horsleys. The 'Southland' aggressors had nine day-bomber and seven night-bomber squadrons, flying Hawker Harts, Boulton Paul

A cartoon of spectators by artist H. H. Harris, which appeared in *The Bystander* magazine for 2 August 1933. In January 1934 the original drawing would be presented to the club by one of their vice presidents, Sir Harry Brittain. (*Illustrated London News Ltd / Mary Evans Picture Library*)

Sidestrands, Westland Wapitis, Fairey Gordons, Vickers Virginias, and Handley Page Hinaidis.

The military objectives were all in the East Midlands and Home Counties—Bicester, Cardington, Halton, Hatfield, Henley-on-Thames, Stratford-on-Avon, Wantage, Warwick, and Wittering. A camera obscura at each target site recorded 'bombing strikes', which the bombers mimicked with visual signals rather than by actually dropping anything. Imaginary mountain ranges kept London, Norfolk, and northern Suffolk out of bounds. On the morning of 19 July, seven bomber squadrons raided Wantage, Bicester, Hatfield, and Wittering. Three of the raids were intercepted by the fighters as they approached, and four were caught as they made their getaways.

John Stroud remembered how, on other occasions at Hatfield, the Virginia bombers would 'drop in sometimes so that their crews could use the swimming pool, after which they draped their swimming things and towels around the rear gun position to dry'.

Adolf Hitler's National Socialist German Workers' (or 'Nazi') Party had come to power in January. While the RAF was at play, the Nazis were accelerating the development of Germany's aircraft and other industries. Arado's Ar67 biplane fighter prototype first flew in 1933, powered by a Rolls-Royce Kestrel. The Reichs luftfahrtministerium (RLM—Reich Air Ministry) published requirements for new bomber and fighter aircraft, and invited various manufacturers to offer designs.

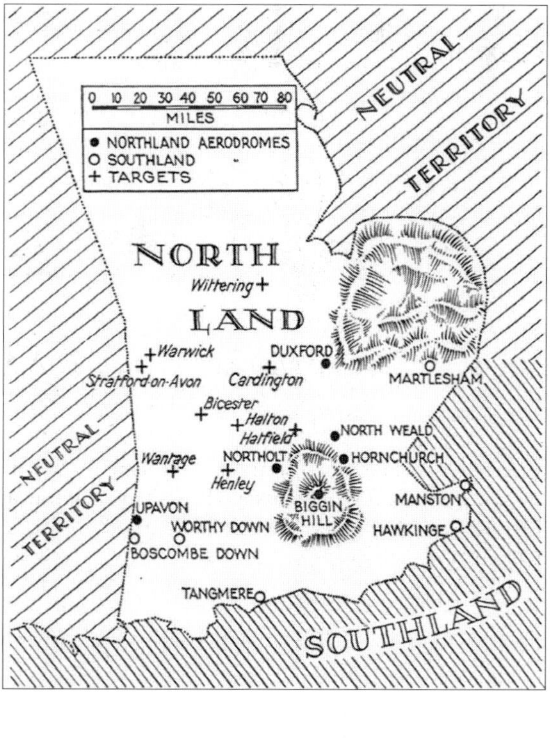

Map for the RAF's air exercises of 17–20 July 1933, showing Hatfield as one of the 'targets' for the bomber force—shown in *Flight* for 27 July. (Flight, *via aviationancestry.com*)

Junkers started developing a new dive-bomber, initially with the Kestrel as its intended powerplant. This would be designated as the Ju87.

Senior British figures were being entertained by their German counterparts. In early June a fleet of eleven private British aircraft had flown to Staaken airfield, on the west side of Berlin. Among them was Linsday Everard, with his Dragon; he had organised the trip, and was accompanied by Air Vice Marshal Borton, Sqn Ldr Leslie Runciman, and Lt-Col. Andrew Hamilton Gault (Member of Parliament for Taunton, Somerset). Gault had lost a leg in 1916, and his decorations included the Russian Order of St Anne and the Belgian Ordre de Leopold. He had flown a Gipsy Moth in the 1930 King's Cup. Runciman was commanding officer of 607 (County of Durham) Squadron, Auxiliary Air Force, since 1930—and would be so until 1939. They spent several days in the Rhineland around Düsseldorf, and visited the Junkers factory at Dessau. They met Erhard Milch, managing director of airline *Deutsche Luft Hansa* since its creation in 1926, who was now appointed as Secretary of State at the RLM. They also met Hermann Göring, Reich Commissioner of Aviation, and Chancellor Adolf Hitler. From 1940 to 1943, Runciman would be the first Director-General of the British Overseas Airways Corporation (BOAC).

From mid-1933 even Hatfield got a glimpse of revitalised German industry at 12 Fore Street—de Havilland was no longer the only aviation-related business in the town. Among the newly registered companies listed in *Flight* for 6 July was this one:

> WILLIAM RICHTER, LTD., Goodrich House, Fore Street, Hatfield. Capital, £2,000 [£125,000 today] in £1 shares. Manufacturers and distributors of, agents for and dealers in Junkers Diesel engines, both British and German, and all parts thereof, agricultural machinery and parts thereof; manufacturers of and dealers in aeroplanes, locomotives, oil, petrol and other engines, motor cars, etc. Directors: William R. Richter, engineering contractor (director of Nene Valley Sand and Gravel Co., Ltd.); Mrs. Ida R. Richter, both of 'Dornhurst,' Roe Green Lane, Hatfield.

The couple had been listed in Kelly's 1931–32 Directory for the St Albans area, and their business would also be listed annually from 1933.

The Mollisons Cross the Atlantic

In November 1932 Amy had broken her husband's England-to-South-Africa record. She used Puss Moth G-ACAB, named *The Desert Cloud* and fitted with a Gipsy Major. She had taken blind flying lessons beforehand, in preparation for if she became disorientated over the Sahara or if there was no moon to navigate

The RAF Reserve Flying Club's first Gipsy Moth, G-AAEO, with the Stage & Screen Aero Club's Gipsy Moth, G-AADI, and the Hatfield hangars behind. (Flight, *via aviationancestry.com*)

The Tudor, Georgian, Regency, and Victorian charm and grandeur of Old Hatfield's Fore Street in the 1930s. No.12, Goodrich House, is nearest to the camera. From 1933 this was the address of William Richter Ltd, importers of German machinery—including Junkers engines. (*Architectural Press Archive/RIBA Library Photographs Collection, no. 72301*)

by. She reached Cape Town in just under four days and seven hours. She made the return flight, the following month, in just over seven days and seven hours—the first solo return flight—and was awarded the Segrave Memorial Trophy for 1932. On Lake Windermere, in 1930, Segrave had set a new world water-speed record of 98.760 mph (158.939 km/h), in a boat powered by a Rolls-Royce R racing aero-engine. He crashed, fatally, on a follow-up run. The trophy was awarded annually, in his memory, to a British national who had achieved an outstanding accomplishment in demonstrating the possibilities of transport on land, on water, or in the air. The previous winners were Charles Kingsford Smith and Bert Hinkler. Hinkler was killed on 7 January 1933, when he crashed in Italy, attempting to break Charles W. A. Scott's England-Australia record of the previous year. Amy's friend, pilot Winifred Spooner, died of pneumonia that month.

Jim had his Puss Moth, *The Heart's Content*, fitted with a Gipsy Major. In February, he took off from Lympne in Kent and became the first to cross the South Atlantic from east to west (via Barcelona and Senegal). He landed at Port Natal, Brazil, after three days and just over ten hours. He then wanted to become the first pilot to cross the Atlantic twice; he and Amy would be the first husband and wife team to make the crossing. They were regular visitors to Hatfield in the summer of 1933, and prepared there thoroughly for the flight. Their aircraft for the crossing

Jim and Amy Mollison prepare for their flight across the Atlantic with DH.84 Dragon G-ACCV, named *Seafarer*. They spent a lot of time at Hatfield before the flight. (*Actualit, Bruxelles, courtesy of Carl Guderian*)

would be Dragon G-ACCV, which they named *Seafarer*. It was registered to Amy at Stag Lane on 7 March. *Seafarer*'s passenger cabin was taken up by three 200-gallon (909-litre) fuel tanks. The press termed the all-black aircraft the 'Flying Petrol Tank'; Jim called it the 'Flying Coffin'. They did a ten-hour test flight from Hatfield on 31 May, and *Seafarer* received its Certificate of Airworthiness on 2 June.

They intended to fly from Croydon to Pendine Sands in South Wales, but the Dragon's undercarriage was damaged after taking off on 8 June. While they waited for it to be repaired they returned to Hatfield. John Stroud was there, on June 28, to witness their arrival in Hillman's Airways' Dragon G-ACEU. Amy used this to practice take-offs with a full load. *Flight* for 27 July would report that they had 'spent a lazy afternoon swimming and sunbathing, which, as a contrast to the anxious waiting for weather, they seemed to thoroughly enjoy'.

Seafarer was repaired and delivered to Pendine Sands on 3 July. After waiting for good weather reports, they set off from Pendine on 22 July; Geoffrey de Havilland filmed their take-off himself. After 3,300 miles (5,311 km) and 39 hours, they were running out of fuel. Suffering from 'extreme fatigue' according to Jim, they crashed, in the dark, at Bridgeport airport in Connecticut. They were only 56 miles (90 km) short of their destination at Floyd Bennett Field, Brooklyn. After recovering from their injuries they were taken to New York, and were given a tickertape parade down Wall Street. They then lunched with President Roosevelt and Amelia Earhart, who was now married to publisher George Putnam. Amelia had been the first woman to cross the Atlantic as an air passenger in 1928, and the first woman to fly it solo in 1932. By 1935 she would set seven women's speed and distance records but, in 1937, she would be lost over the Pacific—while attempting to circumnavigate the globe.

The London Aeroplane Club Arrives

Founded by de Havilland at Stag Lane in 1925, the London Aeroplane Club now needed a new home as much as the company's flying school did. Hatfield's enhanced facilities—including the extended hangars, squash courts, swimming pool, and an additional 90 acres (36.4 hectares) of flying ground—were actually created in readiness for the arrival of the club. The National Aviation Day air display was held at Stag Lane on the weekend of 5–6 August, so the club gave its pupils a foretaste of Hatfield by providing flying lessons from there for a few days. They finally relocated at the end of September, celebrating with a dinner and a dance. Members found the long runways, now over a mile from east to west, to be a great improvement.

Their fleet was updated with the transfer of Gipsy Moths from the School of Flying, plus two others built by the Stag Lane apprentices. They also acquired two Puss Moths, and they were looking forward to getting their hands on a Tiger Moth. The chief flying instructor was now Flt Lt J. A. Harris—Herbert Travers did not remain with the club for the move to Hatfield. Geoffrey de Havilland Jnr, now aged 23 and married, was assistant flying instructor.

Meanwhile, the School of Flying continued to operate as it had done for the past three years. Almost as if to compete for customers with the London Aeroplane Club (which charged lower prices for flying lessons), the school advertised in *Flight* every week from June until December. Movietone News made a film about a first flying lesson at Hatfield; *Flight* for 27 July described it as depicting Eddie Fulford 'giving lessons to a young and pretty lady pupil, and the photography is good, although the film is too short to be really instructive'. In August, Fg Off. G. S. 'Wizzie' King arrived from Egypt to become the sixth instructor on the School's staff. Officials from the Japanese Civilian Flying Schools also visited. Maj. Kondor, Chief Instructor, and Maj. Okumono, Chief Engineer, received a demonstration of the training methods used. In September, RAF Gipsy Moth K1111 had a blind flying hood fitted for military testing.

The de Havilland Service Department also moved to Hatfield, offering routine checks, refuelling, cleaning, general maintenance, and repairs. They published a scale of standard charges for servicing de Havilland models, much like car owners would be familiar with—possibly the first in the world to do so. Private owners could even pay for regular maintenance by 'standing order' instalments. The company spent a further £24,000 (£1.5m today) on buying up more of the surrounding land. A property was also purchased to provide overnight accommodation for those flying in and out. 'Lock-ups' were also added, next to the hangars, for owners to garage their aircraft.

Col. Christopher H. Miskin—a member of the London Aeroplane Club—had served in Egypt with the Bedfordshire Regiment in 1916, and won the Military Cross in the Third Battle of Gaza in 1917; he became Commanding Officer of the Regiment's 5th Battalion in 1928. He kept a Gipsy Moth at Hatfield until July 1933. He then acquired a Moth Major, and despite moving his new aircraft to the Cinque Ports Flying Club at Lympne, in Kent, he remained a member at Hatfield.

In late September Col. Miskin joined Kenneth H. F. Waller (one of the Cinque Ports flying instructors) and other members of that club on a visit to Cologne. The flying club there was a branch of the Deutscher Luftsportverband (DLV, German Sports Flying Association), established by the Nazi Party in March. The organisation followed the British example for encouraging civilians to train as pilots—but to military standards. Its chairman was Hermann Göring. The Cinque Ports club had held an international meeting in July, and the Cologne club now returned the favour. It was extremely well-organised, and customs requirements were waived. The guests' every need was attended to free of charge, including hotels, meals, cabaret shows, a cruise on the Rhine, and a visit to a hunting lodge in the Eifel mountains. They were presented with souvenirs, with the Cinque

Chief instructor at the London Aeroplane Club, Flt Lt J. A. Harris, explains to a pupil how to use the compass in Gipsy Moth G-ACMF. The club owned the aircraft from November 1933, when it was brand new, until 1937. (*LNA Photos Ltd, Hatfield Aerodrome booklet, 1935—BAE Systems, via Roger de Mercado, DHAeTS Association*)

Lock-ups were built next to the hangars for private owners to garage their aircraft. (*LNA Photos Ltd, Hatfield Aerodrome booklet, 1935—BAE Systems, via Roger de Mercado, DHAeTS Association*)

Swimming and flying at Hatfield Aerodrome on 9 August 1933. (*IMAGNO/Austrian Archives (S), via TopFoto.co.uk, Image no. 138101*)

Ports club receiving two old Bibles—they were beautifully bound, and contained valuable prints by famous artists.

The Mollisons' transatlantic flight was only intended as a prelude to an attempt on the non-stop distance record, with a course back across the Atlantic and on to Iraq. In early August, Frenchmen Paul Codos and Lt Maurice Rossi beat them to it by flying 5,657 miles (9,104 km) from New York to Rayak, Syria—staying airborne for 55 hours with their Blériot 110.

But the Mollisons decided to try again—this time from Canada. An identical second Dragon, registered as G-ACJM, was built for them at Stag Lane, thanks to the generosity of Lord Wakefield (encouraged by the opportunity to publicise his Castrol products). The wreck of *Seafarer* had been stripped by souvenir hunters, but the engines and fuel tanks were recovered and fitted to the new aircraft by the Hatfield Service Department. In September, Jim accompanied *Seafarer II* across the Atlantic on the Canadian Pacific liner *Duchess of York*. The aircraft was reassembled by de Havilland Canada, who helped the Mollisons prepare for a flight from Wasaga Beach, Ontario. Unfortunately, the undercarriage was damaged during take-off on 3 October. They decided to abandon the attempt, and shipped *Seafarer II* back to England—giving it the dubious honour of being the first aircraft to cross the Atlantic twice by sea. But this would be neither the end of the *Seafarer* story nor its connection with Hatfield.

Hitler demanded the right to develop military capabilities equal to that of France. France insisted that maintaining German weakness, according to the Treaty of Versailles of 1919, was their only assurance of security. The Geneva Disarmament Conference (which had started in 1932) started to break down in October 1933, when Hitler withdrew Germany from the talks. Air Chief Marshal Sir John Salmond and Lord Londonderry wisely opposed British politicians who were arguing for complete aerial disarmament in the UK. Even more alarmingly, Germany withdrew from the League of Nations (forerunner of the United Nations). Rolls-Royce could not have imagined how important the first bench test of its new 'Private Venture' V12 engine (PV-12), on 15 October, would turn out to be. It was soon named the *Merlin*, and de Havilland's factories in Hatfield and elsewhere would use thousands of them.

Three new Leopard Moths were resident at Hatfield from that autumn. One was registered to Peter de Havilland (now 20 years of age), although it was sold to a buyer in France in December. Another, G-ACKP, was registered to Geoffrey de Havilland. This was one of his favourite aircraft, and he would keep it until it was commandeered by the RAF in 1940. A third belonged to Sir Pyers G. J. Mostyn, 11th Baronet of Talacre in Flintshire, North Wales. He had been awarded the Military Cross in 1915 for gallantry on the battlefield, and also received the Russian Order of St Anne. He was a keen airman, a big-game hunter, and a polo player. He had flown from Kenya to Croydon in 1928, with a German pilot, in a Fokker. He would be killed in a riding accident in 1937.

The London Aeroplane Club advertised its facilities in the 30 November 1933 edition of *Flight*:

> THE LONDON AEROPLANE CLUB, de Havilland Aerodrome, Hatfield, Herts, on the Barnet by-pass, sixteen miles from West End. Large fleet of open, closed and aerobatic machines maintained by Makers' engineering staff. Country Club with Dormy House, restaurant, American bar, summer swimming pool, and squash courts.—Enquirers welcomed.

At the club's first Christmas lunch at Hatfield, on 17 December 1933, Secretary Harold Perrin said he hoped that they would continue, at Hatfield, with the enthusiasm and cheerfulness that they had known at Stag Lane.

9

Construction and Challenge

An architect was needed, for we wanted attractive buildings as well as efficiency. Hearle as Works Manager, in company with several others, motored about the Great West Road district [of London] where there was a number of good-looking modern factory buildings. He fixed on one that satisfied all our conditions and found out the name of the architect. We told him our requirements and he produced plans for the various buildings which, even after twenty-five years, are still considered efficient and attractive.

Geoffrey de Havilland, 1960

The Last Days of Flying at Stag Lane

Once the de Havilland Service Department and the London Aeroplane Club had moved to Hatfield in late 1933, it was time for flying at Stag Lane to draw to a close. The aerodrome at Stag Lane was now prime development land for Edgware's continuing suburban expansion, and was much more valuable than when de Havilland had bought it twelve years before. On 30 December the company held its last annual general meeting at Stag Lane. Chairman Alan Butler drew attention to a contract, to take effect on New Year's Day, for the sale of the aerodrome. The developers were paying £105,000 for the land (£6.5m today). This would go a long way to financing the building of a new factory and headquarters in Hatfield.

The company now employed 1,200 people at Stag Lane. Plans to relocate the majority of them to Hatfield would need to be carefully thought through, and the management would do everything they could to minimise the impact of the move on workers' domestic lives. The company would be left with the 14 acres at Stag Lane on which the factory stood, where production of aero-engines and propellers would continue for some years.

The 3 January 1934 edition of *The Aeroplane* carried a full-page advert, using an aerial photograph of the Hatfield site taken by Aerofilms, which stated:

> Owners and operators of de Havilland aircraft and Gipsy engines are cordially invited to make the fullest use of the new headquarter depot of de Havilland Service at Hatfield Aerodrome.
>
> The standards of honest workmanship, uncompromising inspection, speedy delivery and moderate charges which prevail at Hatfield are those which have built up the reputation of Moth and Gipsy Service all over the world.
>
> The new service depot at Hatfield is, like its predecessor at Stag Lane, under the direct supervision of the designers of DH aircraft and engines and it is backed by all the resources, staff, works and plant of the de Havilland factory.

The services listed were 'Advice, Housing (Private Lock-ups), Repairs, Overhauls, Maintenance'—although the aerial photo had been taken in August 1933, before the lock-ups were built.

The Air Ministry issued Notice to Airmen No.4 of the year, stating that 'The aerodrome at Stag Lane ... is closed and no personnel or facilities are available', and that its public aerodrome licence had been withdrawn on 5 January. *The Aeroplane* commented:

> Stag Lane is the hereditary home of the Moth and may therefore go down in history as the birthplace of private flying. Perhaps the future occupants of the villas which will shortly cover this historic aerodrome will be reminded of past achievements by ghostly flutterings in the linen chest.

Only factory flights and specially-arranged events would use the aerodrome in the final months, until building work finally took over the site. The technical school students produced their own magazine, *Pylon*. In an article for the January-March edition—entitled 'Good-bye, Stag Lane!'—apprentice W. Philip C. Hagger described the factory as 'an oasis in a desert of bricks'.

The last maiden flight of a new design at Stag Lane happened on 14 January, when Hubert Broad took off in the new DH.86. This was a four-engined, twelve-seater biplane with tapered wings, initially known as the *Express Air Liner*. It had been hurriedly developed from the Dragon since September 1933. Queensland & Northern Territory Aerial Services Ltd ('Qantas') and Holyman's Airways wanted a new aircraft to tender for the Singapore and Tasmania legs of a new British Empire airmail and passenger route. Frank Halford's new *Gipsy Six* engine, a development of his four-cylinder Gipsy Major, would power the aircraft—but this was still in development when the DH.86 orders were placed. Amazingly, the *Express* obtained its Certificate of Airworthiness the day before the closing date for tenders of 31 January. The aircraft for Australia would actually serve with Qantas Empire Airways Ltd, a new company jointly created by Imperial Airways and Qantas.

And so the industrialisation of Hatfield that had been gradual now surged ahead. The architects appointed by de Havilland were James M. Monro & Son of Glasgow. Since the 1870s Monro had concentrated on hotels, industries such as bakeries, and (since the 1920s) on department stores—particularly for Marks & Spencer. They had developed an Art Deco style, which they employed again to create very attractive 'Administration Block' offices, a canteen, and a restaurant for de Havilland. The main construction contract was awarded to Holland, Hannen & Cubitt. Fabrication of steelwork would be undertaken by Redpath Brown & Co. They would build a single-storey factory covering 190,000 sq feet, fronted by a large, modern, two-storey office (from where global administration for the company would be conducted), all connected by a site road network. Initial estimates put the cost at £117,000 (£7.3m today). Building work started without delay. The sign below the displayed Tiger Moth monoplane racer now read: 'Site for new de Havilland factory'.

Also in January, the de Havilland Aeronautical Technical School transferred to the new Hatfield assembly shop—the first of the planned buildings to be completed. From then on, only engine and propeller-related training would be provided at Stag Lane.

It's early 1934, and the first steelwork, fabricated by Redpath Brown & Co, has been erected for de Havilland's new Hatfield factory. (*BAE Systems*)

An Impossible Task?

A decision was made at Hatfield in January 1934 that would not only enhance de Havilland's reputation, but would also have a significance for the town that remains to this day. In March 1933, Australian industrialist Sir Macpherson Robertson had announced his intention to put up the prize money for a grand, long-distance air race from England to Australia. Its purpose would be to celebrate the centenary of the founding of the State of Victoria and its capital, Melbourne—Australia's most south-easterly territory. Robertson was a benefactor of exploration, education, and philanthropy, through the success of his MacRobertson Steam Confectionery Works.

In August 1933 competitors of any nationality were invited to register for the race, which was over a distance of around 11,300 miles (18,200 km). The first entry to reach Melbourne would receive £10,000 (£624,000 today) and a gold trophy. There was no limit on aircraft specification for the main race, but there was also a 'handicap' competition with a first prize of £2,000 (£125,000 today). Any entrant that did not reach Melbourne within sixteen days would not be given a final placing, whereas all those who did would receive a gold medal.

The closing date for entries to be sent to Melbourne Town Hall, or to the Australian High Commission in London, was 1 June 1934. The start date was set for 20 October, with the initial intention of using various English aerodromes as starting points. Control points would be at Baghdad, Allahabad, Singapore, Darwin, and Charleville, where pilots would be required to report to officials and would be able to collect meteorological updates. There would also be several intermediate check points that they were free to use, and search and rescue services would be on hand along the route. This was essentially the route used every week by Fokkers of Koninklijke Luchtvaart Maatschappij NV (KLM Royal Dutch Airlines). Competitors were expected to arrange their own refuelling, supplies, spares, and accommodation. There was no limit to crew or passenger numbers, but each aircraft had to carry 'sufficient food and water to maintain life for three days, and approved flotation gear for the pilot and each member of the crew, in addition to not less than six smoke signals'.

The clock was ticking. Martin Sharp relates how the idea for a new, competitive de Havilland aircraft took shape:

> 'You know, we can't stand by and let this race be won without any British effort.' This remark was made by de Havilland in his Hatfield office on a darkening January afternoon in 1934 when he was chatting with Hearle and Walker, Halford, Nixon, and St Barbe ... everyone on the technical side was at top pressure to get the DH.86 out and certified by January 31, 1934, to fulfil the Qantas contract. The production men were turning out Dragons and Fox Moths and Tiger Moths against urgent orders.... But gradually the thought of doing nothing at all became

> more and more insufferable.... There was great promise in the new Gipsy Six ... everybody felt the same.
>
> From that moment the scene changed. In nine months a monoplane could be 'done' ... by the end of September, three weeks before the start. At least three aircraft should be built, to spread the cost ... £50,000 [£3.1m today]? It could be as much as that, Nixon pondered. How much would an entrant be willing to pay to buy a racer ... which could not have much other purpose? £5,000? St Barbe said nobody would pay more....

The DH.88 design, to be named *Comet*, would be kept 'top secret'; details would not even be revealed to customers. Arthur Hagg settled on a twin-engined, low-wing monoplane. He was assisted by R. E. Bishop, who had left de Havilland during the economic slump and nearly took a job with Junkers in Germany—but his absence had only lasted a few weeks. The Comet's sleek fuselage would be formed from a wooden frame, covered with spruce plywood. It would seat a crew of two in tandem, to keep the frontal area to a minimum. A thin, tapered wing, also wooden, would have trailing-edge flaps for low-speed control, but would have no capacity for fuel tanks—these would be placed in the forward fuselage. The engine nacelles would also house de Havilland's first retractable undercarriage. This would be manually operated by a wheel in the cockpit that wound cables around a drum. There was no time to develop an automated mechanism.

Variable-pitch Propellers

The racer would need propellers that were more efficient than anything available in Britain, something that Amy Mollison would campaign for in her *Daily Mail* column—she would be appointed as the newspaper's Air Editor in April. Martin Sharp continues the story:

> ...the Americans had pitch-control mechanisms coming along ... and there was a French one worth considering.... Not only prestige would come of this, [Charles] Walker argued; actual experience with the variable-pitch airscrew...would be valuable for the future ... Hearle was to go to America, and if the general arrangement drawing could be agreed quickly Hagg had better go with him.... They went to Hamilton first, at Hartford, Connecticut ... even before leaving the works felt that they would like to do business with these people—get their propellers ... into production in England as well, by some licence agreement...

Licenced production of the Hamilton mechanism would indeed be secured, and would be announced in June. But it wasn't as simple as that, as Martin Sharp explains:

> Propellers for the DH.88 were not an easy problem. The smallest model was too large ... contact was made with Ratier in France, who were developing a propeller with a very simple pitch change. It was a small propeller, better suited to the Gipsy.... Frank Halford hurried over to Paris.
>
> Unfortunately ... once in coarse pitch it could not be returned to fine pitch before landing the aircraft.

Aerodrome Activity

The de Havilland Company Secretary, Wilfred Nixon, joined the London Aeroplane Club in January. Clem Pike returned from Cairo, having delivered a Dragon to Wilson Airways. George Cox flew to Catterick on 31 January to collect Seafarer II for the Mollisons, who would now keep the aircraft at Hatfield. Richard Shuttleworth visited in a Desoutter—he won the Brighton Speed Trials, in a Bugatti Type 51, in 1934. Capt. Monohan and Capt. Bristol, of the US Embassy, did some flying in their Puss Moth. Col. Miskin flew to Lympne and Sir Derwent Hall-Caine, an actor and former Labour MP, took his Leopard Moth up for a spin. He had founded The Readers Library Publishing Co. Ltd in the mid-1920s to make great literature more affordable. His brother, Gordon, was Conservative Member of Parliament for East Dorset. Their father was the Manx novelist, playwright, and politician, Sir Thomas H. Hall Caine.

On 14 February, the Stage & Screen Aero Club held a 'Grown-Up Kids' party', for which various facilities were renamed as 'the pram park', 'boys' and girls' cloak rooms', the 'nursery' and a 'dolls' house'. A 'doctor' provided cod liver oil, gripe water and 'poisons'. Dinner menus were written on school-style slates, and 'bibs' replaced napkins. The ladies dressed in romper suits, or short frocks with socks. Some of the men also wore rompers, and some were in shorts. Ovaltine, Glaxo, Nestlé, Bovril, Yardley, and other family product posters were displayed. Dinner was followed by a cabaret. A dance, supported by the Red Peppers band, went on until a very 'grown-up' 2 a.m.

Fg Off. V. R. 'Reggie' Moon joined the School of Flying as an instructor in February, just as Eddie Fulford went away for two months. Fulford accompanied Sir Malcolm Campbell as his pilot for an expedition along the Luderitzbucht-to-Spencer Bay stretch of South Africa's west coast (now in Namibia). Sir Malcolm had recently been awarded the Segrave Trophy for 1933, in recognition of his seventh successful attempt on the Land Speed Record in February. A year on, he was now searching for treasure which had been lost when an East Indiaman cargo ship had run aground many years before.

The School of Flying's chief ground engineer, Bob Hardingham, would also leave Hatfield in 1934, but he would not return as he joined the Air Ministry. Don Lawrence had fond memories of him: 'Everyone got on with Bob and I was sorry to see him go. The day he left he gave me his tool chest, which I still have.' Sid Weedon, who had been with the company since 1921, was promoted to fill the vacancy.

The Royal Aero Club passed to de Havilland its ownership of the London Aeroplane Club, which became a limited company. The club formed a squash team, which hosted visiting teams at Hatfield. They won their first match 3–1 on 22 February, against Trinity Hall Cambridge's White Elephant Club, but the RAC beat them 4–1 on 14 March, and Guys Hospital beat them 3–2 on 21 March. While some members were busy playing squash, others were flying far and wide. Lady Margaret Loch left on 21 February, in her Gipsy Moth, for a three-week flying tour to the south of France and Sicily, and brought the aircraft home on 16 March. In May, the club would receive Tiger Moth G-ACSK, which they had been waiting for to replace a Gipsy Moth, which they were selling. The RAF Reserve Flying Club also formed a squash team. More significantly, the club's remit was expanded to cover the serving RAF, retired personnel, and former members of the Royal Naval Air Service and Royal Flying Corp. It was renamed, simply, as the RAF Flying Club. By May 1934, Hatfield would be home to twenty-six aircraft.

After dusk pilots could not easily use landmarks or follow railway lines and

Steel-and-glass 'lantern', built on the roof of Hatfield Aerodrome's new squash courts in mid-1933, seen here in the autumn of 1934. Night beacon apparatus had been installed in March. It was removed in 1988, when the old building was demolished. (*Frank Stewart*)

roads. Hatfield Aerodrome was one of several airfields that installed beacons built like coastal lighthouses. The steel-and-glass 'lantern' that housed Hatfield's example had been constructed in mid-1933, on the roof of the then-new squash courts building. The beacon apparatus within—believed to have been made by Plessey—was installed in March 1934. A revolving lower lens emitted a high-powered beam, angled just above the horizon, and a low-powered beam shone vertically. Its white light flashed for 0.92 of a second every five seconds. From half an hour after sunset it was switched on for one hour, although this could be extended on prior request. On a clear night, the high-powered beam could be seen at up to 38 miles (61 km) away.

Just because the beacon was lit did not mean that the aerodrome was available for landings, for which night-landing flares would need to be requested in advance; but the beacon doubtless guided many an anxious pilot. The development of radar meant that such beacons soon fell out of use, and they would have been an undesirable attraction to enemy aircraft in the Second World War. However, Hatfield's lantern remained in place until 1988, when it was removed to North Weald airfield. Fundraising enabled the beacon to be restored and returned to Hatfield in 2011. It sits in front of the University of Hertfordshire's 'de Havilland Campus', a stone's throw from where it previously stood for 55 years. It may be the last of its kind.

Birkett Air Services Ltd, of Heston, specialised in rapid, airborne deliveries using a small fleet of Puss Moths. One of their aircraft took off from Hatfield at 5.26 p.m. on 23 March 1934, and flew to Liverpool, with copies of a national newspaper's evening edition. The remarkable thing was that this particular edition contained photos of the Grand National horse race, which had been taken less than two hours before, at the Aintree course on the north side of Liverpool. The photos had been 'wired' to London by telephone line. The edition immediately went to print and the copies were rushed to Hatfield; they were on sale in Liverpool just after 7 p.m., thought to be a record at the time.

On 17 April, a new development of the Dragon and Express took to the air at Hatfield for the first time, in the hands of Hubert Broad. It was Hatfield's first hosting of a maiden flight. With tapered wings, and powered by two Gipsy Sixes, it was initially known as the *Dragon Six*. A charming design classic, it became the most successful 'short haul' airliner of the 1930s. Over 200 would be built at Hatfield for civilian use, and they would serve around the world.

On 9 May 1934 Geoffrey de Havilland, now aged 52 and still keen to be involved in flight testing, gave the prototype DH.87 its first flight from Stag Lane. Initially named the *Coupé Moth*, and registered as G-ACTA, it was powered by a Gipsy Major, and was a cabin tourer biplane similar to the Leopard Moth monoplane. Its side-by-side seating enabled passengers to try taking the controls and to have a normal conversation with an instructor. Renamed as the *Hornet Moth*, production would begin at Hatfield, alongside Tiger Moths, the following year.

Above and below: Capt C. C. Larsen of the Danish Army Air Corp collected a DH.84 Dragon from Hatfield on 26 February. In late March he was back, with a group of well-dressed officers, to collect another Dragon and seven Tiger Moths with 'blind flying' hoods. The Dragons would be used for troop transportation, aerial surveys, and general liaison. Note the steelwork of the new factory at top-centre. (The Aeroplane, *via aviationancestry.com*)

The Return of Bulldog Drummond

In 1934, Walter Summers wrote and directed *The Return of Bulldog Drummond*, produced by Walter C. Mycroft, for British International Pictures at Welwyn Studios. Summers placed fellow members at Hatfield's Stage & Screen Aero Club in leading roles: Ralph Richardson as Drummond, and Joyce Kennedy as the villain's beautiful assistant. Richardson had gained his 'A' flying licence at Hatfield in February.

Fifteen minutes into the film, Saunders Roe A17 amphibian G-AAIP is seen taxiing at Hatfield in the dark. Built in 1929 and named *Cutty Sark*, she was the first of twelve examples. Alliott V. Roe had left Avro that year, and had acquired flying boat builder S. E. Saunders Ltd. Saunders' earliest amphibious design, when

Saro A17 G-AAIP, named *Cutty Sark*, at Hatfield Aerodrome in a scene from *The Return of Bulldog Drummond*, filmed in mid-1934. Having climbed out of the cockpit, the villain, played by Francis L. Sullivan, leans forward to reveal the name of the aircraft's former owner—Clyde Flying Boats. (*Copyright © STUDIOCANAL Films Ltd. All rights reserved*)

Interior of the Hatfield squash courts. Ralph Richardson is playing at top-right, in a scene from *The Return of Bulldog Drummond*. (*Copyright © STUDIOCANAL Films Ltd, (1934). All rights reserved*)

By May 1934, erection of steelwork for the factory was complete, roofing was well underway, and, facing the Barnet Bypass, the footings for the new admin headquarters had also been finished. Note the tennis courts being laid at bottom right, between the squash courts building and the airframe assembly shop. (*BAE Systems, via Philip Birtles*)

he was working with Tom Sopwith, had been first flown in 1912, by the 23-year-old Harry Hawker.

G-AAIP had been used from May 1933 by Clyde Flying Boats Ltd, based at Loch Lomond. They operated services between islands off the west coast of Scotland. The Clyde name is clearly visible in the film, below the cockpit side windows. From May 1934 Clyde no longer owned the 'Saro', which was brought to Hatfield, possibly for the very purpose of appearing in the film. She would not fly again.

In the final minutes of the film, Drummond's vigilantes—the 'Black Clan'—race in cars and on motorbikes to save him and Mrs Drummond (played by Ann Todd). Two Clan members arrive by Gipsy Moth. A model was used for a landing in the dark, followed by a real Moth taxiing.

England Expects

In 1929 Albert Edwards had opened the Grosvenor House Hotel in the City of Westminster; he was now the first to buy one of the Comet racers. In their edition of 1 March 1934, *Flight* announced that:

> A DH *Comet* has been entered for the MacRobertson race to Australia by Mr A. O. Edwards, the Managing Director of Grosvenor House, Park Lane. The 'Comet' has a minimum speed of 200 mph guaranteed by the makers. The pilots will be Mr C. W. A. Scott and Mr Campbell Black.

The 14 March edition of *The Aeroplane* published a photograph of RAFC secretary Harold Perrin receiving the entry form for the MacRobertson race from Edwards, flanked by Scott, Campbell Black, and de Havilland business manager Francis St Barbe.

Jim Mollison, too, had put down a £1,000 deposit (£62,000 today) for one of the Comets, although he didn't then know that this was its name—never mind what it would look like. He had used Amy's savings, but did not confirm until May that she would be his flying partner in the race; they quickly became favourites to win. Their entry was soon followed by the third Comet, from former Bentley racing driver Bernard Rubin. Intending to fly it himself, Rubin gave the other seat to Ken Waller. They had even gone to the trouble of flying from England to Australia over fifteen days in late March, in a Leopard Moth, to gain experience of the route. In late April, they made the return journey in an unofficial time of eight days and twelve hours—more than seven hours faster than Jim Mollison's 1931 Australia-England record.

Geoffrey de Havilland's 1933 King's Cup-winning Leopard Moth prototype was modified to accept a new racing engine for flight testing. With an increased 'compression ratio', the Gipsy Six 'R' was developing an encouraging 230 bhp (171.5 kW)—45 bhp (33.6 kW) more than the standard engine. However, the maiden flight of the first Comet was still months away, and there were still many challenges to solve. The Tingey family—pronounced locally with a hard 'g'—were shopkeepers in Hatfield. Successive generations had a bakery, a grocery shop, a furniture business, and a glass and china business; they also ran the post office. They were also ironmongers, and on one occasion engine installation designer John E. Walker had to visit them to buy a spring for a lawn mower—in order to determine the dimensions they needed for a similar item on the Comet engines.

A single starting point for the MacRobertson race was now expected, and a rumour was circulating that Hatfield would be the venue. The world altitude record for aeroplanes (balloons could ascend much higher) had been held by American and French aircraft for the last thirty years. The exception was in 1932, when on 16 September Bristol test pilot Cyril Uwins took a Vickers Vespa, with a supercharged Bristol Pegasus, to 43,976 feet (13,407 m). A year later Gustave Lemoine restored French honour, reaching 44,819 feet (13,661 m) in a Potez 506. But it was Italian aircraft and pilots who were now bringing pride to their country (which had been led by Benito Mussolini's National Fascist Party since 1922). They had already taken the world air speed record from Britain in 1933, and, on 11 April 1934, Renato Donati achieved a height of 47,354 feet (14,433 m) in a

Caproni Ca.113. If Hatfield was going to host the start of the Australia race, could de Havilland recover British pride at the Melbourne finish?

And how fast might the winning race time be? The England–Australia record time, usually to the Northern Territory's capital of Port Darwin, had been steadily dropping since 1930. Charles Kingsford Smith had flown a Gipsy-powered Avro Avian Sports over the 10,000 miles from Heston in 9 days, 21 hours, and 40 minutes. In 1931, Charles Scott had covered the distance from Lympne, in a Gipsy Moth, in 9 days, 4 hours, and 11 minutes. Later that year, Cecil A. Butler did the same flight just one hour and forty-two minutes faster, with a Pobjoy-Comper Swift. Scott took his record back in 1932, again in a Gipsy Moth, with a time of 8 days, 20 hours, and 47 minutes, and was awarded a knighthood for services to aviation. He did it again in October 1933, this time arriving at Wyndham, Western Australia, after 7 days, 4 hours, and 44 minutes. This solo record would stand for two years, but a faster time was set eight days later when Charles Ulm successfully led a new crew in an Avro Ten, named *Faith in Australia*. They flew from Harmondsworth, west London, to Derby, Western Australia, in 6 days, 17 hours, and 45 minutes.

Then, in the second half of May 1934, Jean Batten flew Gipsy Moth G-AARB (fitted with a concealed 'toilet tube') from Lympne to Port Darwin. This was her third attempt to complete the flight, and she did it in 14 days, 23 hours, and 25 minutes—breaking Amy's women's record from 1930. As Geoffrey de Havilland put it, '"Try Again Jean" or "Third-Time-Lucky Jean"—how the Press loved these soubriquets—was the youngest and surely the smallest and most game of the London Aeroplane Club girls'.

10

A Summer of Fun and Progress

> Seventy visiting aircraft at Flying Club display—On Saturday, Prince George flew from Reading to Hatfield in twenty minutes and watched a marvellous display of flying by Britain's crack flyers.... There was not a single mishap to mar a perfect day, which ended with joy rides for the public from 5/- each.
>
> Welwyn Times, *21 June 1934*

Leisure and Pleasure

The Air League of the British Empire held their first annual 'Empire Air Day' on 24 May 1934, with events hosted at aircraft factories, RAF bases, and civilian aerodromes around the world. Hatfield was one of eighty host locations around the UK. The public were able to watch air defence squadrons, flying schools, and clubs operating first-hand on a normal working day. As with the promotion of 'air mindedness' in the 1920s, the intention was to increase public interest and understanding, to encourage flying, and to promote air links across the British Empire. Funds were raised for the RAF Benevolent Fund through ticket prices of 1*s* for adults, 6*d* for children, and 3*d* per head for groups. Amy Mollison used a Tiger Moth, loaned to her by de Havilland, to make special visits to some of the aerodromes. They also provided a DH.86 Express for members of the press to tour the country.

By June two clay tennis courts, behind the squash courts building, had been constructed to championship standard by En-Tout-Cas Co. Ltd. Horse-riding lessons and hacking could be arranged. Snooker matches were played in the clubhouse, and a nine-hole putting green was also laid out. There is also evidence of a much older, larger golf course, with bunkers on the south side of what became the aerodrome. Reg Sutterby had joined the ground staff in 1933, and he and his family moved into de Havilland-owned housing next to the aerodrome. His daughter, Jill Beresford, played in the surrounding fields as a child. She remembered a small building with semi-circular windows, which they called 'the golf hut'. Its derelict remains were removed in 2010.

On 3 June the London Aeroplane Club held a garden party. The pool, now maintained at a pleasant 58 degrees by steam injection, was the setting for a bathing costume parade. A swimming demonstration was given by Miss Betty Blanks, the 1932 100-yards (91-m) breast stroke champion for the Southern Counties. Other entertainments included dancing, novelty races, and competitions. Visitors were also able to get up close to over forty aircraft parked on the aerodrome. Flt Lt William E. P. Johnson gave an impressive aerobatic display in a Tiger Moth. Hawker test pilot Flt Lt Philip G. Lucas flew a Hawker Hart, treating the crowd to the roar of its Rolls-Royce Kestrel engine. Also that day, in preparation for the RAF Hendon Display, practice exercises were conducted over Hatfield by 18, 57, 600, and 601 Squadrons.

Fg Off. Reginald A. C. Brie, of the Cierva Autogiro Co. Ltd, demonstrated their C.30—amazing spectators with its very short take-off, hovering, and a vertical landing. Powered by an Armstrong Siddeley Genet Major, the C.30 was one of a series of autogiros designed by Spanish engineer Juan de la Cierva. It would be produced by Avro in England, Liore et Olivier in France, and Focke-Wulf in Germany. Maj. Albert A. Nathan would keep an Avro-built example at Hatfield from November. A single Cierva C.24 had been built by de Havilland at Stag Lane in 1931, using the cabin of a Puss Moth and a Gipsy III engine. This can still be seen at the de Havilland Aircraft Heritage Centre at Salisbury Hall, near London Colney, in Hertfordshire.

The RAF Flying Club held their second annual air display at Hatfield on 16 June. HRH Prince George arrived with Maj. H. Butler in the Prince of Wales's DH.84 Dragon. His welcome party included Lord Trenchard and his successor as Marshal of the RAF, Sir John Salmond, Lt-Col. Shelmerdine, Capt. de Havilland, club founder Plt Off. Robert Brittain, and his father, Sir Harry Brittain. Frederick Handley Page, Sir G. Hubert Wilkins (the Australian polar explorer), and Lord and Lady Brockett, from nearby Brockett Hall, were also there. Imperial Airways set up an exhibition of photographs and diagrams in one of the hangars. Music was provided by the RAF Band from Henlow, Bedfordshire.

The new Short L.17 39-seat biplane airliner had recently entered service with Imperial Airways. One of only two built, named *Syrinx* and registered as G-ACJK, landed during the display while on its way to Singapore with the mail—600 and 601 Sqns also gave a formation flying display. High-performance, aerobatic, and comical flying displays, including 'car bombing', were provided by Avro Tutors, Tiger Moths, 1 Sqn's Hawker Furies, and the RAF's new standard day-fighter: the Bristol Mercury-powered Gloster Gauntlet. Gerry Sayer demonstrated its amazing manoeuvrability, including tight turns at around 200 mph (322 km/h). Hawker Aircraft Ltd had announced their purchase of Gloster Aircraft Co. in January, with Tom Sopwith being appointed as chairman of both companies. Several of the display pilots were instructors from the civilian flying schools, including Hatfield's Wizzie King and Reggie Moon. The *Flight* reporter likened George Bullman's

Left to right: Lt-Col. Shelmerdine, Sir John Salmond, and Lord Trenchard welcome HRH Prince George and Maj H. Butler to Hatfield on 16 June. They had just arrived in the Prince of Wales's Dragon, G-ACGG, to attend the RAF Flying Club display. (Flight, via aviationancestry.com)

steep climb in a Hawker Hart to its deer family namesake jumping a fence—appropriately enough for flying over Hertfordshire. Reginald Brie was back with the C.30 Autogiro, which could be bought for £1,250 (£78,000 today).

At around 5,000 feet (1,500 m), John Tranum jumped out of the four-seater cabin of a Stinson businessman's monoplane, being flown by Leslie L. Irvin. As usual Tranum delayed pulling the ripcord of his Irvin parachute, and fell for about a thousand feet (300 m) before the crowd could sigh with collective relief. He tried to land inside the aerodrome by controlling the chute, but ended up in a chicken coop beyond the new factory construction site.

On 26 June, Geoffrey de Havilland went to Buckingham Palace to receive the OBE from King George V for his services to aviation. Also in June, the Spanish Government sent a special commission to Britain to explore airline development opportunities, including a visit to Hatfield.

In early July a Swedish Royal Commission visited Hatfield for a similar purpose, accompanied by Maj. Oliver G. G. Villiers of the Royal Aero Club. They met the Prince of Wales, who happened to land while they were there. The Swedish Commission was studying civil aviation across Europe, particularly because the government subsidy for their national airline (AB Aerotransport) would expire in 1936, and they needed to establish a more commercially-viable operation. The commission was led by Torsten K. V. Nothin, Over-Governor of Stockholm, and Capt. Carl Florman, Managing Director of A. B. Aerotransport. Lt-Col. Francis Shelmardine met them at the Air Ministry, and they were entertained by Imperial Airways at the Royal Aero Club. They were also given an opportunity to inspect Croydon airport before they left.

A Spanish government commission visited Hatfield in June 1934. They were accompanied by de Havilland's agent in Spain, Señor Escario (far left), and hosted by Capt. Hubert Broad, seen here leaning against the wing of a Dragon. (Flight, *via the Norman Eastaff Collection*)

Stag Lane had become dangerous as the builders encroached, and the new local residents were increasingly complaining about the few aircraft that were still flying in and out. In later years, Geoffrey de Havilland looked back: '...the take-off area had already been reduced to a narrow landing strip when, with a certain sense of sadness, I made my last take-off in July 1934 and flew the few miles north to Hatfield'. He was flying the prototype Hornet Moth. The street built over the Stag Lane runway would be named *Mollison Way*.

Gipsy Moth G-AASL, which Geoffrey de Havilland had flown in the King's Cup of 1930, had joined the School of Flying's fleet, and it was operated by the London Aeroplane Club from July 1934. It was joined by Moth Major G-ACCW, which Richard Westenra had flown in the 1933 King's Cup—now owned by Charles A. MacDonald. Two new Leopard Moths also became Hatfield residents that summer. One belonged to Lt-Col. Andrew Hamilton Gault, who had visited Germany in 1933 with a party led by Lindsay Everard. The other was registered to a Mr A. Tucker of the Sperry Gyroscope Co. They made advanced aircraft navigation equipment, including the Sperry Gyroscope and the Sperry Radio Direction Finder for assisting with blind flying. The Comets would be fitted with their Artificial Horizon and Directional Gyroscope, as would some of the other MacRobertson entrants. Lady Loch would also keep a new Leopard Moth at Hatfield, from January 1935.

The 1934 King's Cup

For Hatfield's second hosting of the King's Cup, the arrangement of rounds and heats would be the same as in 1933—except that the first two rounds would be held on Friday 13 July, and the semi-final and final would be on Saturday 14 July. There were forty-one entrants, the largest field that would be seen at Hatfield. William Morris, now Lord Nuffield after the New Year's Honours, entered three Wolseley-powered Hawker Tomtits, as he had a year before. Four very fast Percival Gulls were entered. Two were using the new Gipsy Six—including a Mew Gull, sponsored by HRH Prince George and flown by Edgar Percival. Comper was represented by six entries and there were three Miles Hawks, one of which also had a Gipsy Six. The Hawks were built by Phillips & Powis Aircraft at Woodley airfield, near Reading, for Frederick G. Miles—who soon joined the company as technical director and chief designer. It was at Woodley, in 1931, that Douglas Bader had the accident which lead to the amputation of his legs.

In 1931, after the loss of the R101 airship and the cancellation of the R100, Nevil Shute Norway founded Airspeed Ltd with A. Hessell Tiltman. Tiltman had joined Airco in 1916, transferred to de Havilland in 1920, and worked on various designs, including the Moth. Alan Cobham was one of Airspeed's directors, and Amy Johnson was an early shareholder. Tiltman's AS.5 Courier design had made its first flight in April 1933, and was the first British production aircraft with a retractable undercarriage. An example was entered in the 1934 King's Cup by Air Vice-Marshal Borton; he would also be the pilot. This particular aircraft was Napier's testbed for their 325-bhp (242-kW), sixteen-cylinder Rapier IV engine. This was a development of Frank Halford's first design for Napier, which powered the DH.77 intercepter protoype in 1929. The cylinders were arranged around two crankshafts, in an 'H' pattern.

Geoffrey de Havilland and his sons, Geoffrey Jnr and Peter, all competed. Father would fly the prototype Hornet Moth, 'Junior' would be in an experimental aircraft (the TK.1.), and 'little brother' would use a Tiger Moth, entered by their father just before the closing date for registrations. The TK.1 began life as the unsuccessful DH.81 *Swallow Moth* monoplane. It was rebuilt, as a biplane, by apprentices at the de Havilland Aeronautical Technical School at Stag Lane—supervised by Marcus Langley, of the school's Drawing Office. The 'TK' designation arose when Dutch student Juste van Hattum wrote 'Technisch Kollege No.1' on the drawings. The aircraft was entered for the King's Cup by Sqn Ldr Owen W. Clapp, school principal from 1932. Hubert Broad would fly the second built example of the new DH.89 Dragon Six, G-ACPM. Five Leopard Moths, three Gipsy Moths, a Fox Moth, and Puss Moth G-ABLS—still flying today—completed de Havilland's line-up. One of the Leopard Moths was Alex Henhaw's G-ACLO. Another, entered by Sir Derwent Hall-Caine, was G-ACHC—in which the late Bill Styran had come third, the previous year.

Geoffrey Jnr's TK.1 on the end of the line-up for heat one of round one. Officials delayed the start from 8 a.m. until 9.30 a.m. due to concerns over the weather—which proved entirely justified. (*Sport & General Press Agency Ltd—Royal Aero Club Trust, 0751-0173*)

The course for Round One was 232.5 miles (374 km) over the south-west of England: Hatfield to RAF Upper Heyford in Oxfordshire; to Bristol Municipal Airport at Whitchurch, in north Somerset (home of the Bristol & Wessex Aeroplane Club); to RAF Old Sarum in Wiltshire, just north of Salisbury; and back to Hatfield. The cloud base was down to 800 feet (244 m) or less. To the south-west of the aerodrome, the Smallford radio masts were only just visible. Gabrielle Patterson won her heat in one of the Hawks. Peter de Havilland won his heat, but his father was eliminated. Two of the five Leopard Moths also failed to qualify for round two—one of them was Alex Henshaw's. The Gulls flown by H. H. Leech, Wally Hope, and Edgar Percival were all knocked out. Even Percival's average of 191 mph (307 km/h), a King's Cup record, was not enough to overcome their disadvantageous handicaps. One of the Tomtits made a forced landing in a field, and hit a tree to avoid some cows. The Courier was also eliminated, as were two of the Gipsy Moths, one of the Hawks, and two of the Compers—one flown by Nick Comper himself.

The course for round two was exactly the same distance as that for round one: Hatfield up to RAF Waddington in Lincolnshire; down to Upper Heyford; and back over to Hatfield. Low cloud, wind, rain, and even thunderstorms, with canvas-ripping hail, made flying very difficult. Several entrants had to pull out mid-course, including Hubert Broad and Peter de Havilland. Nonetheless, some very fast times were put in by those who got round. Also out were another Leopard

A. George Reynolds, the Rayla Aero Club's official timekeeper and starter, seen here at the 1934 King's Cup. (*Sport & General Press Agency Ltd—Royal Aero Club Trust, 0654-0189*)

Moth, Gabrielle Patterson's Hawk, the fourth Gull, two more Compers, Carill Napier's Hendy, the 1933 fourth-placed Desoutter, and George Lowdell's Tomtit—it suffered a fuel supply problem and had to land in a field, near the Smallford radio masts.

The semi-finals on the Saturday used a 64-mile (103-km) course, from Hatfield to RAF North Weald, in Essex, over to RAF Henlow, and back down to Hatfield. Three circuits enabled spectators to see the racers not only at the start and finish, but twice banking hard around the Hatfield pylon. The last two Compers, another Leopard Moth, and a General Aircraft Co. Ltd (GAL) Monospar ST-6—flown by Charles E. Gardner—all went out. Gardner would be back for the next three years. As an additional display before the final, several of the faster aircraft which had been eliminated the previous day took to the air to provide an exciting aerobatic show.

The final provided even more action, with six circuits of a 23.5-mile (37.8-km) course entirely within Hertfordshire: Hatfield to the village of Watton-at-Stone; to Luton Hoo, on the Bedfordshire border; and back to Hatfield. The starting line-up was filmed for the usual Pathé Gazette newsreel.

The race was won by Flt Lt Harry M. Schofield, in his GAL Monospar ST-10 powered by two Pobjoy Niagaras. He carried the aircraft's designer, Swiss engineer and GAL managing director Helmuth J. Stieger, as a passenger throughout the race. The new prototype Miles M.2F Hawk Major, G-ACTD, was flown into second by First World War 'Ace' Tommy Rose. Laurence Lipton fared much better than he had the previous year, bringing Gipsy Moth *Jason IV* home in third place. He was also

Owen Cathcart Jones banks Puss Moth G-ABLS around the Hatfield pylon. This was typical of the second day's racing at the 1934 King's Cup, as the routes involved several short circuits—enabling spectators to see lots of action. G-ABLS is still flying today. (*Sport & General Press Agency Ltd—Royal Aero Club Trust, 0751-0081*)

awarded the Siddeley trophy as the highest-placed private entrant, representing the London Aeroplane Club. A Blackburn B.2 was fourth. Geoffrey Jnr was fifth, in the TK.1. Plt Off. Hugh R. A. 'Jumbo' Edwards came sixth, in a Southern Martlet—he was an Oxford rowing coach, and the younger brother of 1931 King's Cup winner Cecil Edwards. Tomtits G-AASI finished seventh, flown by W. H. Sutcliffe, an instructor at the Midland Aero Club. Australian Harry F. 'Jim' Broadbent was eighth, in the Fox Moth. Lt Owen Cathcart Jones—a former Fleet Air Arm pilot and the first to land on an aircraft carrier at night—was ninth, in the Puss Moth. Broadbent and Cathcart Jones were filmed by Pathé while banking around the Hatfield pylon. Leopard Moth G-ACHC was disqualified for missing a turning point.

The cash prizes were, again, donated by Lord Wakefield. Lord Londonderry presented the main awards. Pathé captured Harry Schofield's short but gracious acceptance speech:

> Well, I'm very proud to have won this cup, but I think the man who should be speaking is Mr Stieger who built the machine. I couldn't have done it without the machine, and I think a lot of people could have won it in the machine; and that's all there is to be said about it, really.

To the left is Helmuth J. Stieger, a Swiss engineer, managing director of General Aircraft Co Ltd and designer of the Monospar ST-10. Pilot Harry Schofield carried Steiger as a passenger in the ST-10 for the 1934 King's Cup, and they won it together. With him stands William Sempill, acting as a race steward. He became 19th Lord Sempill that year, upon the death of his father. He was rightly suspected of passing secrets to the Japanese in the 1920s, and would be so again in 1941. He avoided prosecution due to his royal connections and high profile. (*Sport & General Press Agency Ltd—Royal Aero Club Trust, 0398-0154*)

Monospar ST-10 G-ACTS, winner of the 1934 King's Cup. It is seen here outside the Midland & Scottish Air Ferries Ltd hangars at Renfrew Airport, just west of Glasgow. Note the 'King's Cup' marking under the rear cockpit window. (*Copyright acknowledged, via the A. J. Jackson Collection*)

Lord Londonderry presents the King's Cup to Harry Schofield. (*Sport & General Press Agency Ltd—Royal Aero Club Trust, 0398-0120*)

Geoffrey de Havilland Jnr (centre) with the experimental TK.1, built by the pupils of the de Havilland Aeronautical Technical School. He had just taken fifth place in the final. He is seen here flanked by his brother Peter and their father, who had both been eliminated in the previous rounds. After the race, TK.1 was sold to Royal pilot Edward Fielden. (Flight, *via the Norman Eastaff Collection*)

Schofield was appointed director and general manager of General Aircraft Ltd in the October.

Although de Havilland had not been as successful as in the 1933 race, four of their aircraft had made the final. The commemorative menu for their annual dinner in December 1934 proudly noted that 'not a single mechanical failure' was suffered by the twenty-five Gipsy and Gipsy Major engines used by participating aircraft.

Another Atlantic crossing

Jim Mollison relinquished his share of *Seafarer II* to Amy in April. In May she sold it to Alan Butler's brother-in-law, Leonard G. Reid—a Canadian aircraft engineer, who had learned to fly with the London Aeroplane Club at Hatfield. He was fortunate to not be seriously hurt in December 1933, when he crashed into trees at the edge of the aerodrome. He intended to attempt the same flight that the Mollisons had abandoned, from Wasaga Beach to Baghdad, to capture the world non-stop flight record. Reid teamed up with Englishman James R. Ayling, a former RAF Flying Officer. They both did a blind flying course with Air Service Training at Hamble, which turned out to be a very wise decision.

They re-named the Dragon as *Trail of the Caribou*, and, after a complete overhaul by de Havilland in June, they shipped it back to Canada for its third Atlantic crossing by sea. They were again assisted by engineers from de Havilland Canada. After 3,700 miles in 30 hours 50 minutes—much of which they did, indeed, have to fly blind—they landed at Heston, unannounced, on 9 August. They flew the Dragon to Hatfield that evening, arriving at around 7.30 p.m.

The media was there to interview them the following day. *Flight* reported that 'both engines and cowlings were as clean as if the Dragon had just left the erecting shop'. Pathé recorded Reid's reflections on their flight:

> Naturally, Jimmy and I are very disappointed that we didn't succeed in flying from Wasaga Beach to Baghdad. However, we have the consolation of knowing that we have done the first flight from Canada to England. Being a Canadian myself, and this specimen being an Englishman [he nods to Ayling], we are particularly glad to have linked up the Dominion of Canada and England by air.

Pathé footage not released at the time also captured Ayling's thoughts:

> We did strike a good deal of bad weather which made us use up much more petrol than we had scheduled for.... When we came in sight of land, we realised that we had not enough petrol to do more than 6,000 miles. We worked it out on paper and were very disappointed, but we came to the conclusion that, in the interests of aviation, it would be a miles better thing to make a safe landing in England

Leonard G. Reid and James R. Ayling with their DH.84 Dragon *Trail of the Caribou*, at Hatfield in August 1934. They were interviewed by the media after completing the first non-stop flight from Canada to England. (*Nederlands Instituut voor Militaire Historie, Ministerie van Defensie*)

> and, therefore, make a real flight of it rather than go ahead and not accomplish anything in particular. We therefore landed at Heston for customs clearance ... and then we carried on from Heston to Hatfield, the home of the Dragon.

Reid added:

> At all times, we had complete confidence in the machine and its engines, and it behaved like a dream. It flew beautifully the whole time. Flying blind in this machine is no trouble at all. It just flies itself.

Flight also commented that 'more and more work is being carried out on the new DH buildings at Hatfield, and machines are now being brought from Stag Lane for assembly and testing'.

Standard Telephones & Cables received a new Puss Moth in August, no doubt fitted with their radio equipment for demonstration to customers. The London Aeroplane Club acquired another Tiger Moth, fitted with night and blind flying equipment, bringing their fleet to seven aircraft. Charles Scott appeared in a Pathé film shot at Hatfield, flying the London Aeroplane Club's Tiger Moth G-ACSK, which had been

The administration block, under construction in the summer of 1934. Note the scaffolding around the power house chimney. (*BAE Systems, via Mill Green Museum, Welwyn Hatfield Museum Service*)

registered to the club on 5 May that year. The film is entitled: 'Like to Fly? Have a "lesson" with Mr C. W. A. Scott, famous Pilot, and holder of various England–Australia record flights.' First, Scott points to each of the cockpit instruments and controls as the narrator describes them. He moves the control stick, and the camera captures the movement of the port wing's aileron and the tailplane's elevators. In the background are other aircraft. The then-new radio masts at Smallford are visible beyond the aerodrome boundary. Scott then points out the fuel tank, set in the middle of the upper wing, and then opens the front cowling to reveal the fuel filter, carburettor, and engine. A 'prop swinger' removes the wheel chocks and starts the engine for him. Scott takes off, and the camera swings round to show the aerodrome buildings as he climbs over the hangars. He demonstrates left and right turns, and then we are airborne beside him over rural Hertfordshire, being filmed from another aircraft. Scott lands, and the film ends with him smiling in the cockpit. G-ACSK would go to the Royal New Zealand Air Force in December 1939.

The MacRobertson Field Takes Shape

The closing date for entries of 1 June had passed. Rumours about Hatfield hosting the start of the race had become expectation, with *Flight*'s 7 June edition feeding the excitement: 'With the fastest machines in the world on the line, "zero hour" at Hatfield on the twentieth of October will be a moment in a million.' Speculation that Leonard Reid might enter with his *Trail of the Caribou* proved unfounded. Wally Hope registered with a Moth Major, as did Alan Bulter, who intended to use a Dragon—with

The factory under construction in the summer of 1934, looking west. The horse at bottom-left is in a field that had been separated from the Harpsfield Hall estate when the Barnet Bypass was built in 1927. (*Sport & General Press Agency Ltd—BAE Systems, via Hertfordshire Constablulary)*

its long-range fuel tanks, *Trail of the Caribou* was thought to be his chosen aircraft, but it was damaged beyond repair on landing at Hamble on 12 August. Twenty-year-old Australian Charles J. 'Jimmy' Melrose would fly a modified Puss Moth. A Dragon Six would be flown by New Zealanders Sqn Ldr James D. Hewitt and Fg Off. Cyril E. Kay. Photographer Frank Stewart would be their passenger.

Airspeed had four entries. An AS.5 Courier was entered by Sir Alan Cobham, to be flown by an RAF crew—Sqn Ldr David E. Stodart, and his distant cousin Sgt Kenneth G. Stodart. Capt. Neville Stack, the 1933 King's Cup entrant, entered an AS.8 Viceroy built to his own specifications. Sidney L. Turner would be in the cockpit with him, and James H. G. McArthur would join them as radio operator. Two Wolseley-powered AS.6 Envoys were also entered: one by Lady Cobham, and one by Lord Nuffield, to be piloted by George Lowdell. The very attractive Pander S.4 *Postjäger*, from the Netherlands, would also start the race. Nicknamed the *Panderjäger*, this was an all-wooden trimotor monoplane. It would be piloted by Gerrit J. Geysendorfer and Dirk L. Asjes, with Pieter Pronk as their navigator.

Sir Charles Kingsford Smith and Patrick G. Taylor signed up with their Lockheed Altair, *Lady Southern Cross*. So did Wiley Post, with his 1931 round-the-world record-breaking Lockheed Vega, *Winnie Mae*. There was also talk of an entry by Howard Hughes, but this did not materialise. Another notable entry was the Granville Brothers' last racing design, the Gee Bee R-6H, named *QED* (Quod Erat Demonstrandum), and crewed by Jacqueline Cochran and Wesley Smith. Jackie had come from obscurity and poverty in northern Florida, developed a career as a beautician, and moved to New York. There she began an affair with the millionaire lawyer and industrialist Floyd Odlum, who was married with several children. He financed her way into the world of glamorous aviation.

However, the strongest competition was expected from two other American aircraft. A Douglas DC-2 was entered by KLM. Developed from the DC-1 of 1933, this was a beautiful, all-metal, fourteen-seat, low-wing monoplane airliner with retractable undercarriage and variable-pitch propellers. It had first flown on 11 May. The KLM entrant was named *Uiver*, a variation in spelling of the Dutch word for 'stork'. It would carry four crew members—Capt. Koene D. Parmentier, Jan J. Moll, Bouwe Prins, and Cornelius van Brugge—and three paying passengers, in comfort! A ten-seat Boeing Model 247D, of similar configuration to the DC-2, was leased from United Airlines by the flamboyant Col. Roscoe Turner. Ironically, it would be named the *Warner Brothers Comet* after one of his main sponsors. Turner would add a '5' in front of its No.7 race number, in honour of his other main sponsor—Heinz. He had broken the trans-America east-west speed record in 1929 and 1930, and had won the Bendix Trophy in 1933. Trans-Pacific flyer Clyde E. Pangborn would be Turner's co-pilot for the MacRobertson race. Turner would win the Thompson Trophy at the American National Air Races on 3 September, before making his way over to England.

Meanwhile, on 21 August, the first Comet to receive its civil registration, G-ACSP, was Jim Mollison's. Bernard Rubin's was registered as G-ACSR two days later. On 4 September, Albert Edwards' aircraft received the registration G-ACSS. There was regret at de Havilland that they were not able to develop a commercial aircraft comparable to the strongest American entries in time for the race, although *Flight* pointed out, in their 30 August edition, that:

> ...there is no earthly reason why after the race, the machines should not be modified slightly ... used as a very efficient, fast and economical mail carrier. We commend it to the attention of air mail operators at home and elsewhere.

There was growing concern in the British parliament and media about the perceived weakness of the RAF. The Member of Parliament for Epping, in Essex, 15 miles (24 km) east of Hatfield, had been warning that Germany was secretly rearming. He had made a major speech on defence on 7 February, highlighting the need to strengthen the RAF and to create a government department for planning national defence. His name was Winston Churchill. On 13 July, he made another speech on the need for the League of Nations to reassert itself. Hitler became Germany's head of state on 2 August.

This was the context in which German gliding expert Wolf K. E. Hirth and Hermann Illg had registered for the MacRobertson, with an entry from Bayerische

The factory under construction in the summer of 1934, looking south. (*BAE Systems, via Hertfordshire Libraries*)

Flugzeugwerke (BFW)—based in Augsburg, Bavaria. Their aircraft was a single-engined, low-wing, cabin monoplane with retractable undercarriage, designed by Wilhelm E. Messerschmitt. It had first flown in the spring. Under its designation system for all German aircraft, civilian and military, the Reichsluftfahrtminist erium (RLM—Reich Air Ministry) designated Willy Messerschmitt's creation as the Bf108. It would be named as the *Taifun*, the German form of 'typhoon' (the tropical cyclone that develops in the north-west of the Pacific Ocean). His Bf109 fighter had been 'on the drawing board' since March.

Three Bf108s were entered in the *Challenge International de Tourisme*, held from late-August to mid-September in Poland. Polish, Italian, and Czeckoslovak teams also entered. A British pilot joined the Polish team with his Puss Moth. A variety of trials included fuel consumption and a technical evaluation—comfort, controls, convenience, safety, construction, and so on—in which the Bf108s were the top scorers. Only one other design had a retractable undercarriage. A rally across Europe and North Africa, of 5,926 miles (9,537 km), was held 7–15 September; the Bf108s led for much of the route. The Puss Moth dropped out. Back in Warsaw, the 108s also took the first three places in a speed trial on 16 September. The Poles took the first two places for the overall competition with their RWS-9S design. A German Fieseler Fi97 was third. The Bf108s were placed fifth, sixth, and tenth. Wolf Hirth was thirteenth, in another Fi97. What might he be able to do with a Bf108 in the MacRobertson?

11

Autumn Frenzy

> Aeroplanes are seldom ready for delivery on the promised day. But this Comet had to be ready ... or all the work and time and money we had put into them would be wasted. I don't think any of us would care to live again through the weeks of agony that preceded the start of the race...
>
> *Geoffrey de Havilland*

Construction and Test Flying

Work was progressing well on the new buildings. Partly-constructed aircraft were being brought from Stag Lane for final assembly, weighing and flight testing from Hatfield Aerodrome; this included the last six of 154 Fox Moths built. DH.82 Tiger Moth production was relocated in its entirety. The little DH.71 Tiger Moth monoplane racer of 1927, which had been on display outside, was now hanging inside the roof of the airframe assembly shop.

Under Fred Plumb's supervision and still 'top secret', construction of the first Comet airframe was taken to an advanced stage at Stag Lane—then the whispers started at Hatfield. Don Lawrence remembered that 'there was a rumour that a secret racing monoplane was being built'. The 44-foot (13.4-m) wing, the 29-foot (8.8 m) fuselage, and a pair of engines had been quietly taken to Hatfield by road.

A new Fox Moth had been registered on 28 May as G-ACRU, based at Hatfield, to the British Graham Land Expedition. Graham Land is the northern end of the Antarctic Peninsula closest to the southern tip of Argentina. It was named after Sir James R. G. Graham, First Lord of the Admiralty, in 1832; due to the surrounding ice, it was thought to be a group of islands. The expedition, which began in September 1934, was one of the last Antarctic missions to be privately sponsored, and would last three years. Using motorised sledges and dog teams, they would establish that the land was connected to Antarctica above sea level. Fitted with floats or skis (depending on the conditions), the Fox Moth would conduct aerial surveys of 1,000 miles (1,600 km) of the Graham Land coast, and would deliver materials for setting up new bases.

A Comet in final assembly at Hatfield in September 1934. Note the DH.71 Tiger Moth monoplane racer of 1927 hanging from the roof. (*BAE Systems*)

Jim and Amy Mollison inspect their Comet during its final assembly at Hatfield. Note the Gipsy Six R engine without its cowlings. (Fox *Photos, Hulton Archive, Getty Images*)

The Hatfield rumours were confirmed for 15-year-old John Stroud, who was 'lucky enough to see the first Comet racer before its first flight'; and for 20-year-old Don Lawrence 'when [he] saw Test Pilot Hubert Broad flying the "Comet" racer'. This was airframe No.1994, the Mollisons' aircraft, which flew for the first time on 8 September. In one of the test flights, Broad nearly came to grief when he wasn't sure if he had hand-wound the landing gear down properly. He flew low over the aerodrome, as if he was about to land, and watched for the reactions of those on the ground. Their frantic gestures included design and production specialist Harold Povey grabbing the spare wheel from his Morris and waving it. Broad had his answer. Adapted Hamilton propellers were used initially, but these did not allow enough cooling air flow to the engines, so Ratier propellers—which could not be adjusted in flight—were adopted, and received the first flight test on 24 September.

Coming in to land during one of these test flights, the Comet banked over, and the tip of one of its slender wings nearly touched the ground. Broad was shaken. On bringing the aircraft to rest, he left it where it stood, walked back to the hangar, and went for a drink. He is believed to have been of the opinion that de Havilland designs had become dangerous, which the company's senior management did not appreciate.

One area of speculation that was brought to an end concerned the venue for the start of the race. A new RAF station outside the village of Mildenhall, in north-west Suffolk, was confirmed as the starting point instead of Hatfield. With only six weeks to go, Geoffrey de Havilland and his team were too busy to be disappointed, and they were far from complacent:

Hubert Broad test-flies the Mollisons' Comet in early September 1934. (Flight, *via the Norman Eastaff Collection*)

> Hubert Broad, our test pilot, was forced to do the work which usually lasted many months in only a few weeks; and instead of prolonged test flights, he had to limit each to ten or fifteen minutes, landing frequently for a series of minor adjustments. This was the only way to get everything right in the short time available ... difficult to believe that the machine could ever be capable of a really long flight. But ... the Comets had a very thorough if unorthodox testing.

Activity at both factories was relentless, and went through day and night. While houses were being built on the old Stag Lane aerodrome, the production lines next door were turning out part-built Dragons, DH.86s for Qantas, various types of Moth, and Dragon Sixes—including the race entry for Hewitt and Kay. These were all being transported to Hatfield for finishing in the assembly shop. Meanwhile, as the new factory neared completion, the permanent relocation of machinery from Stag Lane was also under way. The other two Comets joined their sibling at Hatfield, which averaged 222 mph (357 km/h) over a test course on 18 September. Three weeks into flight testing, Marshal of the RAF Sir John Salmond came to inspect them. He was also shown how construction of the factory was progressing.

Geoffrey de Havilland's brother Hereward, Hubert Broad, and assistant test pilot Bob Waight made test flights with the first DH.86 Express intended for Qantas.

Left to right: Geoffrey de Havilland listens to Hubert Broad share his impressions of the Comet's flight characteristics, with Arthur Hagg, Charles Walker, and Frank Halford. (*BAE Systems, via the Norman Eastaff Collection*)

A Dragon Six being assembled at Hatfield in late September 1934. This aircraft was destined for African Air Transport Ltd, and would begin its delivery flight to South Africa on 29 December. (*Frank Stewart*)

The Mollison's Comet in early testing. (*Frank Stewart*)

Capt. L. J. Brain, the airline's chief pilot, was a highly-interested observer, as he was going to fly the aircraft to Brisbane. With a top speed of nearly 170 mph (270 km/h), the DH.86 was the fastest British-built passenger aircraft in the world at the time. Sixty-two would be produced, initially at Stag Lane and then at Hatfield over the next three years. More interest from 'down under' was shown by Maj. Norman Brearley, Managing Director of West Australian Airways Ltd. His visit to Hatfield, to inspect de Havilland's latest models, was hosted by Francis St Barbe and Hereward de Havilland.

Build-up to the Big Race

Bernard Rubin had become ill, and it was thought that Edward Fielden would join Ken Waller in G-ACSR's cockpit. Rumour was then directed towards George Stainforth, before the final selection of Owen Cathcart Jones—King's Cup finalist in July—was confirmed. The Mollisons did a lot of flying at Hatfield while they were waiting for their Comet to be completed.

At the end of September the Australia–England record was broken, again unofficially, by another two hours. Jimmy Melrose had set off from Darwin in his Puss Moth, and arrived at Croydon after eight days and nine hours; he had made the flight so that he could return by competing in the MacRobertson race. He named the aircraft *My Hildegarde*, after his mother. Noel Pemberton Billing, the former Hertfordshire MP who, in 1913, had founded the company that became Supermarine, was Jimmy's uncle.

Jimmy's fellow Australian Freda Thomson had been keeping her Moth Major at Hatfield since August. She named it *Christopher Robin*. Freda set off from Lympne on 28 September for her own flight to Australia. She was not expecting to beat Jean Batten's record, but she was not against the idea. As it turned out, forced landings near Lyons and Athens were the first of several incidents that would delay her. Six members of the Bombay Flying Club, trainee pilots led by their instructor, Flt Lt Alan K. H. Binley, had arrived at Heston on 26 June, in three Moths, after a fifteen-day flight from India. They set off on their return journey from Hatfield on 29 September. The Sperry Gyroscopes Leopard Moth also left, having been sold to an owner in Poland.

A speed of 230.5 mph (371 km/h) was recorded by the test-flying Comet on 2 October. The next day Albert Edwards' Comet was named in a ceremony at Hatfield, for which the Honourable Richard Linton (Agent-General in Britain for the State of Victoria) and his wife were guests of honour. Mr Linton made a short speech, including the news that Edwards had already left for Australia, and would be there at the race finish to greet his crew. The name *Grosvenor House* can be seen in the film, painted temporarily on the aircraft's nose, as she had not yet received her coat of bright red paint and white stripe. The guests were then shown around the Mollisons' aircraft (seen in the background) by *Grosvenor House*'s crew, Scott and Campbell Black.

Jim Hewitt and Cyril Kay had been at Hatfield from late September, and on 3 October they received their Dragon Six on behalf of the NZ Melbourne Centenary Air Race Committee. *Trail of the Caribou*'s oil tanks, and possibly its long-distance fuel tanks, were fitted to the aircraft. It was painted tangerine and green, with silver wings, and was named *Tainui*—after the first Polynesian ocean-going canoe to reach New Zealand, in around AD 1,200. Hewitt and Kay joined the London Aeroplane Club while preparing for the race. Martin Sharp was also learning to fly with the club—a great time to be there for the assistant editor of *The Aeroplane* and de Havilland's future director of public relations.

In early October, several new aircraft departed from Hatfield bound for their new owners, including a Dragon Six, two Fox Moths for Canada, and the second DH.86 for Qantas. Lt Humberto da Cruz, of the Portuguese Air Force, and Senhor Carlos E. Bleck, de Havilland's agent in Portugal, collected a Leopard Moth. Cruz intended to establish the first aerial service between Portugal and its colony of East Timor, among the South-East Asian islands. He would make the flight in the wake of the MacRobertson racers, accompanied by Sgt Antonio Lobato, using

Richard Linton, Agent-General in Britain for the State of Victoria, as guest of honour at the launch ceremony for Comet G-ACSS, at Hatfield, on 2 October 1934. Standing behind him is Mrs Linton, who had just used a long-handled hammer to smash a bottle of champagne against the airscrew boss of Comet G-ACSS's starboard engine—note the broken glass behind Charles Scott's feet. Between them is Tom Campbell Black. (*British Pathé Ltd*)

Jim and Amy Mollison, with Comet G-ACSP at Hatfield, before it was painted black. (Popular Flying, *via the Norman Eastaff Collection*)

Dragon Six *Tainui*, painted in primer, heading out for a test flight on 8 October 1934. Note the blanked side windows, which obscured extra fuel tanks like those fitted to the Seafarer Dragons. (*Frank Stewart*)

part of their route between 26 October and 11 November. They would then fly back between 13 November and 21 December.

On 5 October, the winner of the 1931 Schneider Trophy, John Boothman, made two test flights of the Mollisons' Comet. This was on behalf of the Aeroplane & Armament Experimental Establishment (A&AEE) at Martlesham Heath, near Ipswich, in south-east Suffolk, and was a 'handling trial' of the aircraft under light loads. Boothman described the controls as 'light and effective at all speeds'. He added that is was 'unstable laterally, and stable directionally and longitudinally', and that its stall 'occurs slowly ... but control can be quickly regained'. On visibility from the cockpit, Boothman commented that, for take-off and landing, 'the view is very restricted owing to the long nose'. He made other notes on the shock-absorbing performance and stability of the undercarriage, which he felt 'posed no great problems' overall.

On 8 October Jim Hewitt began a blind flying course, and the Mollisons made the first flight in their completed Comet. They were impressed with its performance, and Jim made a good landing. Once again he used a macabre sense of humour, describing the long, hinged canopy as a coffin lid; it would be painted black, with a gold stripe. Amy would write to her mother and say that, although it was beautiful and fast, the plane was difficult to fly. It received its Certificate of Airworthiness on the 9th, as did *Tainui*, and Edwards' Comet flew for the first time—with Hubert Broad and then Charles Scott in the cockpit. Also that day, *The Times* reported that the test programme had recorded a speed of 235 mph (378 km/h) in level flight at 1,000 feet (305 m).

On the 12th, Scott flew Edwards' Comet for the second time, Campbell Black had his first opportunity, and the aircraft was given its Certificate of Airworthiness. So was Rubin's, which would be painted, appropriately enough, in 'Bentley Racing Green'. That evening the Royal Aero Club gave a banquet for the race crews at the Grosvenor House Hotel. Among the dignitaries present were Sir John Salmond, Air Marshal Sir Hugh Dowding, Sir Christopher Bullock, and Lt-Col. Shelmerdine. Representing the industry were Lord Nuffield, Charles Richard Fairey, Geoffrey and Louie de Havilland, Frederick Handley Page, the Chairman of Westland Aircraft Sir Ernest Petter, and Sir Alan Cobham—who was experimenting with inflight refuelling.

The toast to the pilots was proposed by Count Gottfried von Bismarck-Schönhausen, the German Charge d'Affaires. He expressed regret that Wolf Hirth, the only German entrant, had been forced to make a late withdrawal—but he assured the gathering that the German nation would follow the race with interest and good wishes. Obviously referring to Amy Mollison and Jackie Cochran, he noted that women had achieved a level of equality with men in aviation that was still unknown in many other pursuits.

The Count was Chancellor Otto von Bismarck's grandson, a Nazi member of the Reichstag, and a friend of Heinrich Himmler. He probably knew that a new

The 'pram' hood on one of the London Aeroplane Club Tiger Moths hides Jim Hewitt, who began his blind flying course on 8 October 1934. The aircraft had joined the club's fleet in July. (*The Jack Meaden Collection, Air-Britain, via Janic the Norman Eastaff Collection*)

Designer Arthur 'Ernie' Hagg with his Comet, G-ACSR, in final assembly at Hatfield. (*BAE Systems, via University of Hertfordshire*)

German air force (the Luftwaffe) had been instituted in secret on 1 October, in direct violation of the Treaty of Versailles. A bomber version of the Junkers Ju52 all-metal transport monoplane had been ordered for the Luftwaffe by the RLM, to serve as a stop-gap with the new bomber units. More modern, purpose-built designs would soon be introduced. The Ju52 was originally powered by three American Pratt & Whitney Hornet radials, which were then developed under licence as the BMW 132. Export models used the Pratt & Whitney Wasp and the Bristol Pegasus. The Luftwaffe would not need their Ju52s for long, as the Ju86 bomber would first fly on 4 November. Dornier's fast, twin-engine mail plane, the Do17, would make its first flight on 23 November; its slim fuselage would earn it the nickname, *Fliegender Bleistift* (Flying Pencil). Development as a bomber would follow.

Other withdrawals from the MacRobertson race had also been announced, including Wally Hope, Alan Butler, Lord Nuffield, Lady Cobham, and Wiley Post. Charles Kingsford Smith also pulled out. Instead, he used *Lady Southern Cross* to make the first west-east aircraft crossing of the Pacific, from Australia to the United States. Back at Hatfield, Charles Scott only had time to conduct five take-offs and landings with G-ACSS. Tom Campbell Black managed only two. To ensure that they did not exceed the maximum permissible weight for the race, the Comets were weighed under the supervision of the Aeronautical Inspection Directorate (AID)—Geoffrey de Havilland and Frank Halford had worked for the AID's predecessor in 1913.

Over to Mildenhall

Bad weather the following week was not the only reason that Hatfield was quieter than usual. All those involved in race preparations were at Mildenhall for either the day shift or the night shift, shuttled back and forth, in a Dragon, by Hubert Broad. Geoffrey de Havilland was with them: 'By the time we arrived at Mildenhall for the start we were half dead from exhaustion; and yet tremendously excited by the tension that built up during those last days'.

On Sunday 14 October the Comets were flown from Hatfield to Mildenhall by their crews. Cathcart Jones and Waller arrived first with G-ACSR, race no.19, having made the 52-mile (84-km) flight in around fifteen minutes—averaging over 200 mph (320 km/h). Scott and Campbell Black were right behind them. *Grosvenor House* was wearing no.34 on her tailfin. Both aircraft were mobbed by an excited crowd, including press reporters and photographers. At lunchtime the Mollisons arrived, in *Black Magic*, no.63. Hearts were in mouths as Jim only landed on his third attempt, due to the Ratier propellers being in unadjustable course pitch. *Tainui* arrived just after midday having flown from Croydon, where a Plessey radio had been fitted.

Jim had the name *Black Magic* painted on the nose of G-ACSP. As preparations progressed, the *Daily Mail* reported that Amy was 'going up and down tirelessly for practice landings'—she damaged the main wheel covers on her first landing. They quoted her commenting on the route's 'mountain, sea and desert hazards'. Scott and Campbell Black were abstaining from alcohol to stay fit; Jim was drinking heavily. The crowds were growing by the hour, abandoning their cars to cross muddy fields, and being kept at bay by the extra police who had been brought in.

The King of Yugoslavia and the French Foreign Minister were assassinated on 9 October as they processed through Marseille. The event was caught on film, and the Mollisons were offered £30,000 (£1.9m today) to take a copy across the Atlantic, in their Comet, so that American audiences could see the horror for themselves. They would have time to return to Mildenhall for the start of the race.

The Pander S.4 Postjäger at Mildenhall. (*Frank Stewart*)

On 17 October, most of the aircraft, including all three Comets, were found to be over-weight under the rules—so their fuel tanks were drained, and refilled with petrol of a lighter specific gravity. It worked. (The Aeroplane, *via the Norman Eastaff Collection*)

They considered it seriously, and even entered negotiations, but then declined.

For practice flights Broad had advised Cathcart Jones to leave the undercarriage down during flight, but also to wind four turns back to avoid disrupting the airflow needed for engine cooling. On the 18th, he forgot to wind the four turns back out again before landing. The gear was damaged, and the propeller blades bent as they struck the ground. The Hatfield mechanics only had one spare propeller; the aircraft was left on the airfield, waiting for a salvage truck. Bonfires were lit and cars were parked nearby, with their headlights on, to prevent any aircraft landing too close to the stranded Comet. Frank Hearle received the bad news over the phone at Hatfield, and assumed that the green Comet was out of the race, but then wondered if they could rescue the situation. Martin Sharp describes the team's response:

> Vivian Holman, in Hearle's office, rushed over to Faireys [Fairey-Reed Airscrews in Hayes, west London] to get the propellers straightened. Percy Bryan at Mildenhall designed a repair scheme on site. [A. A.] Raw rounded up Len Vicarage, Bob Robson and others from their homes, got two hire cars, loaded them with spare engine mounts, undercarriage parts, ropes, jacks and tools, left the factory at 9 p.m. and within hours they were at work with Watson and others at Mildenhall.

Fairey were reluctant to certify and release the straightened blades as they were unfamiliar with Ratier, but a Ratier engineer was happy to sign them off. Then the team decided that they'd better fit the Comets with larger oil tanks, and protective covers for the magnetos and distributors.

Tom Campbell Black had other things on his mind. His actress girlfriend, Florence 'Dessie' Desmond, arrived on Friday 19th to join the spectacle, but did not want to

The green comet was raised on trestles while the Hatfield mechanics worked hard to repair its damaged undercarriage, after an unfortunate landing on 18 October. The bent propeller blades had been rushed over to Fairey for straightening, in time for the start of the race two days later. The Gipsy Six engines are visible with their cowlings removed. (*BAE Systems*)

be there for the start of the race. Tom walked her to the car, got into the back seat with her for a moment, and asked her to marry him—she said she would answer him when he got back. King George V, Queen Mary, and various other dignitaries also visited that day. A famous photo shows them being introduced to the *Tainui* crew by Harold Perrin, standing in front of *Black Magic* with their backs to the Mollisons.

Above: Grosvenor House and *Black Magic*, with *Tainui* on the 'compass swing', on 18 October. (The Times *2122/1/2, via the Norman Eastaff Collection*)

Below: In their hangar at Mildenhall on 19 October 1934, Comet G-ASCR and *Tainui* (left) are seen with the ageing Fairey Fox biplane of Gilman and Baines, and the Gee Bee R-6H of Jackie Cochran and Wes Smith. Note the Comet's missing propellers, which were being urgently repaired. (*Frank Stewart*)

12

The World's Greatest Air Race

Of the many factors to play their part in the high-speed race, the attempt to reach Melbourne from London in something like three days will inevitably call forth, in the highest degree, the skill, resourcefulness and endurance of pilots; the ingenuity and faithfulness of the aircraft and engine construction; the expert mechanical care of engines that must function almost non-stop half-way round the world; the sustained efficiency of refuelling services during day and night; and the close co-operation of wireless and meteorological stations along a course which crosses three continents and spans the seasons from Autumn to Spring.

Sir MacPherson Robertson

And They're Off!

A group of Hatfield apprentices were out polishing the Comets before sunrise on Saturday, 20 October. 'Zero hour' was 6.30 a.m. Vehicles blocked all the surrounding roads. In front of tens of thousands, the Mollisons were the first to take off on the 2,550-mile (4,104-km) leg to Baghdad; Hubert Broad waved frantically to tell Jim that the wheel brakes were still on. They were followed into the air by another aircraft every forty-five seconds. After the Boeing got airborne, G-ACSR swung wildly on its take-off run. Flames shot from the port exhaust and, pouring smoke, Cathcart Jones had to throttle back. The *Panderjäger* was next. Tom Campbell Black changed his mind about his rubber-soled shoes; Fred Plumb threw his boots in just before they closed the canopy and, at 6.34 a.m., *Grosvenor House* was the fifth to leave the ground. They were followed by the DC-2 and the Gee Bee. Cathcart Jones taxied around, and got away two minutes late. *Tainui* was eleventh to leave. Stack and Turner were the last to get off the ground at 6.43 a.m., carrying the canisters of film that had recorded all of the take-offs, to be shown in Melbourne.

And then the 'gladiatorial' attrition of the twenty starters began. Only ten would complete the race. The film canisters would not be delivered by Stack and Turner—

engine trouble forced them to land three times in France, and they would give up in Athens.

Lloyd's of London calculated a one-in-twelve chance of death for the MacRobertson competitors—which, sadly, proved accurate. A Fairey Fox flown by another New Zealand crew, Fg Off. Harold D. Gilman and James K. C. Baines, crashed near Palazzo San Gervasio in southern Italy, killing them both.

Overcome by freezing temperatures over the Carpathian Mountains, Jackie Cochran had to be lifted out of the Gee Bee in Bucharest. They damaged their wing flaps on landing, so Jackie gave instructions that all of the clothes and supplies waiting for her at the checkpoints were now available for Amy to use. Back in the USA Jackie would set a women's national speed record in 1937, and would win the Bendix Trophy air race in 1938. She would join the Wings for Britain campaign before the USA was drawn into the Second World War, and would be the first woman to ferry a bomber across the Atlantic. She would also recruit female American pilots for the British Air Transport Auxiliary (ATA) in 1940, before leading a similar campaign for the US Army Air Force. When she died in 1980, aged 74, she held more speed, distance, and altitude records than any other woman.

The DC-2 landed briefly in Rome and Athens. Only the Mollisons reached Baghdad in a single flight, taking 12 hours and 30 minutes. Greeted by adoring crowds, Amy kept Iraqi officials waiting while she had a bath and sipped tomato juice. Jim drank more alcohol. The red and green Comets both initially missed Baghdad. Scott and Campbell Black 'borrowed' 20 gallons (91 litres) of fuel from the RAF at Kirkuk. Cathcart Jones and Waller reached the checkpoint on little more than vapour, and then had to return with a partial seizure due to low oil pressure—a piston had to be changed, costing them seven hours.

The Mollisons landed next at Karachi, setting a new England–India record of 22 hours and 13 minutes—less than half of the previous best time. When taking off, Jim was not convinced that the undercarriage had fully retracted, and returned to discover that the cables had snagged. *Grosvenor House* passed over Karachi while *Black Magic* was still on the ground. The DC-2, *Panderjäger*, and Boeing landed, and the DC-2 was soon away again. Having lost the lead, Amy took over for Jim to rest—but then lost her way. With inadequate maps, they had to return to Karachi yet again. The Boeing and *Panderjäger* took off ahead of them. Meanwhile, Scott and Campbell Black reached Bamrauli Aerodrome (Allahabad airport today) and allowed themselves a glass of beer.

Compass problems put Jim and Amy off course and they landed at Jabalpur, in central India, 175 miles (280 km) south-east of Allahabad. They had not topped up their fuel tanks after their false starts from Karachi, and the local bus depot could only offer low-octane fuel. They took off with the engines sounding sick. Amy begged Jim to take it gently, but he wouldn't listen. Smoke started streaming from an overheating engine which soon stopped. The ground staff at Allahabad stayed back until the screaming argument inside the cockpit subsided. A tractor towed

G-ACSP to the de Havilland office; three empty whisky bottles lay on the cockpit floor. Pistons were cracked, valves were burned out, and cylinders were scored. It would take four days to get new parts from Hatfield; they had spent all their money, and needed to win the cash prize, but their race was over.

Now in second place, the DC-2 lost valuable minutes when they started their take-off from Allahabad without one of their passengers, who ran to reach the plane. They were 1,000 miles (1,600 km/h) and eight hours behind the red Comet. The *Panderjäger* undercarriage failed to lock down, and was damaged on landing. Two of its three propellers had bent blades, and it was left stranded on the aerodrome. The Boeing left Allahabad in third place. Cathcart Jones and Waller were next to arrive. After leaving, they had to return with propeller pitch control problems, and lost many more hours—but they were now in fourth place.

Scott and Campbell Black reached Singapore, 7,040 miles (11,330 km/h) from Mildenhall, in an incredible new record time of 39 hours and 56 minutes, but one of their exhausts was belching black smoke. They flew the last two and a half hours into Darwin with one engine ticking over, as the oil pressure gauge was reading very low. It was dark, and the Australian soil had been turned to mud by the first rains, but incredibly they touched down safely after 52 hours and 33 minutes. This was less than a third of the previous record. Despite it not yet being 3 a.m., they were mobbed by a large crowd—who slapped the plane alarmingly in their enthusiasm. Scott remarked, 'We've had a devil of a trip.' They still had 2,000 miles to go.

Frank Halford was able to speak to Scott by telephone. He advised taking off with both engines and then allowing the weaker unit to idle to Charleville, but a de Havilland mechanic from Sydney discovered a clogged oil filter. Two cylinders had poor compression, but the engine was flyable. Another big crowd welcomed them at Charleville, where both cylinder heads were changed in case of burned-out valves. The crowd would see them again when they returned, having forgotten their maps.

Victory

They landed at Laverton airfield, after crossing the Melbourne finish line between two pylons at Flemington Racecourse. Albert Edwards and Jean Batten were there to congratulate them, all filmed by Pathé. They were flown the 10 miles (16 km) back to Flemington in a pair of RAF Moths, where more than 100,000 people were chanting and singing. They had covered the distance in 70 hours, 54 minutes, and 18 seconds—also qualifying for the handicap prize. Having proved that the Comet was capable of flying for more than 3,000 miles (4,828 km) at a constant speed of over 200 mph (320 km/h), Scott said, 'It was a dreadful trip, and that's praising it. Neither of us got a wink of sleep the whole time.' Dessie didn't make

Tom wait for her answer any longer; a telephone connection was made for them, and she accepted his proposal.

Later that same day at Desenzano, on Lake Garda in northern Italy, Francesco Agello and the Macchi MC.72 put the world airspeed record further out of reach at 440.678 mph (709.202 km/h); His 1933 title would stand for another five years. The MC.72 is still the fastest piston-engined seaplane ever. Nonetheless, de Havilland had put British aviation 'back on top'. The workers at Stag Lane were given a half-day holiday as thanks for their efforts in building the Comets.

It was now the KLM crew's turn to lose their way in a thunderstorm, landing at Albury in New South Wales. The next day they brought the DC-2 into Flemmington in second place, after a very impressive three days and eighteen hours. They were awarded the handicap prize, simply because the rules did not allow one aircraft to win both prizes. Third, and less than three hours behind the DC-2, were Turner and Pangborn in the Boeing. Cathcart-Jones and Waller claimed fourth place, after four days and just over 12 hours. Housing developments around Mildenhall in later years would include streets named de Havilland Court, Comet Way, Scott Avenue, Douglas Park, Boeing Way, and Melbourne Drive. Many Dutch babies were named *Uivertje* (Little Stork), in honour of *Uiver* and the tradition that babies are delivered by stork.

The Mollisons joined the *Tainui* and *Panderjäger* crews for breakfast at Allahabad on the morning of day four. The *Panderjäger*'s race would also end there—but much more dramatically. After repairs it took off in the dark, and struck an ambulance with a blinding searchlight mounted on its roof. A fuel tank ruptured, and sparks from the exhaust turned the stricken aircraft into a fireball. The crew escaped, but Dirk Asjes burned his left hand as he dragged the badly-injured driver out of the ambulance.

New Zealanders Sqn Ld. Malcolm C. McGregor and Henry C. 'Johnny' Walker arrived at Melbourne with their open-cockpit, Gipsy Major-powered Miles Hawk in fifth place, after 7 days and 14 hours. They had broken the England–Australia record for light, single-engined aircraft. The Stodarts arrived in sixth, after 9 days and 18 hours in their Courier. Ken Stodart explained their relationship to the Western Mail newspaper from Perth, Western Australia: 'Our grandfathers were first cousins. Work it out for yourself. It's too much for me.' Jimmy Melrose finished seventh (and second on handicap), in 10 days and 16 hours. The Danes, Lt Michael Hansen and Daniel Jensen, finished eighth with their ageing Desoutter—the slowest aircraft in the race. On day ten *Tainui* collided with a fence at Cloncurry, Queensland, and was delayed while the delivery of spares was arranged by de Havilland in Sydney. They finally reached Melbourne after 13 days and 19 hours, the last entry to finish within the rules of the race, and were awarded ninth place.
Unbelievably, the Comets' record-breaking in connection with the event was still not over. Cathcart Jones and Waller were prepared to race anyone who was up for the challenge back to England. They settled for returning with canisters of ciné

Comet G-ACSS *Grosvenor House* taxis at Laverton airfield, west of Melbourne, on 23 October 1934—having just won the MacRobertson England–Australia air race. (Melbourne Argus, *Troedel & Cooper Collection, State Library of Victoria*)

KLM's Douglas DC-2 Uiver at Laverton. (Melbourne Argus, *Troedel & Cooper Collection, State Library of Victoria*)

The Boeing Model 247 arrives at Laverton airfield on 24 October 1934, in third place, less than three hours behind the Douglas DC-2. (Melbourne Star, *Troedel & Cooper Collection, State Library of Victoria*)

Black Magic languishes at Allahabad. Jim had pushed the engines too hard, which were running roughly due to the low-octane fuel that they had been forced to use. (*John P. Fielder, Charles M. Daniels Collection, San Diego Air & Space Museum*)

Tom Campbell Black and Charles Scott receive the trophy from HRH the Duke of Gloucester. Sir MacPherson Robertson is standing behind the Duke. (Melbourne Star, *State Library of Victoria*)

Ken Waller (left) and Owen Cathcart Jones with the green Comet, in a hangar at Laverton airfield. G-ACSR was loaded with canisters of ciné film, recording the Australian stages of the MacRobertson air race, and flew them back to England. (*State Library of Victoria*)

Tainui at Laverton, having arrived in ninth place after 13 days and 19 hours. (*RAAF Museum, via Janic Geelen*)

film recording the Australian stages of the race, and set off at 7.05 a.m. on 26 October. At Allahabad, the stranded Mollisons gave them parts from *Black Magic* to overcome more oil pressure problems. Only flying in daylight—in order to demonstrate a potential air mail schedule—they arrived at Lympne on 2 November, in a new Australia–England record time of 6 days, 16 hours, and 10 minutes. Their overnight stops were the reason for the 'slow' time, but they had actually spent less time in the air than G-ACSS had in the other direction. Their total time since leaving Mildenhall was 13 days, 6 hours, and 43 minutes—another record, and half a day before *Tainui* reached Melbourne! Such times would not be achieved by commercial services until 1946.

Mixed Feelings

De Havilland had produced an outstanding racer, and potentially a successful high-speed mail plane which could beat the latest all-metal American airliners in a long-distance race. But so it should have done, all other things being equal. What about the ability of British manufacturers to supply the airlines of the world with competitive aircraft for the future? Francis St Barbe had to admit that building a single-purpose racer was 'an appalling thing to have had to do'. The company was anxious to see the necessary conclusions drawn at government level. The British media was also protesting about the situation, and Geoffrey de Havilland gave a lecture on how a 'scaled-up' Comet could be a very efficient commercial aircraft. A letter dated 8 November was written from Hatfield to the Air Ministry:

> ...the fine performance of the American Douglas and Boeing machines ... demonstrated how far this country lags behind in the use of high-speed commercial aircraft.
>
> The Comets ... have practically no future as a production or saleable type ... do not at present meet any demand of existing Empire Air Routes....
>
> It will not be out of place to mention the heavy cost shouldered by this company over the production of the Comets.... You will understand, therefore, how immensely important it is to us to derive some benefit from the race.... immediate steps must be taken in this country to produce aircraft of better performance and of greater commercial merit...
>
> We are confident that ... we could produce a commercial aeroplane which would acquit itself well with the products of any nation.
>
> ...demand will probably need to be stimulated by some form of government assistance if our national prestige is to be maintained. We therefore venture to enquire whether some form of financial assistance could be extended to us....

Black Magic was repaired, and the Mollisons headed home, but Amy could stand Jim's company no more. At Athens, she swapped seats with a passenger on a KLM flight to Amsterdam. Jim landed the racer at Lympne on 11 November, the same day that Freda Thomson finally reached Australia. The Mollisons put their racer up for sale without delay, and a price was agreed with the Portuguese government in December. Carlos Bleck and Lt Carlos C. Macedo, aerobatic expert and chief instructor at the Portuguese School of Military Aviation, planned to attempt a diagonal crossing of the Atlantic, from Lisbon to Rio de Janeiro, in a record time.

Contacts within the Air Ministry and Imperial Airways appeared to suggest that de Havilland's high-speed commercial aircraft proposal had been received favourably, but no progress was made despite a reminder being sent from Hatfield on 22 December. Their cause had not been helped when the second Qantas DH.86 crashed, fatally, at Longreach, Victoria, on 15 November. The tail fin twisting system, intended to balance the aircraft if two engines failed on one side, may have been incorrectly installed. Another tragedy followed on 4 December, when Charles Ulm was lost off Honolulu, in an Airspeed Envoy, while attempting a trans-Pacific flight to Australia from Oakland, California. Between the 10th and 24th of December, the first airmail service from Australia to England was flown by a succession of British aircraft that now looked decidedly obsolete—the Australians certainly thought so.

After a celebration cavalcade through Melbourne, the red Comet and her crew were shipped to Sydney, where the celebrations were repeated. She was then

The admin block nearing completion on 16 November 1934. Note the scaffolding around the powerhouse chimney and the curved structure of the restaurant roof. (*BAE Systems*)

The admin block and ornamental pond under construction on 16 November 1934. (*BAE Systems*)

returned to England, again by sea. Scott and Campbell Black were honoured at a dinner for 900 guests on 19 December—once again, at Albert Edwards' hotel. The event was hosted jointly by the Royal Aero Club, the Royal Aeronautical Society (RAeS), the Air League of the British Empire, and the Society of British Aircraft Constructors (SBAC). Geoffrey De Havilland needed complete rest and did not attend, but he sent a message which was read out to the assembly:

> Very sorry to be away tonight. All who helped build the *Comet* have unbounded admiration for the splendid achievement of Scott and Campbell Black, and sincerely congratulate them on their victory.

Lord Londonderry expressed delight that a British company had adopted an 'American' approach to enable them to create three such successful aircraft in a short time. He also referred to how effective the retractable undercarriage, trailing-edge flaps, and variable-pitch propellers had proved to be. Lord Gorell expressed admiration for the other competitors, including the Mollisons' record times to Baghdad and Karachi, and gratitude towards Sir Macpherson Robertson. Lt-Col. Moore-Brabazon was also one of the speakers, in his capacity as President of the RAeS. Since 1931, he had been the Conservative Member of Parliament for Wallasey, on the Wirral Peninsula, near Liverpool.

Queen Astrid

Owen Cathcart Jones was at the dinner on 19 December 1934, but Ken Waller was not; he had flown the green Comet from Hatfield to Brussels that day. In early

The green Comet back at Hatfield after returning from Australia, having been modified to carry mail and named *Reine Astrid* after the Queen of the Belgians. Ken Waller would fly her to Brussels on 19 December, to begin a high-speed Christmas airmail demonstration flight to the Belgian Congo and back. (*BAE Systems*)

December G-ACSR had been modified to have reduced fuel capacity in exchange for a commercial payload. She was also named *Reine Astrid*, after the Swedish-born Queen of the Belgians.

Tragedy struck again just after midnight on the 20th. A new crew were flying the same KLM DC-2 from Amsterdam to Batavia (known as Jakarta from 1942), in the Dutch East Indies (Indonesia). They crashed in Iraq, with no survivors. Meanwhile, Waller was joined in Brussels by Capt. Maurice Franchomme, a former Belgian Army fighter pilot, for an airmail demonstration flight beginning that day. A difficult three days and 4,441 miles (7,147 km) later, they delivered the Belgian Post's Christmas mail to Léopoldville, capital of their colony of Congo, having spent a total of 22 hours and 46 minutes in the air.

Waller and Franchomme began the return trip to Brussels on 26 December, with a fresh consignment of mail, arriving back in Brussels on 28 December after 21 hours and 54 minutes airborne. Waller received the Order of the Lion of Africa, Belgium's highest honour; he would also be awarded the Segrave Trophy for 1934. *Reine Astrid* returned briefly to Hatfield for further modification, and was then kept at Lympne in readiness for more demonstration flights that might be requested. They never were.

13

The Town Would Never Be Quiet Again

The move to Hatfield was much more than a mere geographical one. By the early thirties, the company was large, well-established and a respected one in the British aircraft industry. After only a decade we could look back on some substantial achievements; and in our new location with new, better planned buildings, we looked forward with confidence to a great future. Perhaps a more important reason for our optimism was the good team spirit.... We all got on well together, and there was a sort of family feeling in all departments which was not only congenial but produced good results.

Geoffrey de Havilland

Getting Down to Business

Activity at Hatfield aerodrome returned to normal. An Avro-built Cierva C.30 had been registered there on 20 November, to Albert A. Nathan—he would keep it there until 1937. Actor Ralph Richardson acquired Gipsy Moth G-ABCT from the RAF Flying Club in December; he kept it at Hatfield, although the Stage & Screen Aero Club had closed down by that time. The London Aeroplane Club responded to an increase in demand for blind flying training by having another Tiger Moth equipped with a hood and instruments. On Christmas Eve twelve Moth Majors headed for Spain. They were to be used by the Escuela de Combate y Vuelo (School of Combat Flying) at Alcalá de Henares, north-east of Madrid. The DH.89 which Frank Stewart had photographed during its assembly (now being referred to as the *Dragon Rapide*, or just *Rapide*) was collected on behalf of African Air Transport Ltd on 29 December. It was flown to South Africa to provide special charters for onward journeys and cargo from Germiston airport, east of Johannesburg. Its first charter would be for Safari (Africa) Ltd, which offered 'big game' hunting trips and made documentary films on life in Africa. During the year, de Havilland had opened their own new business at Salisbury, in neighbouring Rhodesia (known since 1982 as Harare, Zimbabwe). Cecil Rhodes and his 'Pioneer Column' of military settlers had built Fort Salisbury in 1890, and named it after the 3rd Marquess—who was the British Prime Minister at the time.

The relocation from Stag Lane to Hatfield was almost complete, and full production got under way. A private bus service was chartered for nine months to enable employees to travel from the Edgware area. The drawing office remained at Stag Lane for a while longer; according to *The Aeroplane,* 'Rumour has it that the drawing office cannot be moved to Hatfield until the gas company, plumbers, electricians, and telephone people have walked out of Mr Hagg's nice new home at Potters Bar'. As for Hatfield, as Martin Sharp put it, 'the rural retreat which the flying school had enjoyed since 1930' had been 'invaded, and regrettably the quiet country town would never be quiet again'.

From the Barnet Bypass, the white Art Deco office building completely obscured the main factory building. To the left stood a similarly-styled white building—this housed the staff restaurant upstairs, complete with ballroom floor, and the works canteen at ground level.

Along the right-hand-side of the main factory building were the test lab, buying office, process area, and tool room, and the experimental, machine, fitting, pressing, and sub-assembly workshops. Across the back were the erecting and paint shops. Along the left-hand side were the dope and fabric and wood detail shops, the stores, and the receipt and dispatch area. The boiler and power house and the plant department were built near the front of the site, to the left of the factory. Behind the power house were the transport department and the timber store, with the technical school at the back.

Delivery and test flights had been constantly mixed with flying school and club activities since July 1934, when Stag Lane aerodrome had become no-longer usable. Pilotless 'drones' are nothing new; on 5 January 1935, the *Queen Bee* made its first flight by radio-control from the ground. This was a development from the Tiger Moth, with a DH.60-type wooden fuselage, so that the navy could conduct real anti-aircraft practice. The control range was up to ten miles, and they could be fitted with floats and catapulted from Royal Navy ships. Like today's drones, it was suggested that they could be armed with bombs or torpedoes. In December, a 'Notice to Airmen' would warn pilots to avoid flying near the 'blind' Queen Bees—which had yellow wings for identification—and not to confuse them with the Tiger Moths of the London Aeroplane Club, which had yellow fuselages. Hatfield would build 320 Queen Bees over the next six years.

Hatfield's significance for the regional and national economy was growing because of de Havilland. Manufacturing businesses were invited, through adverts published in January 1935, to set up production in nearby Welwyn Garden City. And it wasn't just up-to-date facilities, affordable energy supplies, and good-quality housing for workers that were highlighted. Hatfield Aerodrome was listed alongside the A1 and the East Coast Main Line as one of the main transport links. The Demolition & Construction Co. Ltd of Victoria Street, London, were pleased to describe themselves

The administration building of De Havilland's new global headquarters in 1935. (*Newberry 70025—BAE Systems, via Hertfordshire Constabulary*)

Sir Geoffrey de Havilland's new office in 1935, upstairs and to the right of the entrance. (*Fox Photos 29929—BAE Systems, via Hertfordshire Constabulary*)

The new Art Deco canteen and restaurant block in 1935. Following their success, architects James M. Monro & Son would open offices in Hertfordshire—at Leavesden in 1940, before moving to Watford in 1943. (*Fox Photos 26876—BAE Systems, via Hertfordshire Constabulary*)

The staff dining room upstairs, which doubled as a ballroom. (*Newberry T69382—BAE Systems, via Hertfordshire Constabulary*)

as 'Contractors to Messrs De Havilland Aircraft Co., Hatfield'.

The company itself started to refer less to Stag Lane in its advertising, describing its products as 'Manufactured by the de Havilland Aircraft Co. Ltd of Hatfield, England—builders of the Comet—sold and serviced by its world-wide organisation'. Two Comets would soon be sold to France, who envisaged a South-Atlantic airmail service from their colonies in North Africa. Col. Davet and senior Air France pilot Jean Mermoz (who had pioneered commercial flying in South America) visited Hatfield, representing the French Air Ministry. Mermoz was very enthusiastic about his flights in Bernard Rubin's Comet, so they placed an order for it and one other new aircraft, yet to be built.

In the factory, Leopard Moths, Tiger Moths, Dragons, Dragon Rapides, and Express Air Liners were in full-scale production. The sixth and last DH.86 for Qantas was delivered in February 1935. In April, Imperial Airways received one for their Budapest service. The company was proud to advertise that 'Tiger Moths have been selected for the comprehensive flying training of pilots of the military and naval Aviation Services of no less than fifteen nations'. However, there was still no word from the Air Ministry on de Havilland's request for financial support to develop a new, high-speed airliner based on their experience with the Comet. Another reminder was sent from Hatfield on 1 March. A short reply was then promptly received, dated 8 March: the Air Ministry had rejected the proposal, but the company kept the idea alive through personal contacts.

The entry age for new apprentices joining the technical school was reduced to seventeen years, and the course was extended from three to four years. This meant that boys who had completed their school 'matriculation' exams early could begin their apprenticeships immediately. They would spend their first year in the workshops, on woodwork, metalwork, and engines, while learning about machine shop practice. Their second year would cover electroplating, aircraft servicing, and propellers. The final two years would be spent in the drawing office, studying design, stressing and component testing, performance calculations, and test flight observations. Other subjects included costing and procurement. More than 500 ground engineers, trained by de Havilland, had been licenced by the Air Ministry. Their course would also be increased to four years, and would now include production engineering.

The Portuguese were still planning their transatlantic flight to Brazil with the Comet that they had bought from the Mollisons. Similarly to the French, they wanted to promote Lisbon as a European hub for transatlantic commercial flights. The aircraft was overhauled for them at Hatfield; Lt Carlos Macedo and Carlos Bleck joined the London Aeroplane Club when they came to collect the aircraft. They left on 26 February, and battled through bad weather—flying blind at times—but flew the approximately 1,100 miles (1,770 km) to Lisbon in six hours and five minutes. They telephoned to say that they had not used as much fuel as they feared, and that the aircraft had flown very well. She was registered in Portugal as CS-AAJ, and was renamed *Salazar* after their Prime Minister, António de Oliveira Salazar.

The DH.86 production line. (*BAE Systems, via Philip Birtles*)

The Mollisons had sold *Black Magic* to the Portuguese Government in December 1934, and it was prepared at Hatfield for delivery in February 1935. It was renamed *Salazar*, after the country's Prime Minister. (*BAE Systems, via Philip Birtles*)

Opposite: Lt Carlos Macedo and Carlos Bleck arrived from Portugal in February 1935 to collect their Comet, and joined the London Aeroplane Club while they were at Hatfield. They flew to Lisbon on 26 February. They crashed on take-off as they set off on their flight to Brazil on 14 March (*BAE Systems, via the De Havilland Aircraft Heritage Centre*)

However, *Salazar* would soon be back at Hatfield. On 14 March, Macedo and Bleck tried to take off from Granja do Marquês airfield (north-west of Lisbon), home of the Portuguese School of Military Aviation. This was to be the first leg of their flight to Brazil—but the Comet swung to the left, a wing tip hit the ground, and the undercarriage was damaged. A de Havilland engineer was sent to Portugal to oversee its dismantling and shipping back for repairs. It would be five months before the aircraft flew again.

Club and Factory Side by Side

Sad news reached Hatfield concerning the celebrated parachutist John Tranum. He had been training there, using Hawker's Hart demonstrator G-ABMR, before attempting a new world record for the longest delayed drop. During a flight over his native Denmark on 7 March, in which he intended to jump from around 30,000 feet (9,150 m), Tranum never left the plane. At around 27,000 feet (8,000 m), he had signalled to the pilot that something was wrong—a faulty oxygen supply was causing him to lose consciousness. Tranum was unconscious when they landed at Copenhagen's Kastrup Airport, and he could not be revived; he died from heart failure. The Hawker Hart is preserved at the RAF Museum, Hendon.

On Sunday 10 March, five members of a Croydon cycling club flew to Hatfield, with their bicycles, for a ride with the local club. They then flew back to Croydon with five members of the Hatfield club and their cycles, and took them on one of their favourite routes. The Hatfield cyclists then returned home on the same plane. At the end of March, four Moth Majors were flown to Vienna for the Austrian Aero Club by Herr Eltz, the De Havilland representative in Austria, and three other Austrian pilots.

Hugh Buckingham delivered Bernard Rubin's Comet to the French Air Ministry on 11 April, taking the opportunity to set a new London-Paris record (from Croydon to Le Bourget) of 54 minutes. The French renamed it as *Cité d'Angouleme IV*. Jean Mermoz made high-speed test flights during the following weeks, from Paris to Casablanca and Algiers. They were already developing a very similar aircraft for the same purpose—the Caudron C.640 *Typhon*, named after the most fearsome monster in Greek mythology. It too was made of wood, and had first flown in March.

In early May 1935, three Australia–England record breakers visited the London Aeroplane Club together—Harold L. Brook, Jimmy Melrose, and Jean Batten. They were photographed 'taking tea' on the terrace. Jimmy joined the club. Brook had not been awarded a final placing in the MacRobertson race, having arrived in Melbourne outside the minimum of sixteen days. However, he had now beaten Melrose's solo Australia–England time, arriving at Lympne on 31 March—7 days, 19 hours, and 50 minutes after leaving Darwin in a Miles Falcon.

Jean made the same trip two weeks later, in the same Gipsy Moth (now nearly 6 years old) that she had flown to Australia eleven months before. She took off from Darwin on 12 April and arrived at Croydon on the 29th, after 17 days, 15 hours, and 15 minutes. She hadn't set a new record, but she was the first woman to make the trip solo in both directions. She received a stream of invitations from prominent organisations, including the Royal Aero Club, the Royal Aeronautical Society, and the League of Airwomen. She was the Mollisons' guest of honour at Grosvenor House for the League's ball—the Mollisons had lived together at the hotel for a while. Jim was still there, but Amy was now living at the Savoy. Jean

Bernard Rubin's Comet after being prepared for delivery to the French Air Ministry. It was given a modified nose and painted red. It is seen here at Hatfield, waiting to be ferried to Le Bourget airport via Croydon. Hugh Buckingham set a London–Paris record of 54 minutes on the delivery flight. (*BAE Systems, via University of Hertfordshire*)

Australian flight record-breakers Harold Brook, Jimmy Melrose, and Jean Batten, 'taking tea' on the Hatfield clubhouse terrace with D. A. Adkins of de Havilland, on 3 May 1935. (*IMAGNO/Austrian Archives (S), via TopFoto.co.uk, Imagno 634452*)

was also invited to New Zealand House by High Commissioner Sir James Parr, and to Hatfield for lunch with the de Havilland directors, which now included business manager Francis St Barbe and designer Arthur Hagg. She was given life membership of the London Aeroplane Club. Also in May, James Ayling, another long-distance flyer known at Hatfield from the previous year, joined the club as one of their flying instructors.

The Air League of the British Empire organised the second annual Empire Air Day for Saturday 25 May. The League produced a souvenir booklet, in which the foreword was written by Lord Londonderry and articles were contributed by Geoffrey de Havilland, Sir Harry Brittain, and Sir Alliott V. Roe. The Hatfield factory was opened to the public by appointment on the Friday, and was fully open from 9 a.m. on the Saturday. Tours were conducted by apprentices from the technical school, and visitors were able to see the aircraft being built. In the last week of May the factory received orders for eighteen aircraft. The apprentices built Tiger Moth G-ADGO, and handed it to the London Aeroplane Club.

Two Rapides were prepared for the Prince of Wales, painted in the red and blue colours of the Royal Foot Guards. They had extended range, and the plush interiors had comprehensive radio equipment, five comfortable seats (rather than eight), equipment for serving light meals, an electric kettle, a cocktail cabinet, and a writing table. The first one built, G-ACTT, had been intended for the Anglo

Gipsy Moth G-ABHN of the London Aeroplane Club, flying over the Hatfield Aerodrome buildings in 1935. Note the Stonehouse hotel and Waters Garage at top-left. (*Fox Photos—BAE Systems, via Philip Birtles*).

American Oil Co. Ltd but was never delivered. It was refitted, registered to Flt Lt Fielden on His Royal Highness' behalf, and delivered to Hendon on 27 April. However, it wasn't used much and was sold in the October. The other royal Rapide was G-ADDD, again registered to Edward Fielden on 4 March and was delivered to Hendon on 8 June.

The Hornet Moth—first flown in April 1934—finally went into production in July 1935, alongside the Tiger Moth line. Such was de Havilland's reputation that eighty of them were ordered within the first ten days of sale. In early 1935 Alan Butler bought Studham Hall Farm, between Dunstable and Redbourn in Bedfordshire. He had a private airstrip laid out beside the wood next to the farm, and regularly commuted the 10 miles (16 km) to Hatfield for many years. He used a Hornet Moth until he sold it in March 1938. The design was intended as an enclosed-cabin military trainer, potentially to replace the Tiger Moth, but it only attracted private buyers—and some of them criticised its handling, due to its finely tapered wings. The wings were redesigned for an Indian government order with parallel leading and trailing edges, and squared tips to give full aerobatic and recoverable spinning characteristics. The new wings were then made available to private owners. Hatfield would build 164 Hornet Moths, and many of them would be requisitioned by the RAF as liaison aircraft during the Second World War.

The Prince of Wales' Dragon Rapide G-ADDD on the compass swing at Hatfield. The Prince would become King Edward VIII when his father, King George V, died on 20 January 1936. The next day G-ADDD would be the first aircraft to carry a reigning British monarch. It would be a founding aircraft of the King's Flight from 21 July 1936. (*BAE Systems, via Philip Birtles*)

Above: The Hornet Moth finally went into production in July 1935. In the background, on the right, is the new pavilion-style clubhouse—which Alan Butler presented to the company on Saturday 4 May, for use by the Sports & Social Club of the de Havilland workforce. (*BAE Systems, via the Norman Eastaff Collection*)

Below: Hornet Moth production began alongside the Tiger Moth line in mid-1935. (*BAE Systems, via Philip Birtles*)

14

Engaging with the Town

I have made it an invariable rule to show no favours to relatives or friends either in connection with their appointment or their future progress ... in these days the average shop workers, who are nearly always a good lot, will not stand for this type of favouritism; and they are absolutely right.

Geoffrey de Havilland

Accommodation

If Hatfield was going to flourish in partnership with businesses moving to the area—de Havilland had over 1,700 employees by 1935—more housing would be needed for their workers. Development had already started in 1919, with the building of Cecil Crescent and then Stonecross Road at the northern limit of the town. Beyond that, the northern limit of the Civil Parish of Hatfield was brought closer in 1927, when Welwyn Garden City became a separate district and parish. The population of the Victorian 'Newtown' area, south of the St Albans Road, had been around 4,500 in 1921. The building of Dellfield Road began its expansion in 1933, and by 1948 its population would double—and it would keep on growing.

An article had appeared on the front page of the Welwyn Times for 26 October 1933, entitled 'Housing estate for aerodrome workers—Birchwood Farm to be developed':

> At a special meeting of the Hatfield RDC [Rural District Council], the Chairman, Mr W. Clarke, reported an informal interview with representatives of developers who were considering the erection of houses on land at Birchwood Farm, to accommodate employees of the de Havilland Aircraft Co., on the transfer of the Company's workshops and factory to Hatfield. The Council gave instructions to Balfour & Sons, Consulting Engineers to the Council, to survey and report on the sewering of this area, having regard to the proposed transfer to Hatfield of the adjacent area in St Peter's Parish, and future development generally.

A large part of Birchwood Farm, owned by Hatfield House, was indeed acquired by developers in 1934. They built the Crawford Road estate, partly private and partly council housing, between Stonecross Road and the Barnet Bypass.

The Harpsfield Hall farm site, developed by de Havilland, was within the St Albans Rural Parish of St Peters. With the building of the Selwyn and Ellenbrook housing estates to the south, in 1935 Hatfield Rural District Council and Development Corporation changed the boundary to bring the entire area into the Civil Parish of Hatfield—as suggested in the *Welwyn Times* article.

The building of 'Hatfield Garden Village', to the north of the de Havilland site, was started that year—although de Havilland raised many objections to it. The development was next to where Green Lanes met Manor Road, to the east of the Barnet Bypass. The houses were sold by estate agents Drage & Towersay and Robert Tidey & Son.

There was also a residential development on the stretch of the bypass immediately opposite de Havilland, later named Comet Way. Four blocks of flats were built in the Art Deco style, to match the de Havilland admin block that faced them. The blocks were named Altham Court, Cumberland Court, Haddon Court, and Rodney Court.

Fifteen-year-old George A. Frodsham had been working at Stag Lane since 1933. He worked in the print room, where engineering drawings were reproduced for the workshops to use. The Hatfield factory clocked on at 7.30 a.m., like Stag Lane, but—rather than moving to Hatfield—George used the temporary de Havilland bus service from Edgware for several months, until it was no longer available. He then got a lift with draughtsman George Fawcett, for a while, in his little Austin Seven. Later, he cycled the 13 miles (21 km) to Hatfield in all weathers, even outside of daylight hours, using the Barnet Bypass. An easier option, when he had the chance, was to put his bike on one of the company's 'flatbed' trailers when aircraft, components, and engines were delivered between Stag Lane and Hatfield. He had to hold onto the bike to stop it sliding off.

An 18-year-old apprentice, who had just joined the technical school, moved into one of the new blocks of flats. He had been to Stag Lane for an interview. Owen Clapp, the school principal, told him that his training would begin at Hatfield if he was successful. He would pay for his training using an insurance policy that his father had set up when he was born, and his mother gave him a small allowance for his living expenses. His name was John Cunningham:

> I joined three other students sharing a flat with J. P. 'Phil' Smith. We had a landlady who looked after us. Living was cheap, and I could get by on a few shillings, or maybe a pound a week.... Working life at Hatfield was gentlemen's hours in the morning because we started at half past eight.

Hornet Moth G-AEET was registered to Capt. George E. P. Palmer of Andover, in Hampshire, on 18 March 1936. He kept the aircraft at Heston, and also became a member of the Wiltshire Flying Club. G-AEET is seen here in use by the London Aeroplane Club at Hatfield. In the background are the houses on Manor Road, which were built in 1935. (*BAE Systems, via Philip Birtles*)

Three of the 'Four Courts' had been built next to the Barnet Bypass opposite de Havilland when this picture was taken, by Aerofilms, in June 1935. Houses on Selwyn Avenue, Selwyn Drive, and the old St Albans Road West can be seen at top-left. The spaces around and beyond them would soon be filled in, including Ellenbrook Lane and Bramble Road. (© *English Heritage, Aerofilms Collection, image EPW047565*)

Cumberland Court, as seen in the *Come to Hertfordshire Official Guide of 1948*. (*Photo by Studio Lisa, The Simmath Press Ltd, courtesy of Alan Cash*)

Clubs and Businesses

A thirty-page booklet, entitled *Hatfield Aerodrome*, was published in 1935 by G. W. May Ltd of Caledonian Road, London. It describes the venue in glowing terms:

> Within easy access of London, yet situated amid delightful Hertfordshire country surroundings, Hatfield Aerodrome is undoubtedly the largest and finest private flying ground in Great Britain ... virtually free from fog and the influence of London smoke.

The booklet mentions de Havilland's credentials as a manufacturer and promoter of private flying around the world. It also briefly relates the history of their move from Stag Lane with the School of Flying and London Aeroplane Club, and the development of the new aerodrome. The company now had 200 acres (81 hectares) of flying ground, after Harpsfield Hall and its farm buildings were demolished. They also owned 300 surrounding acres (121 hectares), which was kept clear for aircraft flying in and out. They would continue to buy parcels of adjoining land until 1947.

The members of the London Aeroplane Club's committee are named, including Frank Hearle, Francis St Barbe, Wilfred Nixon, J. Vivian Holman, and Capt.

Harpsfield Hall and farm on 10 March 1934. The buildings were demolished in 1935, and the site was most cleared for further expansion of the aerodrome. (*BAE Systems*)

Alfred G. Lamplugh—chief underwriter and principal surveyor of the British Aviation Insurance Co. Ltd. Lamplugh said that 'Aviation in itself is not inherently dangerous. But to an even greater degree than the sea, it is terribly unforgiving of any carelessness, incapacity, or neglect.' One of the assistant flying instructors under Flt Lt J. A. Harris was Geoffrey de Havilland Jnr, who was now 25 years old. After a brief history of the club, the availability of aircraft is described as 'a large fleet of the most modern touring and training aeroplanes ... maintained in perfect condition by the Manufacturer's own Service Department'. It goes on to list membership and flying fees, and provides a membership application form.

The School of Flying is described purely as an RAF-associated organisation, and the RAF classified it as an Elementary & Reserve Flying Training School (ERFTS) from 4 August. As it had been the first of its kind to open in 1923, the school was designated as No.1 ERFTS. They had their hands full training service pilots, and decided to leave civilian flying to the private clubs. Therefore, whereas Geoffrey de Havilland's older sons had learned to fly with the school, his youngest son—John—would learn with the London Aeroplane Club in 1937, when he was 19 years of age. As a civilian organisation, the RAF Flying Club bridged the gap between the two.

Facilities available to military and civilian visitors are proudly described:

> ...the atmosphere and attractions of a country club of the highest class.... No expense or effort has been spared at Hatfield to make it the finest private

> aerodrome in the country; to provide the best possible facilities for those who fly or wish to learn, and to cater to the comfort and recreation of those using it.

Fifteen of the booklet's pages, plus the inside covers, carry adverts for local businesses. These are accompanied by a generous and unreserved endorsement, encouraging the many 'air-minded' visitors to make use of mostly local services:

> The attention of the Members of the [London Aeroplane] Club is respectfully drawn to the advertisements appearing in this issue.
>
> - The advertisers in every case are fully equipped to render excellent service, and can supply every need at reasonable prices.
>
> - Not only are they all local traders but they are especially desirous of proving their ability to give adequate attention to requirements in any part of the country.

Clothing and footwear businesses included S. B. Miles & Co. on St Albans Road, A. E. Evans and The Express Boot Repairing Factory in Newtown, The Wool Shop on London Road, 'Lilian' on Batterdale, and The Hatfield Laundry. Food

Adverts printed in the Hatfield Aerodrome booklet of 1935. (*BAE Systems, via Roger de Mercado, DHAeTS Association*)

and drink could be provided by F. J. Hollier & Sons dairy in Brookmans Park, J. Tingey grocers in Newtown, and A. W. Saye bakers on Fore Street. Butler Bros butchers, 'Purveyors to the de Havilland Flying School Club', had shops in Fore Street, North Road, and St Albans Road. The Salisbury Arms Temperance Hotel, on London Road, provided alternative beverages to the Whitbread ale and stout sold in the aerodrome clubhouse.

Building, decorating, and utility services were available from J. Naden on French Horn Lane, Francis Dunham on London Road, and W. J. Richardson & Son on North Road and Park Street, who were also stonemasons and funeral directors. E. T. Tingey & Son, at The Corner Houses, dealt in furniture and furnishings, removals, chimney sweeping, window cleaning, ironmongery, ceramics, and silver plate. They also had a branch in Potters Bar. G. D. Lovell & Sons, blacksmiths on St Albans Road, produced wrought ironwork and dealt in lawn mowers. Modern transport could be provided by Gray's garage on London Road and at South Mimms, which sold Ford and Morris cars. Harry Lawrence, at Station Yard, was a haulage contractor and horse-dealer. Other adverts were for Alexandra House boarding and day school, and Mervyn Powell Photography on North Road.

Services from further afield—for the more 'discerning' guest—included March Brown antiques of Ripley, in Surrey, S. Lewis flying & motoring clothing of Carburton Street, in London, and (for hunting with dogs and falconry) the British Field Sports Society, headquartered at St James's Square in London.

15

Summer Shadows

Ten Years of Club Flying

By 1935 the London Aeroplane Club had been in existence for ten years, which they celebrated on Saturday 8 June with their now-annual garden party. Tickets were 5*s* for visitors and 4*s* for members, which included use of the swimming pool and tea from the restaurant. The flying display was reduced due to bad weather in the morning.

However, an insect-like glider, assisted by a buzzing motorcycle engine and known as the *Drone*, was demonstrated impressively. It was built by the British Aircraft Co. (BAC)—not to be confused with the British Aircraft Corporation, formed in 1960. The pilots were Robert Kronfeld and Capt. E. D. Ayre, who smoked his pipe in flight. Ayre had finished fourth in the 1933 King's Cup, in one of the first Leopard Moths. Kronfeld was an Austrian Jew who had fled Germany, in 1933, after the Nazis banned Jews from flying; he came to England and took over the British Aircraft Co. Germany would enact 'Nuremberg Laws' from September of that year, denying basic rights to Jews. Their wealth would be confiscated, they would not be allowed to marry non-Jews, and they would be prohibited from holding professional status in law, medicine, or education.

As Kronfeld would have been well aware, the re-organised Luftwaffe had been announced in February with Hermann Göring as its Commander-in-Chief. That same month, Rolls-Royce's new, powerful Merlin engine was flight-tested for the first time in a Hawker Hart biplane. In March, Hitler was claiming that the size of the Luftwaffe was a match for the RAF. It was certainly expanding faster. The first prototype of Junkers' new dive-bomber, the Ju87, had been secretly built in Sweden and transported to Germany, for completion in late 1934. The power plants intended for this and a number of new German designs, the Junkers Jumo 210 and the Daimler Benz DB600, were not ready. Therefore the RLM acquired Rolls-Royce Kestrels in exchange for a sleek, elliptical-winged airliner—the Heinkel He70 *Blitz* ('Lightning'). As a Kestrel testbed, it proved to be faster than existing British fighters. The new Messerschmitt Bf109 fighter took to the air for

This photo was used for a full-page advert in a supplement to the 27 June edition of *Flight*. It had this invitation, in English, French, German, and Spanish: 'Visitors to England interested in aviation are cordially invited to visit the new de Havilland factory at Hatfield'. (*Fox Photos 26877—BAE Systems, via Hertfordshire Constabulary*)

The de Havilland site on Saturday, 8 June 1935, during a break in the weather. The marquee erected for the London Aeroplane Club's tenth-anniversary garden party can be seen at mid-left, beyond the tennis court and squash courts building. (*BAE Systems, via Hertfordshire Constabulary*)

the first time on 29 May, powered by a Kestrel. The British Government would respond slowly over the next few years, but a new expansion programme had been announced in May. The RAF's home defence capability would be trebled to protect the country against its newest, strongest opponent. This would require an additional 1,500 aircraft.

Just as William Richter Ltd (of 12 Fore Street, Hatfield) was importing German machinery (now listed in Kelly's 1934-35 Directory for the St Albans area), so too were British gliding clubs importing German gliders (ironically for Kronfeld). In order to attend the garden party on 8 June, G. Eric Collins (Chief Instructor of the London Gliding Club at Dunstable, and holder of British gliding distance records) was towed in his Rhönadler 'sailplane' by an Avro 504N, from a field near Dunstable. After a little over 10 miles (16 km) in a south-easterly direction, he was released near Hatfield, where he landed. The Rhönadler was designed by Hans Jacobs and built by Alexander Schleicher GmbH & Co., under the control of the state-owned Deutsche Forschungsanstalt Für Segelflug (DFS, German Research Institute for Sailplane Flight). The DFS provided gliders and sailplanes to the Deutsche Luftsportverband for civilian pilot training. Collins would be killed on 30 July, at Sir Alan Cobham's Air Display at Upwood, near Ramsey, in Huntingdonshire. He was attempting a forward loop in his Grunau *Baby II* when most of the left wing broke off. The *Baby* had been designed with assistance from Wolf Hirth—who had withdrawn his Messerschmitt Bf108 from the MacRobertson race—and was the standard type of sailplane being used for pilot training in Germany.

Reginald Brie was back, with a Cierva C.30, to amaze the spectators with more hovering and flying backwards. The afternoon was pleasant enough for the planned swimming and diving demonstrations by Betty Blanks, members of the Highgate Swimming Club, and Edward H. Temme—who also gave a short talk. Temme had become the first man to swim the English Channel in both directions—to England in 1927, and to France in 1934.

A 'Pathé Pictorial' film compilation, which included the event, was released—entitled: *Peeps Through the Window of the World*. At the beginning of the clip, the BAC Drone and Dragon G-ACNA (of Olley Air Service Ltd, based at Croydon) are seen in front of the hangars with their propellers spinning. The Drone is then seen flying comically, under the control of Robert Kronfeld.

The commentator calls it 'the beauty of movement', just as the film cuts to a bathing costume parade around the pool—like the year before—which he describes as 'the movement of beauty'. After more comments of that kind, we see the Cierva hovering. After a brief glimpse of the clubhouse and terrace, the film shows Jimmy Melrose and others sitting on the ground in a hat-trimming competition.

A close-up aerial view of the London Aeroplane Club's tenth anniversary garden party. Eric Collins can be see dismantling his Rhönadler sailplane at bottom left, ready to pack into the trailer parked next to it. (*BAE Systems, via Philip Birtles*)

Cierva C.30 G-ACWR, demonstrated by Fg Off. Reginald Brie, at the London Aeroplane Club's garden party on 8 June 1935. (Flight, *via aviationancestry.com*)

A picture of the pool and squash courts used in the Hatfield Aerodrome booklet of 1935. (*LNA Photos Ltd, BAE Systems, via Roger de Mercado, DHAeTS Association*)

The swimwear models at the garden party on 8 June 1935 have a picnic in the shade of Dragon G-ACNA, of Olley Air Service Ltd at Croydon—registered to them on 25 January 1934. (*Fox Photos, Hulton Archive, Getty Images*)

The 1935 RAF Flying Club Display

The other big event of the summer was the RAF Flying Club display. In April they had acquired Puss Moth G-AAYA from Lady Bailey, who had used it in her attempt to set a record to South Africa in January 1933 and had flown it in the King's Cup that year. The Puss Moth gave many RAF pilots their first experience of flying in an enclosed cabin. The Prince of Wales became patron of the club that year. The display took place on Saturday, 15 June; bad weather again limited the day's enjoyment, but plenty of impressive flying was provided. Sir Philip Cunliffe-Lister had replaced Lord Londonderry as Secretary of State for Air on 7 June. Sir Philip arrived in RAF Dragon Rapide K5070. This had been delivered from Hatfield to 24 Squadron at Hendon a few weeks before, for use as a communications aircraft. Many of the usual dignitaries were also there, including Sir Christopher Bullock, Air Marshal Sir Hugh Dowding, Lord Trenchard, and Lt-Col. Shelmerdine.

The flying displays involved Bristol and Hatfield instructors in Tiger Moths, a Brough instructor in a Blackburn B.2, Hawker Furies of 25 and 43 Squadrons, and the Auxiliary Air Force's 600 and 601 Squadrons. Bullock was working hard to lay the foundations of RAF expansion, supplying Winston Churchill with information on the growth of the Luftwaffe. The RAF would come to regret placing such a high value on aerobatic skills rather than developing combat tactics. They did, at least, stop releasing public reports on the RAF Flying Club's activities.

Taking the place of the late John Tranum was Frederick C. Coveney, who jumped from Leslie Irvin's Stinson SR-5 Reliant. His Irving Airchute brought him down perfectly in front of the spectators' enclosures. Individual aircraft on show included the tiny, semi-tailless Granger Archaeopteryx G-ABXL (with its V-shaped 'parasol' wing, like a hang glider), a Saro Cutty Sark, an Airspeed Envoy, a Miles Hawk Major, and Amy Mollison's black Beechcraft B17L 'Staggerwing' demonstrator, G-ADDH. The band from RAF Henlow was there, again, to close the rainy day with music.

Amy had taken up the position of sole distributor in the UK for American manufacturer Beechcraft. Her contract was dated 28 June 1934, and she received the aircraft in February 1935. She advertised it as 'The luxury motorcar of the air'. For £2,400 (£149,000 today), privileged buyers would get a 175-mph (282-km/h) aeroplane with a four or five-seat cabin, an electric engine starter, and a pneumatically-retractable undercarriage. Amy gave her business address as Grosvenor House, London. High import taxes made the Beechcraft poor value for money, and she didn't get much interest.

The Last Comets

The Comet obviously had military potential. G-ACSS *Grosvenor House* had been on a show tour, by land and sea, to celebrate her MacRobertson victory, and had finally returned to Hatfield in April 1935. She was then sold to the Air Ministry for

£7,000 (£434,000 today). Painted silver, and given the RAF serial K5084, she was prepared for trials with the Aeroplane & Armament Experimental Establishment at Martlesham Heath, near Ipswich, in south-east Suffolk. Meanwhile, the second Comet for France, newly-built and registered as F-ANPZ, was ferried by Hubert Broad on 5 July, again from Croydon to Le Bourget. He couldn't resist beating Buckingham's time by two minutes.

The fifth and final Comet flew for the first time in late July, and was completed for delivery over the first weekend of August. Cyril A. Nicholson, a Sheffield stockbroker, paid £10,000 for it (£620,000 today)—double the 1934 price. Nicholson had created a new airfield at Firbeck Hall, on the Yorkshire-Nottinghamshire border. He intended to base the Comet there, and use it for a new series of attempts on the major long-distance records. England-South Africa would be first, and a transatlantic flight would be next, plus competing in the King's Cup in early September. It was painted in a striking blue and silver livery, and was registered as G-ADEF.

Tom Campbell Black would attempt the record to Capetown, joined in the cockpit by James H. G. McArthur as navigator. McArthur had been Neville Stack's radio operator, in the Airspeed Viceroy, when they had failed to deliver the film of the MacRobertson race start to Melbourne. Campbell Black and McArthur departed from Hatfield at 5.30 p.m. on 8 August, after a ceremony presided over by Cyril Nicholson. A Union Jack flag was draped over the aircraft's nose, which Lady Kathleen Feilding (Countess of Denbigh and Desmond) pulled away to reveal the Comet's name—*Boomerang*. She had suggested it to Nicholson in the expectation that the aircraft would always come back. Tom's wife, Dessie, was there to wave him off this time. They had got married on 30 March, and held the reception at Grosvenor House, where Sir MacPherson Robertson toasted them with his race-winner's gold cup.

Tom had only flown the aircraft once. James had flown it with Hubert Broad, but Broad had made the landing. They reached Cairo after a non-stop flight of 2,240 miles (3,605 km), in a record 11 hours and 18 minutes. But they had to abandon the attempt, yet again, because of oil circulation issues. However, they did make the return flight in 12 hours and 15 minutes, setting a new 'London–Cairo–London' record.

Salazar's troubles were still not over. Geoffrey de Havilland gave it a test flight at Hatfield on 13 September, and when he tried to land the undercarriage was wrecked once again. They were learning about retractable undercarriage the hard way.

Campbell Black and McArthur made a second attempt to reach Cape Town with *Boomerang*, setting off on 22 September. Tom had never used a parachute before, but this time Dessie persuaded him to take one. *Boomerang* reached Cairo nine minutes faster than on the previous occasion, but ironically it would be the one Comet that did not come back.

Above and below: Tom Campbell Black and James McArthur taxi and take off from Hatfield, heading for Cairo, following *Boomerang*'s naming ceremony on 8 August 1935. (*CEGES/SOMA Collections, Brussels - Nos.596529 & 596530*)

The next day, south of Atbarah in north-eastern Sudan, and around 100 miles (160 km) north-east of Khartoum, they had a propeller problem. Realising that the aircraft was doomed, Tom and James escaped from the narrow cockpit and made use of their Irving parachutes. With two Comets in France and *Salazar* still grounded, the RAF trials with K5084 would now be the only Comet flights taking place in Britain.

Campbell Black got a message back to England:

> I am cabling from Atbara. You should see Atbara and live in it for a day. A day would be enough. They tell me it is one of the hottest places on earth. Undoubtedly they speak the truth. But Atbara is Paradise. At least, it was Paradise to McArthur and I when we came rolling in on a camel train last night. The camels are going to Kassala for dispatch to Eritrea. The Italians want them in their preparations for war.

After a long-running international dispute, Mussolini would order Italy's *Regio Esercito* (Royal Army) and *Regia Aeronautica* (Royal Air Force) to invade Abyssinia (Ethiopia) in October. Both countries were members of the League of Nations, but the League would do little to restrain Italy or to support Abyssinia.

James McArthur would compete in the 1936 King's Cup. Tom Campbell Black would be tragically killed that year in a taxiing accident at Speke Airport, south of Liverpool (known as Liverpool John Lennon Airport since 2002). In 1937, Dessie would be married to another pilot seen at Hatfield—Charles F. Hughesdon. They remained together until she died, in 1993, aged 87.

Boomerang back at Hatfield in September 1935. As she sits on her Dunlop tyres, refuelling is conducted with a fire extinguisher at hand. A de Havilland Aircraft Co. lorry passes, towing a Hornet moth on a 'flatbed' trailer—its tapered wings carried on the lorry. (*BAE Systems, via the Norman Eastaff Collection*)

Above and below: In stark contrast to the matter-of-fact way in which Jim and Amy Mollison sometimes bade each other farewell before long-distance flights, Tom and Dessie Campbell Black left the crowd and members of the press far less doubtful about the romance in their marriage. James MacArthur took the rear seat. As Tom climbed into the front seat, Dessie handed him a small silver horseshoe for good luck. He also took photographs of her with him. (*Topham Picturepoint—TopFoto.co.uk, EU045577 & EU045718*)

16

A Fleeting Peace

We cannot tell whether Hitler will be the man who will once again let loose upon the world another war in which civilization will irretrievably succumb, or whether he will go down in history as the man who restored honour and peace of mind to the great Germanic nation and brought them back serene, helpful and strong, to the European family circle....

It is enough to say that both possibilities are open at the present moment. If, because the story is unfinished, because, indeed, its most fateful chapters have yet to be written, we are forced to dwell upon the dark side of his work and creed, we must never forget nor cease to hope for the bright alternative.

Winston Churchill, 'The Truth about Hitler', Strand Magazine, *November 1935*

The 1935 'Jubilee' King's Cup

Instead of holding the event in July as usual, the Royal Aero Club chose 6–7 September, which they announced in March. They wanted to avoid clashing with the summer celebrations of King George V's Silver Jubilee. There would be just two rounds: a long-distance elimination round on the Friday, and a multi-circuit race on the Saturday. The entry fee was £10 (£620 today) if paid by 15 July, or £20 for late entries up to 30 July. They also chose September to increase the chance of better weather for a much more northerly course on the Friday than had been used before. This would be 953 miles (1,534 km), starting and ending at Hatfield.

Checkpoints and turning points would be all around the United Kingdom: up to Newcastle and Edinburgh; over to Renfrew Airport, west of Glasgow and Stranraer; over the 21.5-mile (34.6-km) wide Northern Channel of the Irish Sea to Newtownards Aerodrome, east of Belfast, on Northern Ireland's Ards Peninsula; back across to Dalbeattie, south-west of Dumfries; down to Blackpool's Stanley Park Aerodrome and Avro's Woodford Aerodrome, south of Manchester; and further south to Cardiff Municipal Airport, at Pengam Moors Aerodrome, south-east of the city. Competitors would be in two classes—those with less and those with more than

150 bhp (110 kW). The fastest ten in each class on the Friday would make up the field for Saturday's final—seven laps of a 50-mile (80-km) triangle, via the Herts & Essex Aero Club's aerodrome at Broxbourne and RAF Henlow.

The two most exciting de Havilland entries should have been Cyril Nicholson's Comet (*Boomerang*, flown by Tom Campbell Black) and the next development of the Dragon family—the scaled-down, Gipsy Major-powered DH.90 Dragonfly. Both *Boomerang* and the Dragonfly were withdrawn before the race. The Comet was being spared for its second, doomed attempt on the Cape Town record. This meant that the only de Havillands competing in a field of twenty-nine starters were two Leopard Moths and a new racer from the technical school.

The Dragonfly was a five-seat cabin biplane built from spruce and plywood. The prototype would have been entered by Geoffrey de Havilland and flown by his sons, Geoffrey Jnr and Peter. It had been first flown on 12 August, by Hubert Broad and Bob Waight. Broad had been fired in July, apparently due to his outburst in the Comet racer almost a year before and his perceived poor judgement in approving the Hornet Moth's tapered wings—which had cost de Havilland a lot of money to redesign. Frank Hearle had to break the awkward news to Broad, who had been their chief test pilot for thirteen years. Bob Waight replaced him, but Broad remained employed by de Havilland as a freelance pilot. He also worked as a test pilot with the Royal Aircraft Establishment.

As with TK.1, Marcus Langley supervised work by the de Havilland student design team on another racing plane—this time an all-new design. A competition was held, and the best ideas were selected by Langley and Geoffrey de Havilland. TK.2 was a low-wing, cabin monoplane, built mostly of wood by the students. Nearby, John Cunningham was busy on his first project—making his own wooden tool box. TK.2 was powered by a race-tuned Gipsy Major of 140 bhp (103 kW), keeping it within the lower of the two classes. The rear seat position would be occupied by an extra fuel tank for the race.

Hubert Broad was hired by the technical school to fly TK.2 in the race, and got TK.2 into the air for the first time on 16 August. He registered it as G-ADNO. He would be its pilot in the race, sponsored once more by Lord Wakefield.

Reflecting the trends in aviation by that time, most of the competitors in the 1935 King's Cup were monoplanes. Most of those were 'low-wing', and many had enclosed cabins. Miles was represented by ten Hawks. Their pilots included Owen Cathcart Jones, Hugh Edwards, and Alex Henshaw. A Miles Falcon would be flown by Lawrence Lipton, carrying the owner and sponsor—Samuel Harris, of the Redhill Flying Club in Surrey—as a passenger. Another Falcon would be piloted by Tommy Rose, sponsored by Lady Wakefield.

Another of the Hawks would be flown by a 24-year-old mining engineer and Flying Officer in the RAF Special Reserve, named William 'Bill' Humble. Bill was a flying instructor at the York & County Aero Club, and had been a founder member of 504 (City of Nottingham) Squadron, Special Reserve, in 1928.

Technical School students test the strength of TK.2's wing by standing on it. (*BAE Systems, via Ken Watkins, DHAeTS Association*)

The part-painted TK.2 out on the aerodrome for testing. It was painted bright yellow, although the 'colour subtraction' phenomenon in photographs of the time made her appear black. (*CEGES/SOMA Collections, Brussels—No.596679*)

Ruth Fontés clearly had a sense of humour to match her beautiful Brazilian smile, registering her Gipsy Six-engined Hawk G-ADOD under the name of 'Miss R. Slow'. Her brother Luis entered with a similar aircraft, although Ruth's was powered by the 'R' engine. The siblings were both born in England. Luis had won the Le Mans 24 Hours motor race in June in a Lagonda, with John S. 'Johnny' Hindmarsh, breaking Alfa Romeo's domination since the last Bentley win in 1930. Frederick Miles himself would fly a Sparrowhawk. They all arrived on the Thursday, and made an impressive line-up for official inspection.

Percivals were the next most numerous: six Gulls—Cecil Edwards, Ken Waller, and Jimmy Melrose were in three of them, and Charles E. Gardner (an aeronautical engineer with his own aerodrome in Surrey) was in another. Edgar Percival was in a Mew Gull, sponsored once more by Prince George—who had been made Duke of Kent in 1934. The days of 'Moth-eaten' events had passed. Nevertheless, most of the engines were Gipsys, and most of the Miles and Percival entries were using Gipsy Sixes, so they would not be short of assistance at Hatfield. Two de Havilland engine mechanics, with spares, would also be placed at each control point.

Many of the aircraft arrived at Hatfield on Thursday, in good time for official inspection. The only other multiple entry was from the British Aircraft Manufacturing Co. (BA)—not to be confused with the British Aircraft Co. (BAC)—with two Eagles and a Cupid, flown by Jack Armour. BA had been formed at Hanworth as the British Klemm Aeroplane Co., to produce a German design under licence from Klemm Leichtflugzeugbau GmbH. The other three entries were an old Avro Avian, a Comper Swift flown by Richard Shuttleworth, and a GAL Monospar ST-12.

Wally Hope was going to fly a Comper Swift, but ended up flying Sir Derwent Hall-Caine's Leopard Moth, G-ACHC, in its third year of competing. Hope's passenger was Sir Derwent's mistress, actress and racing driver Paddie Naismith. She had become England's first air hostess, and was serving aboard a British Air Navigation Co. (BANCO) charter from Heston to Liverpool, for the Grand National horse race, on 23 March 1934—the day that Birkett Air Services had rushed the London-printed evening papers from Hatfield to Liverpool with pictures of the race. Sir Derwent and his brother, Gordon, established the short-lived Hall Caine Airport on the Isle of Man in 1935, named after their father. Sir Derwent would become 1st Baronet Caine of Greeba Castle in 1937.

The weather was perfect. The crowds at Hatfield were more than double that of 1934, with 4,100 tickets sold at 5*s* and 1*s*, plus another 1,500 non-paying visitors. There were 900 cars in the car park, each charged 2/6, and motorcycles were 5*d*. Smith's Instruments, Dunlop, BTH, Bendix, and Titanine were among the service providers present. Fifteen thousand programmes were printed. Sir Philip Cunliffe-Lister had written the foreword, in which he stressed the importance of Empire air routes and increases in speed. He was sure that the King's Cup would further these aims by encouraging private flyers to support the development of civil aviation.

Bill Humble's Hawk G-ACTE and Frederick Miles's Sparrowhawk G-ADNL on the starting line. (*CEGES/SOMA Collections, Brussels—No.596455*)

Ruth Fontés with her Gipsy Six-engined Hawk G-ADOD, named *Jabbawocky*. (*CEGES/ SOMA Collections, Brussels—No.596454*)

Flight was still a little disappointed that such events were not even better-attended, but there was a sea of picnics with brightly-coloured umbrellas across Hatfield's grass. An article in the *Sunday Times* the next day described the scene:

> ...as soon as the flying started, and the cheerful, gossiping young people—for none seemed much more than 30—craned their necks and screwed up their eyes in tense apprizement of banks and turns, one felt that here was an epitome of our air-minded age.

Edgar Percival was first away, as his machine was the fastest. The starting order, with the slower aircraft last, ensured that the field would spread out. Wally Hope's take-off was alarmingly untidy. Before TK.2 got away, the Hatfield apprentices were crawling all over it, polishing everything. After fifteen minutes all the starters had gone, and it was time for a good breakfast in the clubhouse restaurant. The only noise was from a Gipsy Six being ground-tested in Harpsfield Hall woods; although, if the hall was still there, it was about to be demolished for further expansion of the aerodrome. Ruth and Luis Fontés were both eliminated—she was disqualified for missing a turning point, and he had to make a forced landing near Durham. Jack Armour, Cecil Edwards and Richard Shuttleworth also retired. He had more success in motor racing that year, winning the Brighton Speed Trials for a second time, the Donnington Grand Prix, and the Brooklands Mountain Championship—all driving an Alfa Romeo. Alex Henshaw had to 'ditch' in the Irish Sea, 6 miles before reaching the Northern-Irish coast. He had just seen the mail steamer *Ramsey Queen*, and touched down near her; he was thrown out of the cockpit, and had to swim back to the floating plane before being picked up. Wally Hope and Jimmy Melrose circled until they saw that Alex was safe.

The Hatfield spectators were excited to see Frederick Miles coming in first, while Edgar Percival was spotted a few miles north, having missed the aerodrome. They arrived almost together, but from opposite directions. The *Flight* reporter wondered how Percival had not noticed the large de Havilland factory! Then most of the other Hawks, Falcons, and Gulls started arriving, split by TK.2 in eleventh.

The next day the start of the final was ordered by the usual handicap, with the old Avro Avian biplane leaving first and Percival's Mew Gull last. In fact, the Avian was well into its third lap before the Mew Gull even took off. Then the excitement began, as spectators waited to see how many places the faster machines had been able to make up on each lap. Tommy Rose emerged as the unexpected favourite by the end of the fourth circuit, having started in thirteenth but now being in third place. Lapping at over 170 mph (274 km/h), his Miles Falcon was 20 mph (32 km/h) faster than the handicappers had predicted. The Miles racers were cheered on by busloads of the Phillips & Powis employees from Woodley, near Reading, who had built them.

Phillips & Powis, makers of Frederick Miles's designs, bussed its workers up from Woodley for the final of the King's Cup on 7 September 1935. As Falcons and Hawks improved their placings throughout the race, their supporters made their feelings known. (Flight, *via the Norman Eastaff Collection*)

By the end of the fifth lap Rose had gained the lead that he would hold to the end. Owen Cathcart Jones, Hugh Edwards, and Jimmy Melrose were behind him. Hubert Broad had got TK.2 up to fifth, and Wally Hope was next. However, the order was changing constantly as the fastest machines gradually scythed their way through the field. By the start of the final lap Broad had gained one more place. Percival was now lapping at 211 mph, and was up to twelfth, but those with slide rules had already calculated that he could not catch Rose—who dived Lady Wakefield's Falcon over the line, to a chorus of car horns. He had averaged 176.28 mph (283.7 km/h).

A tense 6 minutes and 38 seconds passed before Edwards claimed second place. Another 17 seconds later Cathcart Jones arrived in third, securing a Phillips & Powis 1–2–3. Broad nearly caught him, however, with TK.2 finishing one place better than TK.1 had done the year before—much to the delight of the Hatfield apprentices. Lipton and Harris were fifth, with Edgar Percival screaming up behind them to take sixth. He had averaged 208.91 mph (336.21 km/h) over the whole race, and his fastest lap was 211.178 mph (339.86 km/h). His Mew Gull was the

Tommy Rose winning the 1935 King's Cup in a Miles Falcon Six, sponsored by Lady Wakefield. This photograph hung in the Link Miles boardroom at Lancing, in Sussex, and was going to be thrown away when the operation was merged with Thomson-CSF in 1990 and moved to Crawley. The picture was rescued by Terry Jago, nephew of Bill Tucker—who worked for Miles at Woodley in the early 1930s, before moving to Supermarine in 1936. (*Courtesy of Trevor Jago*)

first aircraft in the history of the King's Cup to average more than 200 mph. What might *Boomerang* have done on its home ground?

Four more of Percival's racers completed the top ten, including Gardner in seventh—he would do much better over the next two years—and Ken Waller in ninth. Frederick Miles was eleventh, Jimmy Melrose was twelfth, and Bill Humble was thirteenth. Wally Hope's Leopard Moth, now totally outclassed, was fifteenth. The Avian finished seventeenth, and the Monospar (in view of GAL's win the previous year) was a disappointing nineteenth.

Sir Philip Cunliffe-Lister presented the trophy to Tommy Rose, who had it filled with alcohol and took it over to the Reading employees, who took turns drinking from it. Frederick Miles was awarded a £50 prize (£3,100 today) for the best the lower-powered class performance in Friday's round. Gardner was awarded the equivalent prize for the higher-powered class, in recognition of his 163.2 mph average around Britain; he was also awarded the Siddeley Trophy, for the best placing of a private-club entrant in the final. He would do even better in the next two King's Cups. A telegram was sent from Balmoral Castle to the Royal Aero Club, and said: 'Please convey the warm congratulations of the King to Viscountess Wakefield on winning his cup, and also to the pilot'. Once again, high praise was directed at de Havilland for their organisation of the event.

The company held a sports day for its employees the following Saturday, to end the summer season. Departments competed against each other for a trophy

Above and below: Tommy Rose receives the King's Cup from Sir Philip Cunliffe-Lister, and Hugh Edwards receives second prize. Beside Sir Philip is Lt-Cdr. Harold Perrin, secretary of both the Royal Aero Club and the London Aeroplane Club. (*Royal Aero Club Trust, 0122-0129 & 0122-0170*)

presented by Geoffrey de Havilland. The day also included a motor cycle 'gymkhana', a model aeroplane display, and other fun activities. Those with 'lucky number' programmes won flights from the aerodrome.

The London Aeroplane Club's fleet was being frequently updated. Between July and October they acquired two Tiger Moths and a Hornet Moth, providing flying lessons with a new level of comfort. They would add another Hornet Moth in February 1936. Shell-Mex & BP Ltd would also keep a Hornet Moth at Hatfield from November 1935. The company was a joint venture between Royal Dutch Shell and British Petroleum; it was formed in 1932 to help both companies market their products and services in Britain during the economic depression, but it would remain active for over forty years.

The increase in all business and pleasure activities at de Havilland's Hatfield site meant that they needed more phone lines coming in, which they announced in the 31 October edition of *Flight*:

> As from Friday next, November 1, the telephone number of the de Havilland Aircraft Co. Ltd will be changed from Hatfield 281 to Hatfield 2345 (14 lines). The Gipsy engine and variable-pitch airscrew works at Stag Lane will retain the old number, Edgware 0171.

Jean Batten Crosses the South Atlantic

For her next big flight, Jean Batten paid £2,000 (£124,000 today) for Gipsy Six-engined Percival Gull G-ADPR. On her twenty-sixth birthday, 15 September 1935, she collected her aircraft from Edgar Percival's factory at Gravesend, in Kent, and flew it to Hatfield. Geoffrey de Havilland had it fitted with another toilet tube. She rented 39 Endymion Road, a semi-detached, late-Victorian house. Joined there by her ever-supportive mother, she planned a flight across the South Atlantic. Endymion Road runs parallel with the main railway line, separated from Hatfield station by Beaconsfield Road. On 25 September Jean was elected as a member of the Royal Aero Club, along with Bill Humble and London Aeroplane Club member Lady Loch.

Jean and her mother kept their address secret to avoid media attention, and all their mail was received via Thomas Cook & Son. Jean regularly travelled to London to collect maps and details of aerodromes along her chosen route; she also obtained flying permits and visas. She went to Shell-Mex House to arrange fuel supplies, where she met a young man with a limp who wished her good luck—it was Douglas Bader. From her test flights from Hatfield, she knew that her 147-gal. fuel tank gave her a flying time of 14½ hours. She also had a 10 gal. oil tank from which she could top up the engine with a hand-operated pump.

On 9 November, Jean made the journey of just over a mile to the aerodrome by bus. When she arrived she was handed a letter from the French aviation authorities, which forbade her to cross the Sahara because the Gull had no radio fitted. After pondering the situation, she went into the ladies room, tore up the letter, and flushed it down the toilet. She then walked out to her shining silver aeroplane 'with the thrill of anticipation and exhilaration that glowed in [her] heart before every big flight'. She then flew from Hatfield to Lympne, and waited for good weather.

That day, Jim Broadbent (who had finished eighth in the 1934 King's Cup) left Croydon in a Mew Gull that he was delivering to a customer in Australia. He took the opportunity to break Sir Charles Kingsford Smith's solo record, set two years before. Broadbent did it in 6 days, 21 hours, and 19 minutes. Sadly, at that moment the RAF were considering abandoning their search for Kingsford Smith in the Bay of Bengal. He had left Lympne on 6 November, accompanied by John Thompson 'Tommy' Pethybridge, in Lockheed Altair *Lady Southern Cross*. They were trying to beat the 1934 England–Australia record which Scott and Campbell Black had set with their MacRobertson race-winning Comet. At Allahabad they were less than three hours behind the Comet's time, but they never reached Singapore. Jimmy Melrose had been flying the same route, and believed he saw the Altair pass above him; he helped in the search, but it was hopeless. Jimmy would also be killed while flying—in 1936 his Heston Phoenix 'air taxi' broke up in turbulence, over the State of Victoria. The crowd lining the streets of Melbourne to honour him would be estimated at over 100,000. He was just 22 years old.

Jean left Lympne on 11 November 1935, and arrived at Casablanca later that day. The next day, after a refuelling stop in Western Sahara, she reached Thiès, near Dakar, in Senegal. On the 13th she set out across the South Atlantic. When she arrived at Port Natal, Brazil, she was the first woman to make the crossing—and in a men's record-beating time of 13 hours and 15 minutes. Her time of 2 days, 13 hours, and 15 minutes from England to Brazil was also a new record. After further flights to Uruguay and Argentina she and the Gull sailed from Buenos Aires on 6 December, arriving in England on the 23rd and rejoining her mother for Christmas in Endymion Road.

France made her a *Chevalier de la légion d'honneur*, and the French Academy of Sports gave her their Gold Medal. Brazil awarded her the Order of the Southern Cross. She received the Harmon Trophy and the Women's International Association of Aeronautics Challenge Trophy from America. The Royal Aero Club gave her the Britannia Trophy for 1935. Messages of congratulation (via Thomas Cook) came pouring through the letter box at Endymion Road. Viscount Swinton and Sir Francis Shelmardine, who had become friendly with Jean, pondered how the British should honour her appropriately—they were uncomfortable with encouraging such reckless risk-taking. The New Zealand government insisted that she be recognised for her achievements at a level equal to Amy Mollison, and so Jean was be awarded the CBE.

Above: Jean Batten poses in front of her Percival Gull Six at Hatfield on 9 November 1935. She was preparing for her record-breaking flight across the South Atlantic to Brazil. She was obliged to carry a revolver by the French Air Ministry, for when she passed over their North-African colonies. (*Planet News—TopFoto.co.uk, EU38946*)

Right: Jean Batten inspects her Percival Gull Six at Hatfield, before taking off for Lympne for her South-Atlantic flight. Note the 'lock up' garages for private aircraft owners in the background. (*Planet News—TopFoto.co.uk, EU38945*)

New Military Flying Schools and Aircraft

January 1935 had seen the launch of another programme to increase the size of the RAF Reserve. Training would be provided, as usual, at the Elementary & Reserve Flying Training Schools (ERFTS) in Bristol, Brough, Hamble, and Hatfield, using Tiger Moths, Avro Cadets, and Blackburn B.2s. The syllabus would include aerobatics, blind flying, and aerial photography. Flt Lt Gordon V. Carey left active service in the RAF in 1935, and joined the Hatfield school as a flying instructor. He had been a Lieutenant in the Devonshire Regiment before transferring to the RAF. He was with 100 Sqn in Singapore when he was promoted to Flight Lieutenant on 5 Jan 1934. He was secretary of the Aero Club of India and Burma from 1 July that year, and was transferred to the RAF Reserve on 19 July. He returned to England permanently in mid-1935, and did it in style. The Bombay Flying Club arranged another long-distance flight for its student pilots; their four Moths flew via Turkey, accompanied by Gordon Carey in his Miles Hawk.

Meanwhile, Germany's technical advances were continuing. The Junkers Ju87 dive-bomber and Heinkel He112 fighter (a scaled-down He70) made their first flights in September 1935. The Henschel Hs122—which led to the successful Hs126 reconnaissance aircraft—and the Focke-Wulf Fw159 and Arado Ar80 fighter prototypes also first flew that year. All of them were initially Rolls-Royce Kestrel-powered.

Hawker and Armstrong Siddeley had announced in July that they were merging, to become Hawker-Siddeley Aircraft Co. Ltd. Sir John Siddeley retired, and Tom Sopwith was appointed as chairman. The group included Armstrong Whitworth, Avro, Gloster, and Air Service Training. The Hawker Hurricane monoplane fighter—powered by the new Rolls-Royce Merlin—would make its first flight on 6 November in the hands of George Bulman, who had flown at Hatfield in the 1933 King's Cup. N. Michael Daunt also left the RAF in 1935 to become an instructor at Hatfield. He would join Hawker as a test pilot in 1936, and in 1937 he would transfer to Gloster.

With the expansion of British home air defence now under way, the RAF would need many more ERFTS centres. These would need fleets of mostly Tiger Moths from the Hatfield factory. Older aircraft became surplus, and two Gipsy Moths were donated to the RAF Flying Club in July 1935. The Air Ministry invited tenders from civilian organisations to establish several of the schools. Bristol, Blackburn, Brooklands Aviation, Air Service Training, and Phillips & Powis—now a public company, with Rolls Royce as a major shareholder—were among the successful bidders. The contract for No.13 ERFTS was awarded to de Havilland, who bought 200 acres (81 hectares) at White Waltham, near Maidenhead, in Berkshire. The airfield opened in November 1935, and Bob Reeve left Hatfield to become White Waltham's chief flying instructor. Clem Pike took Reeve's place at Hatfield.

Also from November, Hatfield started supplying Dragon Rapides to the RAF, modified as 'airborne military classrooms' and coastal patrol aircraft. The navigator had a map table, as did the radio operator—who also had a transmitter, receiver, and switchboard. If the aircraft had to ditch, a cylinder of compressed carbon dioxide would automatically inflate a Youngman flotation dinghy and keep the whole machine afloat. Parachutes, flares, fire extinguishers, and a first-aid box were also carried. They could also be used as troop carriers or ambulances.

The 'self-defending reconnaissance bomber' version had a Vickers machine gun positioned in the starboard fuselage. This was belt-fed from a box under the pilot's seat, which contained 400 rounds. The pilot had a forward-firing Vickers gun, a Very light pistol (flare gun), and a bomb-release control. Two 100-lb bombs, carried in the fuselage, were released through spring-loaded trap doors in the floor, which closed automatically. A sliding hatch revealed four 20-Ib bombs. An ingenious ring mounting for a Lewis machine gun was also added, in the roof of the fuselage; the gunner sat in a swivelling seat. When not in use, the whole assembly could be stowed away in a few seconds and covered by a sliding hatch. The gunner had eight drums of ammunition to hand, each containing ninety-seven rounds.

Thirty new Tiger Moths for RAF pilot training, lined up at Hatfield on 26 September 1935. Those in the front row were destined for the Phillips & Powis-run No.8 ERFTS at Woodley, whereas the second row would stay at Hatfield with No.1 ERFTS. (*BAE Systems*)

The militarised Dragon Rapide of November 1935, as advertised in de Havilland's 'General Information' booklet of 1937. (*BAE Systems, via Ian Grace*)

British government support for de Havilland's new high-speed commercial aircraft proposal would finally be confirmed in January 1936. Arthur Hagg and his Hatfield design team got started on what would be named the *Albatross*. But its future was by no means secure, as Martin Sharp explains:

> ...a statement was made in the House of Commons on November 18, 1936, that a British operator was to negotiate for American airliners for a mail service which the British taxpayers were to subsidize. This was an unexpected blow ...
>
> The Albatross should have been built in 1934, to win the England–Australia race and go straight into airline service....
>
> The Government policy was robbing de Havilland of world airliners markets, the company's legitimate business. Rearmament gave plenty of production work to do, and it was work that must be done, but it was holding up the one already belated airliner project, the Albatross, and the airline policy allowed no prospect whatever of British orders for a more advanced metal successor. If, as all hoped, rearmament was to prove a temporary phase, de Havilland would have no civil business to which to return.

The 'Golden Years' had lost their lustre.

Epilogue

The Long-Distance Flyers

Amy Mollison set up a short-lived luxury charter flight business in March 1936, with a Dragon G-AECZ based at Hatfield. It was requisitioned by the RAF in 1940, and was sold to a customer in Ireland in 1950; it is still flying today, as EI-ABI. Amy competed in the King's Cup at Hatfield in July 1936. Jean Batten beat her women's record to Australia in October, and flew on to New Zealand for another new record. That December, Jim Mollison set a new east-bound transatlantic record of 13 hours and 17 minutes; he named his aircraft after an actress who he was friendly with. Amy and Jim divorced in 1938, and Amy reinstated her Johnson surname. She was based at Hatfield in 1940, making delivery flights for the Air Transport Auxiliary (ATA); Jim also joined the ATA as a ferry pilot. In January 1941 Amy lost her life on one of those flights. The Civil Aviation Authority revoked Jim's pilot's licence in 1953, due to his excessive drinking.

Charles Scott took over Sir Alan Cobham's company, National Aviation Displays Ltd, for the 1936 season. Tom Campbell Black and Jean Batten were directors. They then closed the company down. That year, Scott raced in the King's Cup and won the England–South Africa Schlesinger Air Race. In the Second World War, he initially served as a civil defence ambulance driver before joining the Royal Naval Volunteer Reserve (RNVR). He later became a factory test pilot, instructor, and transatlantic ferry pilot with de Havilland Canada, flying newly-built Mosquitos. Sadly, while working for the United Nations in Germany in 1946, he committed suicide. He was 43 years old.

Comet G-ACSS was immortalised in Hatfield in December 1936 with the opening of the Comet hotel, at the junction of the Barnet Bypass and the St Albans road. It was fronted by a model of the aircraft on a stone column, which remains to this day. The real aircraft had ironically been wrecked in a landing accident a few weeks beforehand, during trials with the RAF. It was sold as scrap to architect Frederick E. Tasker, and was rebuilt by Essex Aero Ltd at Gravesend in Kent. In 1937, Flt Lt Arthur E. Clouston flew it to fourth place in the Istres–Damascus–

Paris race, and set a new London-Cape Town-London record. Ken Waller raced it in the King's Cup that September. In 1938 Clouston and Victor A. Ricketts used it to set a new England–New Zealand–England record of 10 days, 21 hours, and 22 minutes. G-ACSS has been part of the Shuttleworth Collection at Old Warden, in Bedfordshire, since 1965. It was restored to flying condition in the 1980s but, for the last twelve years, has only been in taxiable condition. Happily, on 1 August 2014, *Grosvenor House* took to the air again and regained its rightful place as one of Britain's top aviation attractions. Restoration of the well-known replica of the aircraft is also underway once more, at the de Havilland Aircraft Heritage Centre.

Ken Waller became chief flying instructor at Brooklands in 1937, returning for the 1938 King's Cup. He became chief test pilot for Miles Aircraft in 1946.

Jean Batten's England–New Zealand record flight of 1936 also beat Jim Broadbent's England–Australia record. He then set an Australia–England record in May 1937—he also competed in the King's Cup that year—but Jean beat his time once more that October. This made her the first person to hold the record in both directions at the same time. Broadbent then set a new Australia–England record in 1938; this was the last record set between the two countries before the Second World War. He flew for Qantas on their Sydney–Singapore route before becoming a ferry pilot during the Second World War, crossing the Atlantic and delivering aircraft to Australia. He returned to flying for airlines after the War. In 1958 he, his passengers, and his crew were lost without a trace off the coast of Portugal. He was 48 years of age.

Lt Carlos Macedo returned to Hatfield in 1937 to collect Comet *Salazar.* On the return journey he reduced the London–Lisbon time to 5 hours and 17 minutes. The derelict remains of the former *Black Magic* were found on a farm in Portugal in the late 1970s, and it was returned to the UK. It is being gradually restored to flying condition by the Comet Racer Project Group at Derby Aerodrome. The two Comets sold to France were destroyed in a hangar fire at Istres, in France, in June 1940.

The Racers and Test Pilots

Bob Waight raced TK.2 in the 1936 King's Cup, and the new TK.4 in the 1937 event. He was killed when TK.4 crashed a few weeks later; Geoffrey de Havilland Jnr succeeded him as chief test pilot. Hubert Broad became chief production test pilot for Hawker in 1940.

Wally Hope competed in the 1936 and 1937 King's Cups at Hatfield; these were his tenth and eleventh entries, having won the event more times than anyone else (in 1927, 1928, and 1932). Charles Gardner won the 1936 and 1937 races.

After sustaining several serious head injuries, 1934 King's Cup winner Harry Schofield gave up flying. He became a farmer during the Second World War, and published two books—one co-written with *Biggles* author W. E. Johns.

1935 King's Cup competitor Luis Fontés served as a ferry pilot with the ATA early in the Second World War. He was killed in a crash in 1940, while delivering a Vickers Wellington to an RAF Aircraft Storage Unit at Llandow in South Wales.

Richard Shuttleworth was badly injured in 1936 when he crashed his Alfa Romeo in the South African Grand Prix, after which he retired from motor racing. He was killed in a flying accident in 1940, when he crashed in a Fairey Battle. His collection of old cars and aircraft formed the basis of the Shuttleworth Collection.

Gerry Sayer moved from Hawker to become Gloster's chief test pilot in November 1934. Hatfield flying instructor Michael Daunt became a Hawker test pilot in 1936, and joined Sayer at Gloster in 1937. Sayer led Gloster's E28/39 and Meteor jet fighter test flying programmes, but Daunt took over after Sayer was killed test-flying a Hawker Typhoon in 1942.

Neville Stack returned to Hatfield to compete in the 1937 King's Cup. In the Second World War he became chief test pilot for the Austin Motor Co. and their licenced production of Fairey Battles, Short Stirlings, and Avro Lancasters. He later commanded the Fleet Air Arm's 742 Squadron in India. His son, also named Neville Stack, become an Air Chief Marshal in the RAF.

In 1936, Reginald Brie returned to Hatfield, with his Cierva C.30, for the London Aeroplane Club's garden party. In 1941, he was sent to the USA to propose the use of autogyros on ships for protecting convoys. He left the RAF as a Wing Commander in 1945, and worked on helicopter development with BEA Helicopters and Westland Helicopters.

Bill Humble competed in the 1936 and 1938 King's Cups. He joined George Bulman's test pilot team at Hawker Siddeley in 1940, initially testing new Hurricanes. He then moved on to prototypes including the Typhoon, Tempest, Sea Fury, and the Sea Hawk jet. TV presenter Kate Humble is his granddaughter.

Alex Henshaw competed in the 1936 and 1937 King's Cups, and won the 1938 event. He beat Clouston & Ricketts' Cape Town-and-back time in 1939—his record stood for seventy years. He joined Vickers Armstrong in 1940 as a test pilot at their Weybridge factory, flying Wellingtons and Walruses. He then tested Spitfires for their Supermarine subsidiary at Southampton, before moving to their Castle Bromwich factory on the east side of Birmingham—where he flew countless more Spitfires and also Avro Lancasters, built under licence. After the Second World War Henshaw became a director of Miles Aircraft in South Africa and gave demonstration flights, but the company soon folded. He never took charge of an aircraft again, and instead managed the family farming and holiday business in Lincolnshire. He did rescue work during the floods of 1953, and was awarded the Queen's Commendation for Brave Conduct. He died in 2007, aged 94.

Hatfield hosted the Isle of Man races in 1938 and 1939. These attracted entries from Czechoslovakia, France, Switzerland, Latvia, the USA, and Germany—

including Messerschmitt Bf108s and a Focke Wulf Fw44. Arthur Clouston, Luis Fontés, Tommy Rose, Alex Henshaw, Hugh Edwards, Bill Humble, and Geoffrey de Havilland Jnr all took part. Geoffrey Jnr won the 1939 race with TK.2. The 61-year-old Lord Londonderry also competed in the race.

John Cunningham joined de Havilland's test pilot team in 1938. He earned the nickname 'Cat's Eyes Cunningham' as a highly-successful night-fighter pilot during the Second World War. John de Havilland was killed while test-flying a new Mosquito from the factory in 1943. Geoffrey de Havilland Jnr was killed in 1946, while flying a DH.108 high-speed experimental jet. Cunningham succeeded him as the company's chief test pilot until 1978.

The de Havilland Men

Hagg left de Havilland in 1937, and R. E. Bishop took over from him. In 1938 Hagg was a design consultant for the Heston racing aircraft project, using Frank Halford's monstrous new 'H form' Napier Sabre. The Second World War thwarted plans for a world speed record attempt. Bishop designed the DH.95 Flamingo, the company's first all-metal aircraft. He then led the design team for the legendary DH.98 Mosquito 'Wooden Wonder' and its scaled-down offspring, the very fast *Hornet*, using techniques developed with the Comet and Albatross. Hagg joined Airspeed in 1943 as technical director, and was responsible for their Ambassador airliner.

Bishop went on to design de Havilland's post-War *Dove*, *Heron,* and *Comet* airliners, the DH.108, and their *Vampire*, *Venom*, and *Sea Vixen* jet fighters. He retired as design director in 1964. Phil Smith, John Cunningham's flat-mate, worked on the designs for many de Havilland aircraft—eventually leading the design team for the Trident jet airliner and the wings for the first Airbus.

During the Second World War Frank Halford developed a simplified version of Frank Whittle's jet engine. His design of 1942 was known as the Halford H.1, developed by de Havilland as the *Goblin* for their Vampire and DH.108. They bought his business in 1944 and appointed him as chairman of the new de Havilland Engine Co. Ltd, with Hugh Buckingham as business director. Buckingham had established de Havilland's subsidiary in New Zealand in 1939. Peter de Havilland, who had been working for the company as a test pilot, accompanied him. Halford then developed his H.2 engine, the *Ghost*, which was first ground-tested in 1945. It was used in the *Venom* and the early Comet airliner. Halford also worked on turboprop and rocket engines. He was president of the Royal Aeronautical Society from 1951 to 1952.

During the Second World War Hereward de Havilland conducted trials using Tiger Moths fitted with bomb racks, in preparation for a possible German invasion. He also travelled the world with Allied air forces, in an RAF liaison role.

Hereward became the company's regional manager for Latin America after the Second World War, and joined Airspeed in 1949; the de Havilland Company had been part-owner of Airspeed since 1941. Many AS.10 Oxfords—used for training in navigation, radio-operating, bombing, and gunnery—were built in the Hatfield factory. Airspeed was absorbed by de Havilland in 1951.

Bob Hardingham, Hatfield's chief ground engineer until 1934, joined the Air Registration Board (ARB) in 1937. He was Chief Executive of the ARB from 1947 and was knighted in 1969, following his retirement. The ARB was replaced with the Civil Aviation Authority (CAA) in 1972.

Lois Butler flew with the ATA in the Second World War and, as Geoffrey de Havilland put it, she was 'a grandmother when she delivered her eighty-second Mosquito'. Alan Butler retired as chairman of de Havilland in 1950.

Geoffrey de Havilland was knighted in 1944 for his services to the war effort. He flew until he was 70 years of age and retired in 1955, but remained as president of the business. Sir Geoffrey died in 1965, aged 82.

A new company, de Havilland Propellers Ltd, was set up in 1946 with Wilfred Nixon as chairman. He also became chairman and managing director of a new de Havilland parent company in 1956. Charles Walker retired in 1954, Frank Hearle in 1956, and Wilfred Nixon in 1959. Francis St Barbe was the last of the 'old guard', retiring in 1961.

The Industry Men

John Stroud left Hatfield in 1935, but returned to witness the 1937 King's Cup. He was back again in 1938, aged 19, as he was involved in designing the Imperial Airways livery for the Albatross.

Nick Comper's company ceased trading in August 1935. He tried to revive an aircraft design and manufacturing business in the late 1930s, but without success. He died, in an accident, in 1939.

William Richter Ltd of Goodrich House, Fore Street, Hatfield, was included again in the local Kelly's Directory for 1937. After the Second World War started, the company was no longer listed.

Sir Alan Cobham set up Flight Refuelling Ltd in 1934, which later branched out into other aeronautical technologies. His company is known today as Cobham plc.

Edgar Percival transferred his production to the newly-built Luton Airport in 1936. He returned to Hatfield to race in the King's Cup that year, sponsored once more by Prince George, Duke of Kent. He also entered the 1937 and 1938 King's Cups, sponsored by Viscountess Wakefield. He developed a military-training version of the Vega Gull, named the *Proctor*. He left his company in 1940 but remained in aviation development, working in the USA, New Zealand, and the

UK. The Luton factory built Airspeed Oxfords and de Havilland Mosquitos under licence during the Second World War.

Germany bought the rights to produce Leslie Irvin parachutes in 1936. In the Second World War they commandeered a German factory which was producing the parachutes; by that time, they were in use all over the world. They saved thousands of lives during the War, and have continued to do so—the company is still producing parachutes today. Irvin also designed and manufactured the iconic RAF sheepskin flying jacket, to protect aircrew from freezing temperatures at high altitude.

Lord Wakefield continued to support private and sports flying, and enjoyed his nickname: 'The Patron Saint of Aviation'. He died in 1941, aged 81.

Harold Perrin remained as secretary of the Royal Aero Club until 1945, by which time he had signed more than 20,000 private pilots' licences.

Glider pilot Robert Kronfeld became a British citizen in 1939. He joined the RAF, and worked on the development of troop-carrying gliders. He reached the rank of Squadron Leader, and was awarded the Air Force Cross; he was killed in a glider accident in 1948.

Rolls-Royce ended its association with Phillips & Powis in 1941, and Frederick Miles took the company over in 1943, under his own name.

Lord Nuffield (William Morris) was placed in charge of the Vickers factory, at Castle Bromwich, to ensure high rates of Spitfire production—but this did not materialise, and he was sacked in 1940. In 1938 he had added Riley (Coventry) Ltd to his car manufacturing group, which included Wolseley and MG. This would merge with the Austin Motor Co. in 1952 to form the British Motor Corporation (BMC).

Tom Sopwith was knighted in 1953, and continued to work for Hawker Siddeley until 1980. He died in 1989, aged 101.

The Politicians and Aristocrats

Lord Gorell, who presented the King's Cup to Geoffrey de Havilland in 1933, assisted in the rescue of thousands of mainly Jewish children from Germany, Austria, Czechoslovakia, and Poland. They were brought out on *Kindertransport* trains in the nine months before the Second World War began. Placed in foster care, many of them were the only members of their families to survive the Holocaust. Gorell relinquished the chairmanship of the Royal Aero Club after the 1935 King's Cup, but he took up the office once more from 1944 to 1946.

Secretary of State for Air Lord Londonderry, who had presented Harry Schofield with the King's Cup in 1934, was a leading member of the Anglo-German Fellowship, which promoted friendship between the two countries. He was nicknamed 'Londonderry Herr', and from 1936–1938 he attempted to secure peace in Europe through diplomacy with Hitler and senior members of his government. He passed his knowledge of Nazi plans for Poland and Czechoslovakia to the British government, some time before those conflicts began, and he refused a German invitation after the occupation of Prague. However, his motives were distrusted and he was naïve about the Nazi philosophy. He served briefly in Neville Chamberlain's government but his second cousin, Winston Churchill, did not employ him.

Following the death of his father in 1934, Lord Sempill took his seat as a Conservative peer in the House of Lords. He joined the Anglo-German Fellowship, and was sympathetic to militarised, right-wing, and anti-Semitic governments. He also joined the pro-Nazi 'Link' group, and The Right Club in the late 1930s. From 1939 he served in the Admiralty's Department of Air Materiel, and gained access to British aviation secrets. In 1941, MI5 and Bletchley Park discovered that the Japanese were paying him for secrets. On 7 December, the Imperial Japanese Naval Air Service (that Sempill had helped to establish) severely damaged the US Navy's Pacific Fleet at Pearl Harbor, Hawaii. They also destroyed 188 US aircraft, and over 2,400 Americans were killed. On the 10th they sank the Royal Navy's HMS Prince of Wales and HMS Repulse, off the east coast of Malaya, with the loss of 835 British sailors. On the 13th, British security raided Sempill's office and found secret Admiralty documents. On the 15th he was caught contacting the Japanese Embassy in London. He escaped prosecution again, but he agreed to resign.

Sir Philip Cunliffe-Lister, who presented the King's Cup to Tommy Rose in 1935, became Minister of Civil Aviation during the Second World War. He served in the government formed by Winston Churchill in 1951, including as Secretary of State for Commonwealth Relations.

Lt-Col. Andrew Hamilton Gault, who kept his Leopard Moth at Hatfield from 1934, retired as Member of Parliament for Taunton in November 1935. He served with the Canadian army in the Second World War, and was promoted to Brigadier-General in 1942.

Sir Christopher Bullock, Vice-President of the RAF Flying Club, was dismissed from his position as permanent under-secretary at the Air Ministry in 1936—he was accused of abusing his position to gain a place on the Board of Imperial Airways. Many in official circles were very uncomfortable with the decision: Lord Trenchard considered him to be 'the man with the finest brain I ever met with'.

Lindsay Everard bought Dragonfly G-ADXM off the Hatfield production line in December 1935, and kept it at his private airfield at Ratcliffe Hall. It was commandeered by the RAF in 1940 but is still flying today, re-registered as G-AEDU and owned by the Norman Aeroplane Trust since 1997. As chairman of the Royal Aero Club's Racing Committee, Everard entered aircraft in the 1936 and 1937 King's Cups. In 1938 he was granted the rank of Honorary Air Commodore with 605 (County of Warwick) Squadron, Auxiliary Air Force. He was knighted, in the 1939 New Year's Honours, for his services to aviation and commerce. Ratcliffe Hall was used by the ATA during the Second World War. Everard also assisted with the introduction of a light aircraft (designed by Taylorcraft in the USA and built under licence in the UK by Auster) which saw service in the Second World War and long after. He was MP for Melton Mowbray until 1945.

Once there was little more to be proved in making dangerous, long-distance flights, Amy Johnson struggled to find sources of income to fund her lifestyle. Sir Francis Shelmerdine, a vice president of the RAF Flying Club, tried to get her a job at the Air Ministry in 1938—but the junior post she was offered did not pay enough even to cover her rent. Shelmerdine approved of admitting female pilots into the ATA in late 1939, and the first all-female unit was formed at Hatfield in January 1940. According to Shelmerdine, Amy was not invited to lead the unit because of her public profile as a 'stunt pilot with all the publicity which is attached to that role'. The job was given instead to Pauline Gower—another of the London Aeroplane Club girls from the Stag Lane days—who had been working as a civil defence commissioner in London, with the Civil Air Guard, since 1938. Shelmerdine continued as Director General of Civil Aviation until his retirement in 1941.

Lt-Col. Moore-Brabazon remained as Conservative Member of Parliament for Wallasey until 1942. He was strongly opposed to war with Germany, and even attempted to co-ordinate activity against it in 1939 with British fascist leader Oswald Moseley. Nevertheless, he was Winston Churchill's Minister of Transport in 1940, and Minister of Aircraft Production in 1941. He became Baron Brabazon of Tara in 1942. From 1943 he chaired the Brabazon Committee for planning the post-war development of the British aircraft industry. The proposals gave rise directly to the de Havilland Dove and Comet, the world's first jet airliner, the Airspeed Ambassador, Vickers Viscount, Miles Marathon, Avro Tudor, and the giant Bristol Brabazon.

Count Gottfried von Bismarck-Schönhausen, who toasted the MacRobertson racers at the Grosvenor House Hotel, reached the rank of Brigadeführer (Major General) in the SS. He became opposed to the continuation of the Second World War, and was in contact with other high-ranking opponents. After the failure of the Stauffenberg plot to assassinate Hitler, his activities were discovered and he was sent to Sachsenhausen concentration camp. Due to his name and friends he was not badly treated, and was liberated by the Russians in 1945.

The RAF Officers

Sqn Ldr Owen W. Clapp continued as principal of the de Havilland Aeronautical Technical School until 1940. He was promoted to Wing Commander in the RAF Reserve in 1942.

Lord Trenchard, president of the RAF Flying Club, used his position and connections to promote and interfere with British military aviation policy for many years. Nevertheless, he refused all offers of a senior position. He was consulted by the Americans concerning their plans to establish the United States Air Force, independently from their army, after the Second World War. They called him the 'patron saint of air power'.

Marshal of the RAF Sir John Salmond joined the RAF Flying Club at Hatfield in 1936. During the Second World War, he was Director of Armament Production at Lord Beaverbrook's Ministry of Aircraft Production, until they fell out in 1941. He then became Director-General of Flying Control and Air Sea Rescue. Salmond retired due to ill heath in 1943, but continued as president of the main Royal Air Force Club until 1966.

Cecil Edwards returned to Hatfield to race in the 1937 and 1938 King's Cups. He reached the rank of Wing Commander, but while leading 53 Squadron in 1940 he was killed in action over Rotterdam, flying a Bristol Blenheim. His brother, Hugh, was promoted to Squadron Leader in 1938, and served with distinction in the Second World War—including commanding 53 Squadron after his brother was lost. In 1946 he retired as a Group Captain, and returned to rowing to high acclaim as a coach. He coached Oxford's Olympic Eight in 1960.

George Stainforth, the first man to exceed 400 mph (644 km/h), served as a Squadron Leader in Iraq from 1936 and as a Wing Commander back home from 1940. He worked with Battle of Britain fighter ace Sqn Ldr R. Robert Stanford Tuck at Farnborough, testing a captured Messerschmitt Bf109 against a Spitfire. Stainforth returned to front-line service from 1941, as commanding officer of 89 Squadron and their Bristol Beaufighters. In 1942, they were posted to Egypt, to patrol the Nile Delta and the Suez Canal, but Stainforth was killed that year when his Beaufighter was shot down near the Gulf of Suez.

Tommy Rose, winner of the 1935 King's Cup, competed in the 1936 and 1937 events. He became chief test pilot of Miles Aircraft in 1939 after the death of Bill Skinner. That year, he was flying while wearing his pyjamas when he was accidentally shot down by a Spitfire. He bailed out, revealing his unsuitable attire. He was promoted to Squadron Leader, but remained as Miles' test pilot until 1946, when he was succeeded by Ken Waller.

Prince George, who sponsored Edgar Percival's entries for the King's Cup, was granted the rank of Group Captain in 1937. He was also made Honorary Air Commodore of 500 (County of Kent) Squadron, Auxiliary Air Force. He was promoted to Air Vice-Marshal in 1939, but relinquished the rank in 1940 out of respect for more experienced officers. He also briefly held the rank of Rear Admiral, serving in Naval Intelligence. The Prince was one of fifteen killed in 1942, when the Short Sunderland flying boat that was taking them to Iceland crashed in Scotland. He was 39 years old, and the first member of the Royal Family to die on active military service for over 450 years. The Duchess of

Kent had given birth to Prince Michael of Kent, their third child, just six weeks beforehand.

Robert Leckie, a vice president of the RAF Flying Club, commanded British air forces in the Mediterranean in 1940. He then returned to Canada as head of RAF training, with the rank of Air Vice-Marshal. He transferred to the Royal Canadian Air Force (RCAF) in 1942, and from 1944 he was their Chief of Air Staff, as an Air Marshal.

Air Cdre Christopher Courtney, another vice president of the RAF Flying Club, was appointed Air Officer Commanding, RAF Iraq Command, in 1937. In 1939 he became Air Officer Commanding-in-Chief, Reserve Command. He was then Air Member for Supply and Organisation from 1940 until he retired in 1945.

RAF Flying Club founder Robert Brittain was promoted to Wing Commander during the Second World War, and later to Group Captain. He became the Air Ministry's Deputy Director of Navigation in 1952 (which included responsibility for rescue services), and then the first appointed Inspector of Mountain Rescue until 1954. A keen mountaineer himself, he was responsible for preventing the disbandment, due to economisation proposals, of the RAF's Mountain Rescue Service.

Edward Fielden continued with his duties as the royal pilot. The Prince of Wales became King Edward VIII when his father, King George V, died on 20 January 1936. The next day, Dragon Rapide G-ADDD became the first aircraft to carry a reigning British monarch. It was a founding aircraft of the King's Flight, of which Fielden was appointed Captain on 21 July 1936. Fielden became a Squadron Commander and Group Captain from 1942, and provided direct support for European Resistance groups. After the War he returned as Captain of the Kings Flight until 1962. He retired in 1969 as an Air Vice-Marshal.

The Aerodrome and Factory

The London Aeroplane Club and RAF Flying Club continued until war suspended all private flying. All RAF pilot training was now for active service rather than for reserve organisations, so the de Havilland School of Flying had its RAF designation changed from No.1 ERFTS to No.1 EFTS—Elementary Flying Training School. During the Second World War a new personnel block, added next to the gatehouse, was built in the same Art Deco style as the other buildings fronting the site. The factory was bombed on 3 October 1940, with the loss of twenty-one lives. The School of Flying moved to a 'decoy' aerodrome at Panshanger and continued there, alongside the London Aeroplane Club, until its closure in 1953. The RAF Flying Club was revived at Panshanger in 1948, but lack of interest led to its closure in 1950.

In 1947, concrete runways were laid on Hatfield Aerodrome to cope with the new jet high-performance aircraft. A new flight hangar and a design block were built in the early 1950s for the Comets and other aircraft being produced, and the factory was further extended.

The de Havilland Aircraft Co. was absorbed by Hawker Siddeley in 1960, as part of the Government's rationalisation of the aircraft industry; Hawker Siddeley discontinued the de Havilland company name in 1963. Hawker Siddeley's aircraft division would itself be absorbed through a government-organised merger and nationalisation in 1977, with the forming of British Aerospace. The Hatfield site would close in 1993.

Bibliography

Hatfield & Hertfordshire History

Brown, Gladys M., *Hatfield And Its People, Part Nine: Farming Yesterday and Today*, (Workers Education Association, Hatfield, 1962)

Brown, Gladys M.., *Hatfield and Its People, Part Two: The Story of Roe Green and South Hatfield*, (Workers Education Association, Hatfield, 1960)

Gray, Henry W., *Hatfield And Its People, Part Eleven A & B: Families and Trades*, (Workers Education Association, Hatfield, 1964)

Hutton, Barbara, *Hatfield And Its People, Part One: A Thousand Years of History*, (Workers Education Association, Hatfield, 1959)

Hutton, Barbara, *Hatfield And Its People, Part Ten: Houses*, (Workers Education Association, Hatfield, 1963)

Hutton, Barbara, *Hatfield And Its People, Part Twelve: The Twentieth Century*, (Workers Education Association, Hatfield, 1964)

Hutton, Kenneth, *Hatfield And Its People, Part Five: Roads and Railways*, (Workers Education Association, Hatfield, 1960)

Kirby, Sue, and Richard Busby, *Hatfield—A Pictorial History*, (Phillimore & Co. Ltd, 1995)

Lawrence, Brian, *History of Birchwood*, (Hatfield Local History Society)

Our Own Country: Vol 2, (Cassell Petter Galpin & Co., 1890)

Preston, J. A., *Hatfield And Its People, Part Seven: Churches*, (Workers Education Association, Hatfield, 1961)

Richardson, Robert, *Hatfield—No Ordinary Town*, (1988)

Richardson, Robert, *The Book of Hatfield*, (Barracuda Books Ltd, 1978 & 1988)

Walby, William G., *The Life and Times of William George Walby*, (Hatfield Local History Society, 2001)

www.english-heritage.org.uk/professional/archives-and-collections/nmr/archives/photographs/aerofilms

www.highsheriffofhertfordshire.org.uk

www.bishopshatfieldparish.co.uk
www.britainfromabove.org.uk
www.disused-stations.org.uk
www.domesdaymap.co.uk
www.hatfield-house.co.uk
www.welhamgreen.com
www.ourhatfield.org.uk
www.stalbans.gov.uk
www.smallford.org

de Havilland History

A. J. Jackson—www.ajjcollection.co.uk

Allward, Maurice, and John Taylor, *The de Havilland Aircraft Company*, (The History Press, 1996)

Bill Grace—www.n5490.org

De Havilland, Capt. Sir Geoffrey, *Sky Fever*, (Airlife Publishing Ltd, 1979)

DH Aeronautical Technical School Association—www.dhaetsa.org.uk

Geelen, Janic, *Frank's Flight*, (NZ Aviation Press, 2012)

Geelen, Janic, *Magnificent Enterprises—Moths, Majors & Minors*, (NZ Aviation Press, 2004)

Golley, John, *John 'Cat's Eyes' Cunningham—The Aviation Legend*, (Airlife Publishing Ltd, 1999)

Guernsey history of the de Haviland family—www.havilands.org

Sharp, C. Martin, *DH: A History of de Havilland*, (Airlife Publishing Ltd, 1982)

The de Havilland Aeronautical Technical School at Stag Lane and Kingsbury, compilation by Roger de Mercado, (de Havilland Aeronautical Technical School Association, 2013)

Early Aircraft

Hare, Paul R., *The Royal Aircraft Factory (Putnam's British Aircraft)*, (Conway Maritime Press Ltd, 1990)

Hare, Paul R., "When Aeroplanes Spoiled the War", published in *WW1 Aero: The Journal Of The Early Aeroplane*, No.212, (2012)

Jackman, William J., and Thomas H. Russell, *Flying Machines: Construction & Operation*, (Charles C. Thompson Co., 1910)

Walker, Maj. George Goold, and Col. Geoffrey R. Armstrong, *Honorable Artillery Company 1537–1987*, (the Honourable Artillery Company, 1986)

Franks Pages AKA Goldoni, Aviator's Obelisk—homepage.ntlworld.com/frank.cooke

www.cambridgeshire.gov.uk/leisure/archives/online/worldwar1/army-1912.htm
The Honourable Artillery Company—www.hac.org.uk
www.thosemagnificentmen.co.uk/britain
www.earlyaeroplanes.com
www.ourletchworth.org.uk
www.thebookofdays.com

The First World War

Castle, Ian, *London 1914–17: The Zeppelin Menace,* (Osprey Publishing, 2008)
Der Traum vom Fliegen: Johann Schütte, Ein Pionier der Luftschifffahrt, (Stadtmuseums Oldenburg, Isensee, 2000)
Evan-Hart, Julian, *War-torn Skies: Hertfordshire*, (Red Kite, 2007)
Griehl, Manfred, and Joachim Dressel, *Zeppelin: The German Airship Story*, (Weidenfeld Military, 1990)
Jones, H. A., *The War In The Air, Vol V, (Clarendon Press, Oxford, 1935)*
Robinson, Douglas H., *The Zeppelin in Combat: History of the German Naval Airship Division, 1912–18*, (G. T. Foulis, 1962)

Zeppelin crew funeral, Potters Bar, 1916, East Anglian Film Archive—www.eafa.org.uk/catalogue/2473
Brookmans Park Newsletter—www.brookmans.com
Potters Bar History—www.pbhistory.co.uk
www.rafhornchurch.thehumanjourney.net
www.worcestershireregiment.com
www.hellfirecorner.co.uk

General Aviation History

Cadogan, Mary, *Women With Wings*, (Macmillan London Ltd, 1992)
Gillies, Midge, *Amy Johnson—Queen of the Air*, (Orion Books Ltd, 2004)
Mackersey, Ian, *Jean Batten—The Garbo Of The Skies*, (Warner Books, 1992)
O'Brien, Sicele, "Keeping an Aeroplane of One's Own", published in *The Girls Own Paper And Woman's Magazine*, (April 1930)
Schrader, Helena P., *Sisters in Arms*, (Casemate Publishers, 2006)
The Sailplane & Glider, Vol.6, 1935—no.7 (July 1935) and no.8 (August 1935)

Air Britain Researcher's Corner—www.ab-ix.co.uk/firstfiles.html
British air racing between the wars—www.afleetingpeace.org
Aerial lighthouses—www.mycetes.co.uk/a/page16.html

British industrial history—www.gracesguide.co.uk
www.flightglobal.com/pdfarchive
www.aviation-safety.net
www.rafmuseum.org.uk
www.britishpathe.com
tomcampbellblack.150m.com

Hatfield Aerodrome

Birtles, Philip J., *Hatfield Aerodrome—A History*, (British Aerospace Regional Aircraft Ltd, 1993)

Brindle, Jon, 'The Golf Course', published in Newsletter No.75 of the Hatfield Local History Society, Dec 2009

Brittain, Gp Capt. Robert E. G., 'The Royal Air Force Flying Club', published in the *RAF Historical Society Journal*, No.17, (1997)

Franklin, Jack, 'Hatfield aerodrome in the 1930s', published in *Hertfordshire Countryside Magazine*, (March 1983)

Hatfield Aerodrome, (G. W. May Ltd, 1935)

Lawrence, Don, *The Early Days of de Havilland at Hatfield*, (Hatfield Local History Society, 2007)

Simons, Graham M., *Airfield Focus No.45: Hatfield*, (GMS Enterprises, 2001)

Stroud, John, 'Hatfield Memories', article published in *Air Pictorial*, (December 1975)

The de Havilland Legacy—Hatfield Aerodrome Remembered, (University of Hertfordshire Press, 2010)

The Return of Bulldog Drummond, directed by Walter Summers, (British International Pictures, Welwyn Studios, 1934)